DISTRUSTING DEMOCRATS

Distrusting Democrats

Outcomes of Participatory Constitution Making

DEVRA C. MOEHLER

The University of Michigan Press
Ann Arbor

Copyright © by the University of Michigan 2008
All rights reserved
Published in the United States of America by
The University of Michigan Press
Manufactured in the United States of America
∞ Printed on acid-free paper

2011   2010   2009   2008   4   3   2   1

A CIP catalog record for this book is available from the British Library.

Library of Congress Cataloging-in-Publication Data

Moehler, Devra C., 1972–
    Distrusting democrats : outcomes of participatory constitution making /
Devra C. Moehler.
        p.   cm.
    Includes bibliographical references and index.
    ISBN-13: 978-0-472-09993-1 (cloth : alk. paper)
    ISBN-10: 0-472-09993-0 (cloth : alk. paper)
    ISBN-13: 978-0-472-06993-4 (pbk. : alk. paper)
    ISBN-10: 0-472-06993-4 (pbk. : alk. paper)
        1. Constitutional history—Uganda.
    2. Political participation—Uganda.
    3. Democracy—Uganda.
    I. Title.

    KTW172.M64   2007
    342.676102'9—dc22   2007019166

CONTENTS

FIGURES

TABLES

ACKNOWLEDGMENTS

This book is a product of the efforts of many people, and I owe them all my heartfelt thanks. The Ugandan citizens about whom I have written deserve special acknowledgment. Shopkeepers, government officials, farmers, and many others welcomed me into their workplaces and homes and spent hours thoughtfully answering my many questions. The time and opinions they shared with me are precious gifts. I have tried accurately to reflect their views in this book, but I am unable to provide sufficient recompense for their magnanimity.

Long before and long after I went to Uganda, I benefited from the generosity and wise counsel of others. Jennifer Widner has earned my admiration, respect, and gratitude. Her influence on this work is obvious, but she has also affected me in far greater ways. I strive to follow her example as a good teacher, scholar, and friend. I am grateful to Nancy Burns for providing me with skills, knowledge, and the motivation to pursue my research interests. Each time I came to her with a seemingly insurmountable theoretical or statistical obstacle, she managed to turn it into an exciting research possibility. Valerie Bunce, Frederick Cooper, Don Kinder, Muna Ndulo, Jonas Pontusson, Michael Ross, Sidney Tarrow, Mark Tessler, Nic van de Walle, and Chris Way merit warm thanks as well. They read my work at different stages and gave insightful feedback. I am especially indebted to Claudio Holzner, Nick Jorgensen, Darcy Leach, Irfan Nooruddin, and Cihan Tugal of Dissertation Roadkill, who pulled, prodded, and assisted me throughout the writing of this book. Thanks also go to all my friends and colleagues at the University of Michigan and at Cornell University for creating supportive, stimulating, and motivating intellectual environments. I am grateful to several anonymous reviewers and to conference and seminar participants who commented on this work. Where I addressed these scholars' suggestions, the book is better for it. The faults that remain are entirely my own.

During my year in Uganda, I incurred additional debts. I am grateful to the Ugandan researchers who conducted the survey interviews: Suzanne Aroko, Margaret Ateng, Victor Aturinda, Janet Auma, Theresa Awelo, Yolamu Gabula, Ann Gidudu, Mary Gidudu, Gorden Kahwezi, Joseph Kiwanuka, Charles Kyegonza, Hussein Ahmed Malali, Isaac Mukobe, Teddy Namalike, Patience Namanya, Patrick Opio, Nakitende Regious, Lydia Rwaheru, Bob Tumwesigye, Betty Wannyana, and Barbara Peace Wasukira. They endured grueling work schedules yet managed to remain cheerful and professional. I enjoyed their company on the road and learned more about Uganda during our car rides and meals together than from any other source. Paul Bangirana and Joseph Kiwanuka spent long hours diligently entering data into the computer. Thanks go to Frank Ochum, Kate Perry, A. B. K. Kasozi, Ronnie Kasolo, Robert Sentamu, Makerere Institute of Social Research, the Centre for Basic Research, the Electoral Commission librarians, Ronald Atkinson, Jessica Worden, Jeremy Weinstein, Gina Lambright, Laura Johnson, and Yerger Andre for helping me get the most out of my stay in Uganda. I especially thank Richard Kabuye, who remained patient and kindhearted no matter what road we traveled.

Several institutions contributed financially to my studies and research for this book. I thank the National Science Foundation for three years of support as a Graduate Research Fellow. The International Institute and the Center for Afroamerican and African Studies at the University of Michigan funded my predissertation research in Uganda. The University of Michigan's Center for the Education of Women helped me attend a conference on constitutionalism in Africa. A Fulbright IIE Fellowship and a National Science Foundation Research Grant provided for dissertation research in Uganda. A Rackham Predoctoral Fellowship supported my final year of writing. Throughout the process, the political science department and the University of Michigan's Rackham Graduate School granted additional assistance. I also owe much to the staff members at the university's political science department, who were friendly, accommodating, and masterful at negotiating the intricacies of university bureaucracy. Lili Kivisto and Michelle Spornhauer deserve special mention for efforts above and beyond the call of duty. Thanks also go to the staff at the Cornell University Department of Government for all their help.

A sincere and heartfelt thank you go to Mom, Dad, and Becca, who inspired my interest in politics, love of travel, and desire to understand people's motivations and aspirations. At its core, my book is about these things. Thanks also go to Mom for responding to numerous last-minute requests for a fresh pair of eyes when my own were clouded by exhaustion. Finally, and always, I want to express my gratitude to my husband, Wolfgang, who sacrificed more than anyone else for this book. He patiently endured my long absence in the field, my late nights at the computer, and my sometimes distracted or irritable disposition. More importantly, he brought joy and meaning to this endeavor. I dedicate this book to him.

INTRODUCTION

Participation and Distrusting Democrats

In the current wave of democratization, several countries embarked on innovative constitution-making programs designed to develop democratic norms as well as to create formal institutions. The Ugandan process provided for extensive involvement by the general public over an eight-year period. Eritrea, South Africa, and Albania followed with analogous participatory processes. Of late, reformers are advocates for the participatory model of constitutional development in countries as diverse as Iraq, Nigeria, and India.

These and other participatory policies are inspired by a venerable scholarly tradition emphasizing the importance of public involvement in political life. Classical liberal and contemporary participatory theorists optimistically assert that political participation[1] builds democratic attitudes, civic competence, and political legitimacy. In contrast, other scholars are pessimistic about the consequences of extensive citizen involvement in government. They argue that mass participation polarizes the citizenry, frustrates ordinary people, and threatens political stability, particularly during periods of political transition. Although the theoretical literature on the value of participation is extensive, empirical work on its consequences is sparse, especially at the individual level of analysis. How does political participation affect political culture in hybrid systems? Does mass participation invest or disinvest in democracy? This book seeks to answer these questions.

Drawing on survey, interview, and archival data, I identify the individual-level consequences of citizen involvement in the Ugandan constitution-making process. The quantitative and qualitative data indicate that participation was significantly related to attitude formation, but not entirely in the manner

---

1. This book employs the commonly used definition of political participation: "those legal activities by private citizens that are more or less directly aimed at influencing the selection of government personnel and/or the actions they take" (Verba, Nie, and Kim 1978, 46).

or direction predicted by either the optimists or pessimists. In my extensive fieldwork, I found that participation was associated with stronger democratic attitudes[2] as well as higher political and constitutional knowledge, as the optimists would expect. However, participation did not improve feelings of civic competence or directly alter constitutional legitimacy; among those who offered opinions about the constitution, participants were no more supportive of the constitution than were nonparticipants. Instead, participation appears to have indirectly enhanced constitutional support by helping citizens to form opinions about the constitution (most of which were positive) and by compelling people to think in larger and more comparative ways. Most notably, the data suggest that participation contributed to the erosion of institutional trust, an effect more in keeping with the predictions of the pessimists. In short, I argue that participation helped to create distrusting democrats[3]—citizens who are democratic in their attitudes but suspicious of their governmental institutions.

If participation in the constitution-making process generated distrust, then reformers elsewhere might be wary of copying the Ugandan experience. However, the participatory process provided citizens with new tools with which to evaluate critically the performance of their government institutions. In Uganda, as with most states undergoing transition, infant democratic institutions are imperfectly functioning and incomplete; participation seems to have raised democratic expectations and alerted citizens to existing democratic deficits. I contend that political distrust can facilitate democratization, especially when paired with civic engagement, democratic preferences, and support for the constitution, as appears to be the case in Uganda. The implications for other constitution-building countries are evident: short-term risks of disillusionment and instability and long-term advantages from a more sophisticated citizenry with the capacity to monitor leaders and promote democratic governance.

My central theoretical argument is that participation affects attitudes in two ways: (1) by increasing citizen interest in and exposure to political information and (2) by changing the standards by which citizens evaluate that information. The content of the information imparted through participation determines the direction of attitude change; participation can deliver both positive and negative messages about government. Civic activity does not

---

2. Democratic attitudes include support for public involvement in decision making, citizen rights and duties, tolerance, equality, autonomy, freedom, resistance to hierarchy, and respect for the rule of law.

3. The term *distrusting democrats* is similar to Norris's (1999) use of *critical citizens* and *disenchanted democrats*. It is also similar to Pharr and Putnam's (2000) term, *disaffected democracies*.

happen in a vacuum, and people do not mechanically transform information into opinions. Participation must be viewed in context, and participation in hybrid systems that combine elements of democratic and authoritarian rule will have different consequences than will participation in well-performing consolidated democracies. If scholars and policymakers want to predict how citizen involvement will affect democratization, they must examine how participants obtain and interpret information about the processes in which they are involved. This book offers guidance regarding when participation is likely to enhance democratic development and when it might undermine the democratic project.

RESEARCH DESIGN AND METHODOLOGY

This book responds to the debates about the democratic implications of participation in general—and of participatory constitutional reform in particular—by analyzing the individual-level effects of public participation in the Ugandan constitution-making process. The effects of participation are typically small, gradual, and reciprocal and thus are difficult to detect and substantiate with any degree of certainty (Mansbridge 1995). The Ugandan constitution-making process offers a unique opportunity to observe the typically elusive results of participation. Ugandan officials and civil-society activists actively mobilized ordinary people to participate in a variety of activities,[4] over an extended period of time, focused on a highly salient topic—the constitution. Uganda serves as a crucial test case because the effects of participation in the constitution-making process are expected to be more evident than in other instances of public participation.[5]

To examine the effects of citizen participation in constitution making, I employ a multimethod approach that includes an original national survey of 820 Ugandan citizens, in-depth interviews and focus groups, primary materials from public and private archives,[6] case studies of local nongovernmental

---

4. Ugandans engaged in many activities that are common in democratic politics: they attended meetings, contacted government officials, wrote to newspapers, called radio-talk show programs, participated in local associations, attended rallies, campaigned, voted, and lobbied government officials.
5. The difference between participation in the Ugandan process and participation in other programs is a difference in magnitude, not a difference in kind. While the consequences of participation are magnified in the Ugandan case, I expect my analysis to be relevant to other participatory programs.
6. I visited the archives at the Electoral Commission, the Center for Basic Research (an independent research center), the Ministry of Women in Development, Parliament, and several nongovernmental organizations. Collectively, these sites contain: (1) reports from the 899 public meetings; (2) 25,547 memoranda and essays submitted to the Uganda Constitutional Commission; (3) Uganda Constitutional Commission reports; (4) the Constituent Assembly proceedings; (5) newspaper articles, position papers,

organizations (NGOs), and an analysis of media content. The research data were collected during two visits to Uganda—the first in June and July 1999 and the second from October 2000 through September 2001.

The bulk of the evidence comes from two sources: (1) a multistage probability sample survey[7] and (2) in-depth unstructured interviews with citizens and local elites in the locations where the survey was conducted. I designed the survey instrument based on other questionnaires, in-depth interviews, and focus-group discussions with a variety of Ugandans. I pretested the questionnaire instrument in rural and urban locations. To ensure a representative survey, I sampled research sites and respondents according to a multistage area sampling design. The questionnaire was translated into the five languages of the sampled regions and was checked using the technique of translation/back-translation. Five teams of native-speaking interviewers administered the survey. To gain an understanding of the conditions in each location, I accompanied the interview teams in the field. Finally, I cross-checked the survey responses about attendance at meetings, contribution to memoranda submitted to the Uganda Constitutional Commission (UCC), and voting behavior against documents housed at the Electoral Commission Archive to estimate the differences between previously recorded and self-reported participation.

While the survey was under way, I conducted open-ended interviews in the sampled locations with three types of Ugandan citizens. First, I selected local elites based on their positions and the likelihood that they would know about the constitution-making activities that took place in their area. Second, at the Electoral Commission Archive in Kampala, I copied the attendance and signature lists from the memoranda, meeting notes, and seminar transcripts from each of the sites. Where possible, I conducted in-depth interviews with citizens identified on these lists.[8] Third, I conducted in-depth interviews with randomly sampled individuals. Since these in-depth interviews were not done in proportion to the population in any given area, they are not representative of all Ugandans as the survey is, but they do provide a deeper understanding of causal processes and thus facilitate the interpre-

---

manuals, newsletters, and academic analyses written on the constitution; (6) recordings from the weekly NGO radio and TV programs on constitutional issues; (7) reports of NGO-sponsored meetings; and (8) material from programs targeted at women's participation.

7. See Appendix A for details on sampling methodology and survey design.

8. A limited number of citizens participated in these particular activities, so I used the lists to identify and interview a larger number of participants than would have been the case if I had selected respondents only randomly. This approach also allowed me to gauge the completeness and accuracy of the lists, develop a better understanding of the events in that area, and probe the causal influence of participation.

tation of survey results. In the text, I present the English translation of quotations from these interviews, and I cite only the district location and interview date to preserve anonymity.

To assess the effects of public participation on civic knowledge and attitudes at the individual level, I rely on statistical analysis of my survey data.[9] I augment the statistical analysis with qualitative analysis of the indepth interviews of citizens from the same locations.[10] I also examined submissions to the UCC, reports from meetings, and debates in the media during the period 1988–95 for evidence of change over time in the levels and accuracy of public information, understanding of issues, and support for democratic attitudes.

Although mobilization played a large role in influencing who participated, participation in constitution-making activities was voluntary. Therefore, the initial knowledge, attitudes, and behavior of the citizens who participated are not identical to those of the citizens who did not. I use information on determinants of participation to account for the potential reciprocal effects. Although I explicitly model reciprocal effects, it is difficult to determine causation from survey data collected at one point in time. Qualitative analysis of in-depth interviews provides additional leverage to untangle the direction of causation and to delineate the causal mechanisms at work.

OUTLINE OF THE BOOK

The remaining chapters of this book expound my theoretical argument and interrogate the empirical evidence. In the first chapter, I engage the twin debates about whether participation helps or hinders democracy and whether participatory constitution making is a panacea or a poison for democratic constitutionalism. I expose the deficiencies in these debates and address the shortcomings with an alternative theoretical approach. I contend that participation affects political culture by increasing citizen access to political

---

9. Thirty of the survey questions were open-ended response questions. These were postcoded to enable statistical analysis, but the actual answers were also examined for qualitative evidence.

10. I used the Nvivo qualitative data-analysis program to code and retrieve sections of the interview transcripts. I read through the full transcripts several times and assigned codes on key themes. I then reviewed all passages coded on a given theme or at the intersection of two themes. This was done in a reiterative process with the quantitative analysis. My initial readings of the qualitative data helped inform some of the statistical models used in the quantitative analysis. Findings from the quantitative analysis were then cross-checked with the systematic analysis of the qualitative data to ensure that the two were consistent.

information and by adjusting how citizens evaluate that information. The content of the information imparted through participation determines the direction of attitude change.

Chapter 2 confronts Uganda's constitutional and political history and sets the stage for the analysis of participatory constitution making in the rest of this book. It describes the constitution-making exercises, the controversial issues, the debates about the fairness of the process, and leader motivations. Uganda's history influenced the development of the participatory constitution-making program and generated the controversies that emerged during the process. The process design and the controversies in turn influenced who participated and the influences of that participation. Chapter 2 also reviews the democratic performance of the National Resistance Movement government prior to the time I conducted the field research. Uganda is not a democracy. It is a hybrid system that combines considerable amounts of democratic political competition (between individuals, not parties) and public participation with elements of authoritarian rule. Citizens who participated in the constitution-making process ultimately seem to be especially sensitive to their government's democratic shortcomings.

What effect did participation have on the Ugandan participants' attitudes? In chapter 3, I evaluate the hypotheses that political participation contributed to higher democratic values, subjective political capabilities, and institutional trust. In so doing, I use a simultaneous equation system to account for the possibility of reciprocal relationships between participation and attitudes. I first develop a model of the factors that contributed to participation in Uganda. The analysis suggests that elite mobilization drew people into politics. This model then serves as the basis for the subsequent analysis of the consequences of participation. The tentative conclusions about causation from the statistical analysis are further bolstered by qualitative analysis of in-depth interviews. The evidence suggests that participation in constitution making had a positive estimated effect on democratic attitudes—as the optimists would expect—but had no discernable influence on civic competence. In contrast, it appears that participation in the process contributed to the erosion of trust in political institutions—as the pessimists would expect. Paradoxically, we find mixed support for the two opposing perspectives. Chapter 3 reveals the central puzzle of this book: Why were individuals who became involved in the constitution-making process more likely to emerge as distrusting democrats?

Chapter 4 solves the puzzle. Participation in constitution making increased democratic attitudes and raised civic knowledge, while the joint effect of higher democratic attitudes and knowledge of the undemocratic actions of the government provoked a gradual erosion of institutional trust. Participants are distrustful because they want full democracy and know that the Ugandan government is not delivering it. I present statistical and qualitative evidence that is consistent with this argument. In short, chapter 4 argues that participation in Uganda contributed to the creation of informed distrusting democrats.

Did participation generate dissatisfaction with the fundamental rules of the game or just disappointment with the way the game is being played? How did participation in the Ugandan constitution-making process affect public support for the constitution? In chapter 5, as in chapter 4, I argue that participation furnished Ugandan citizens with additional information and changed the criteria by which citizens evaluate that information. The evidence indicates that participation contributed the overall support for the constitution by creating a new class of opinionated citizens, most of whom are supportive. In addition, participation seems to have increased the durability of existing support for the constitution by inducing citizens to evaluate the constitution based on procedural fairness rather than on fluctuating personal fortunes. However, among those citizens with opinions, participants were no more likely to support the constitution than were nonparticipants. In Uganda, as elsewhere, ordinary people have difficulty evaluating the constitution-making process and the constitution itself. Ugandan citizens looked to political elites for cues. Elites also made concerted efforts to influence public opinion on constitutional issues. Both active and inactive citizens seem to have been highly influenced by elite rhetoric. So, while participation may have helped citizens form opinions about the constitution and made those opinions more durable, it appears that the leaders in the area (rather than participation) influenced whether citizens came to view the constitution as legitimate or illegitimate.

The conclusion reevaluates the benefits and drawbacks of participation in light of the evidence. Participatory programs seem able to alter participants' political culture and thus beget a more democratic, knowledgeable, discerning, and engaged citizenry. Skeptical citizens can be beneficial for political development, especially if most remain attached to democratic and constitutional principles, as in Uganda. Unfortunately, such beneficial outcomes of participation are not guaranteed. If we want to understand the effect of mass action on attitudes, we must pay attention to the content of the messages to which participants are exposed as well as the means they use to interpret those messages.

THEORETICAL AND POLICY IMPLICATIONS

The research described in this book has theoretical implications for four key fields of inquiry: comparative democratization, political participation, institutional trust, and constitution making. It also offers lessons on best practices for policymakers involved in these spheres of activity.

For scholars of democratization, this book demonstrates that political attitudes are subject to short-term influences and are not solely the product of long-term socialization.[11] However, this work also warns that political culture is not easily crafted. Promoters of democracy seek simultaneously to raise democratic norms and institutional trust, making new democracies both more democratic and more stable. Scholars of democratization similarly assume that advances in one attitude will spill over into the other: higher trust in government will build support for system norms, and greater attachment to democratic attitudes will foster trust in the new institutions.[12] My research indicates that these goals may initially be incompatible. During transitions, when institutional performance is low, increases in democratic attitudes are likely to create expectations that undermine institutional trust. Only when institutional performance improves will increases in democratic attitudes and knowledge be accompanied by higher trust.

Moreover, elevating political trust not only may be difficult to achieve in new democracies but also may be undesirable. This book calls into question previous assumptions about the constellation of attitudes that are conducive to democratic development. While most scholars presume that distrust threatens the democratic project, I argue that the development of critical capacity is advantageous for democratization, especially in the medium and long term. In the current wave of transitions from authoritarian rule, regimes are less likely to experience dramatic breakdowns that reinstate dictatorships and more likely to stabilize under hybrid systems that fall short of liberal democracy (Bratton, Mattes, and Gyimah-Boadi 2005; Bratton and van de Walle 1997; Diamond 2002; Levitsky and Way 2002).

---

11. This book complements several recent works on democratization, including Bermeo 2003; Bratton, Mattes, and Gyimah-Boadi 2005; Bratton and van de Walle 1997; Carothers 1999; Diamond 1999; Gibson and Gouws 2003; M. Howard 2003; Reynolds 1999; Rose, Mishler, and Haerpfer 1998; Schaffer 1998.

12. Scholars often conflate different types of political support, but democratic attitudes and institutional trust have different referents and need not covary. *Democratic attitudes* refers to support for the political regime or rules of the game, while *institutional trust* refers to support for the existing structures of the state.

Transitioning polities are not well served by naive publics that overestimate the quality of democratic governance.[13] In Uganda, active citizens seem to be more attached to democratic principles and constitutional rules and simultaneously more attentive to the flawed democratic performance of their political institutions. Uganda's informed distrusting democrats are thus more inclined to hold their leaders accountable to constitutional standards and to push for democratic improvements. Institutional distrust, combined with civic engagement, democratic attitudes, and support for fundamental rules, seems to offer the best recipe for furthering democratization, though individual-level attitudes alone are not sufficient to guarantee progress. However, such a beneficial constellation of attitudes is unlikely to emerge from all participatory programs; I offer lessons on when participation might hinder rather than help democratization.

This work also has implications for the study of political participation in both hybrid systems and consolidated democracies. It revises our understanding of political participation by highlighting the critical role that context plays in conditioning the influence of participation on citizen attitudes.[14] By comparing the results in Uganda with the existing studies of developed democracies, I highlight the importance of institutional performance and information environments.[15] In addition to refining our understanding of the consequences of participation, this book imparts a cautionary warning to scholars studying the causes of participation.[16] Conclusions about causation based on cross-sectional survey data are necessarily tentative. Nonetheless, my analysis suggests that participation in Uganda significantly influenced

13. Bratton, Mattes, and Gyimah-Boadi (2005) also suggest that lowered trust might benefit Africa. After noting that the average level of institutional trust in twelve African countries is similar to that found in the Organization for Economic Cooperation and Development's member countries, the authors write, "But, given that the institutions in question often perform abysmally in Africa, one is forced to consider whether Africans are perhaps *too* trusting, or whether they lack the experience or information necessary to arrive at more critical judgments" (229).

14. Numerous theoretical accounts discuss the individual-level consequences of participation. See, for example, Almond and Verba 1963; Barber 1984; Huntington 1968; Huntington and Nelson 1976; Mill 1948; Pateman 1970; Radcliff and Wingenbach 2000; Rousseau 1968; Scaff 1975; Tocqueville 1945; Verba, Schlozman, and Brady 1995. For reviews of literature on participation, see Mansbridge 1995; Nelson 1987; Salisbury 1975; Thompson 1970.

15. For empirical research on participatory consequences in developed democracies, see Almond and Verba 1963; Brehm and Rahn 1997; Clarke and Acock 1989; Finkel 1985, 1987; Jackman 1972; Muller, Seligson, and Turan 1987; Pateman 1970; Rahn, Brehm, and Carlson 1999; Sullivan, Piereson, and Marcus 1982; Verba, Schlozman, and Brady 1995.

16. Examples of recent books on the causes of participation in old and new democracies include Bratton, Mattes, and Gyimah-Boadi 2005; Dalton 2004; Norris 2002; Rose and Munro 2003; Rosenstone and Hansen 1993; Verba, Schlozman, and Brady 1995.

attitudes but that initial attitudes did not determine who participated. Studies of the causes of participation that do not address the possibility of reciprocal effects may generate spurious results.

This study contributes to the growing new institutionalist literature on political trust. The influence of participation on trust is undertheorized and inadequately tested. This book outlines a comprehensive theory linking participation, institutional performance, and trust that is relevant beyond the specific case.[17] In addition, most of the literature on trust focuses on what makes institutions trustworthy. I look to the two understudied components in the new institutionalist perspective: (1) access to information on institutional trustworthiness and (2) evaluation of that information (Hardin 1998, 12; Levi 1998; Norris 1999; Putnam, Pharr, and Dalton 2000, 23–25). I provide empirical evidence that participation is associated with those two components. Moreover, I demonstrate that both citizens' knowledge of institutional performance and their criteria for evaluating performance predict institutional trust. Thus, this work offers valuable theory and evidence on the understudied links between individuals and institutions.

Finally, this book engages the debate between proponents of the traditional elite model of constitution making and advocates of the new participatory approach.[18] The participatory model has the potential to advance a culture of democratic constitutionalism that will support the new system. Citizens who are involved in constitution making are more likely to know and care about the constitution; however, participation does not automatically confer constitutional legitimacy, as advocates have assumed. Most citizens lack the information and skills to evaluate the fairness of the constitution-making process on their own, and they turn to local leaders for guidance. As a result, elites mediate between participation and constitutional legitimacy, especially in places where citizens lack independent sources of information about the constitution. If the elites are divided and debates are antagonistic, then citizens are likely to develop polarized views

17. For example, to explain the decline in institutional trust in the United States, scholars often argue that an expansion of government in the post–World War II period raised citizen expectations (Norris 1999, 22). My theory suggests that participation could also have been responsible for raising expectations. It is possible that new forms of participation that emerged in the 1960s altered participants' ideas about how government should be performing (see Tarrow 2000). Furthermore, new information technologies have expanded the information on government performance that is available to active citizens. In short, changes in citizen engagement with government may have contributed to the decline in political trust in the United States.

18. Some of the more comprehensive and up-to-date examinations of comparative constitution making include Elster, Offe, and Preuss 1998; Greenberg et al. 1993; Hart 2003; A. Howard 1993; Hyden and Venter 2001; U.S. Institute of Peace 2005; Widner 2005a, 2005b.

of the process and the constitution. In a polity with a robust opposition and no consensus, participatory constitution making can reduce constitutional legitimacy. The conclusion suggests possible remedies to minimize the polarization of public views while still providing for public involvement in constitution making.

CHAPTER 1

Prospects and Pitfalls of Participation

Is democracy helped or harmed when previously inert citizens become active and influential in politics? Democracy requires at least a minimum of public participation, but greater participation (more participants engaging in more activities with more influence) is not necessarily good for civic culture and democracy. The debate about participation's influence is enduring, voluminous, contentious, and cyclical. Whereas the pessimistic view that direct and pervasive citizen involvement threatens democracy had more adherents in past eras, today the optimistic view that participation enhances democracy is once again ascendant—perhaps with greater allegiance than ever before. Scholars and policymakers currently advocate mass involvement in domains, such as constitution making, that were previously restricted to lawyers, political leaders, and constitutional experts. In addition, participatory policies are often recommended for poor, transitioning polities despite pessimists' warnings that participation poses the greatest threat in these environments. Does participation in constitution making enhance or impair democratic prospects? Do participants become more supportive of or hostile toward fledgling democratic rules, norms, and institutions? What theoretical approach best explains the effects of participation on participants' political culture?

This chapter begins with the debate about participation's influence on democracy, paying close attention to the hypothesized individual-level mechanisms associated with macro-level outcomes. So far, theoreticians and policymakers rather than empiricists have dominated the debate. The literature lacks empirical verification, causal specificity, and relevance to current discussions of democratization, and these deficiencies impair our understanding of the effects of participation. It is striking that precisely the same problems emerge in assessments of the virtues and vices of participatory constitution making. This finding leads me to develop a revised theoretical perspective on how participation affects individuals.

1.1. MASS PARTICIPATION: HANDMAIDEN OR HINDRANCE TO DEMOCRACY?

Scholars disagree about whether widespread public involvement sustains, subverts, or is inconsequential for democratic politics. This section reviews the optimistic, pessimistic, and intermediate perspectives and then expounds on the shortcomings of the debate thus far.

Participation Helps Democracy

The most prevalent view today is optimistic about the ability of citizens to deepen and strengthen democratic governance through vibrant, expansive, and direct participation in politics. The current optimism about participation is based on a rich literature that extols the benefits of deliberation, consultation, and direct public involvement in government. Scholars argue that participation facilitates the flow of reliable information so that resulting policies are high quality, appropriate to circumstances, and congruent with citizen preferences. Mass involvement prevents tyranny and ensures government accountability because an aggrieved public can penalize incompetent, corrupt, or inattentive leaders. Participation bolsters the legitimacy of rules and rulers and thus engenders compliance and facilitates the rule of law. Finally, citizen inclusion promotes stability by teaching individuals to accommodate opposing views and by channeling potentially disruptive and violent energy into peaceful, institutionalized mechanisms for resolving grievances.[1]

Theorists often assert or imply that system-level benefits (effectiveness, accountability, legitimacy, capacity, and stability) result from changes at the individual level. By participating, citizens acquire political awareness, skills, internal and external efficacy,[2] trust, satisfaction, tolerance, civic-mindedness, attachment to democratic principles, and self-realization. Changes in citizen attitudes, knowledge, and behavior are thought to be essential for democratic development. In addition, these hypothesized

1. For theoretical accounts of the consequences of participation, see Almond and Verba 1963; Barber 1984; Finkel 1987, 2003; Hirschman 1970; Huntington 1991; Mill 1948; Mutz 2002; Pateman 1970; Radcliff and Wingenbach 2000; Rosenstone and Hansen 1993; Rousseau 1968; Salisbury 1975; Scaff 1975; Tocqueville 1945; Verba, Schlozman, and Brady 1995. For reviews of literature on participation, see Nelson 1987; Salisbury 1975; Thompson 1970.
2. According to Clarke and Acock, "Internal efficacy is the perception that one has the requisite skills and resources to influence the political system. External efficacy is the perception that government institutions and elites are responsive to one's attempts to exert political influence" (1989, 552). Subjective political capability, the variable that I investigate in chapter 3, is a crucial component of internal efficacy, while external efficacy is similar to the concept of institutional trust.

changes benefit the individual participant as well as the system. Theorists view human development as a valuable goal in and of itself.

The developmental theory of participation—the idea that participation develops the democratic characteristics of participants—can be traced back to classical democratic theorists such as Aristotle, Rousseau, Tocqueville, and Mill.[3] For Mill (1948, chapter 5), the developmental effects of participation provide the best justification for democratic institutions:

> In many cases, though individuals may not do the particular thing so well, on the average, as the officers of government, it is nevertheless desirable that it should be done by them, rather than by the government, as a means to their own mental education—a mode of strengthening their active faculties, exercising their judgment, and giving a familiar knowledge of the subjects with which they are thus left to deal.

Contemporary participatory theorists revived and built on the developmental perspective from classical liberal theorists. Barber (1984), Mansbridge (1995), Pateman (1970), and Thompson (1970) argue that participation (1) strengthens citizens' commitments to community and government by putting people in contact with their wider surroundings; (2) educates participants to become more knowledgeable about relevant issues, tolerant of opposing views, and realistic about policy interests; (3) legitimizes rules, institutions, leaders, and policy outcomes by allowing citizens to influence decision-making processes; and (4) builds the public's capacity and desire for additional involvement by providing practice, expressive benefits, and social support to those who become involved.[4]

The developmental theory of participation reasons that civic participation, knowledge, and attitudes are interrelated in three ways that create virtuous cycles. First, the hypothesized effects of participation are uniformly positive. Therefore, more participation is always beneficial.[5] Second, participation creates mutually supportive webs of benefits, where one resulting attitude reinforces another. Participation increases efficiency; efficiency re-

3. For reviews of classical literature on participation, see Mansbridge 1995; Pateman 1970; Salisbury 1975.
4. For additional references to developmental effects of participation, see Clarke and Acock 1989; Finkel 1987; Hirschman 1970; Nelson 1987; Nie, Junn, and Stehlik-Barry 1996; Putnam 1993; Radcliff and Wingenbach 2000; Rosenstone and Hansen 1993; Verba, Nie, and Kim 1978; Verba, Schlozman, and Brady 1995.
5. For example, Thompson (1970) has a subsection, "The Desirability of More Participation," in which he argues that citizenship theorists believe that more participation is always desirable (67–72).

inforces social trust; social trust builds support for government institutions; institutional trust fosters attachment to the underlying democratic principles; democratic principles make citizens feel more efficacious; and so on. Third, a feedback loop exists between participation and its individual-level consequences; participation produces changes in attitudes and knowledge that facilitate even greater participation. Pateman (1970, 25) emphasizes the reciprocal effect of participation and developmental change:

> Once the participatory system is established, and this is a point of major importance, it becomes self-sustaining because the very qualities that are required of individual citizens if the system is to work successfully are those that the process of participation itself develops and fosters; the more the individual citizen participates the better able he is to do so. The human results that accrue through the participatory process provide an important justification for a participatory system.

From the developmental viewpoint, public policies should be targeted at encouraging maximum participation as a means of jump-starting a virtuous cycle of democratic development.

Contemporary scholars "rediscovered" the classical writings on participation at the same time that the United States witnessed a flourishing of public and private attention to participation. Both normative theory on participation and the practice of encouraging participation "rose in the 1960s, flourished in the 1970s and waned in the 1980s" (Mansbridge 1995).[6] As it waned in the United States and other advanced industrial democracies, policy interest in encouraging participation shifted to the developing world.[7] As it became apparent that democratization and economic growth required not only new formal institutions but also changes in mass attitudes, knowledge, and behavior, policymakers and activists increasingly looked to participation to induce the desired changes. For example, Stiglitz (2002, 165) argues that participation is especially important because it changes attitudes, not just policies:

6. In the past decade, research on civil society and concern about declining participation rates reinvigorated interest in mass political involvement in advanced industrial democracies.

7. If questioned about whether their theories would apply equally to participation in nondemocratic regimes, some if not all of the participatory theorists mentioned would certainly say no, even though most do not explicitly specify the type of political system in their works. However, most current policy programs and academic writings argue that participation is useful everywhere and especially in the developing world (Sen 1999; Stiglitz 2002). I refer to these current understandings when I evaluate the hypotheses of the optimistic developmental theory of participation.

If a change in mindset is at the center of development, then it is clear that attention needs to be shifted to how to affect such changes in mindset. Such changes cannot be "ordered" or forced from the outside, however well-intentioned the outsiders may be. Change has to come from within. The kinds of open and extensive discussions that are central to participatory processes are, I suspect, the most effective way of ensuring that the change in mindset occurs not only within a small elite, but reaches deep down in society.

Later in the article, Stiglitz (2002, 168) elaborated on participation's benefits for development:

Participation is thus essential to effect the systemic change in mindset associated with the development transformation, and to engender policies that make change—which is at the center of development—more acceptable. And because individuals have had a voice in shaping the changes, in making them more acceptable, change is likely to be accepted or even embraced, rather than reversed at the first opportunity.

Current policy documents on the developing world mirror normative academic arguments on the developmental benefits of participation. Both assert that participation is important not only for its utilitarian benefits at the system level but also for individual self-realization and its effects on citizens' psyches. For example, political participation is the main focus of the *Human Development Report 2002* published by the United Nations Development Programme (UNDP):

Political freedom and participation are part of human development both as development goals in their own right and as means for advancing human development. Political freedom and the ability to participate in the life of one's community are capabilities that are as important for human development as being able to read and write and being in good health. People without political freedom—such as being able to join associations and to form and express opinions—have far fewer choices in life. And being able to participate in the life of one's community—commanding the respect of others and having a say in communal decisions—is fundamental to human existence. (2002, 52)[8]

---

8. This particular policy document most closely reflects Sen's ideas: "Such processes as participation in political decisions and social choice cannot be seen as being—at best—among the means of development (through, say, their contribution to economic growth), but have to be understood as constitutive parts of the end of development in themselves" (1999, 291).

Facilitating participation is not only the concern of international agencies and nongovernmental organizations but also the target of numerous bilateral donor funds and energies. For example, in the strategic plan of the Center for Democracy and Governance of the U.S. Agency for International Development (USAID), two of the seven stated goals are "reinforc[ing] the principles of inclusion, participation, and peaceful competition in all sectors of society" and "facilitat[ing] a deepening of citizen participation and cultural commitment to democratic norms" (USAID 2000, 1). Of the approximately $700 million annual budget for USAID's support for democratic governance, a considerable portion is devoted to widening and deepening participation by promoting high turnout for elections, strengthening outreach by political parties, fostering participatory and active civil society, and decentralizing government decision making (USAID 2000, annex A). In addition, participation of the target population is now a requirement for most economic development projects. In short, many policymakers have adopted the optimistic normative claims of the developmental theory of participation and actively encourage mass public involvement in transitioning states through international, multilateral, bilateral, and domestic programs.

While the international community has recently come to embrace and support participatory campaigns in developing countries, Africa also has a strong historical tradition that extols the benefits of public participation. Drawing on community traditions and late colonial doctrines, independence leaders in states such as Tanzania, Kenya, Zambia, and Ghana initially promoted the idea of participation as central to development. However, following independence, authoritarian leaders increasingly sought to control, contain, and limit public involvement in most of Africa (Kasfir 1976). The 1990s brought the resurgence and reworking of earlier doctrines that emphasize mass participation as the key to economic, social, and political development in Africa.

Participation Harms Democracy

In sharp contrast to the optimistic developmental perspective, some scholars assert that high levels of direct citizen involvement threaten democratic stability and performance.[9] Most of those who are pessimistic about participation acknowledge that democracy requires some citizen involvement (most notably in electing representatives). However, they assert that participation threatens democracy when political activity extends beyond capable

---

9. Nelson groups these scholars under the heading "conservative critics of liberal assumptions" (1987, 114).

and rational citizens periodically exerting mediated influence through formal institutionalized channels. Because ordinary citizens should play only a circumscribed role in politics, programs that increase levels of participation or expand the realms of citizen involvement will do more harm than good. These pessimistic assessments often come from scholars who study nondemocratic, transitioning, and resource-poor polities, and their theories reflect the differences in context. The pessimists are not unified in their arguments about how participation might lead to negative outcomes, so I sort the arguments into four general categories: (1) the elitist outlook; (2) the traditional-modern viewpoint; (3) the instrumental approach; and (4) the focus on institutionalization.[10]

The elitist perspective claims that the typical citizen is ill informed, uninterested, and easily deceived; when too many ordinary people become involved in politics or when their influence on politicians is unmediated, the system is threatened.[11] Not only are most people poorly equipped to make intelligent political decisions, but the act of participating can magnify their initial weaknesses. Citizens are likely to become disillusioned when they are incapable of understanding the political process and fail to realize their expected rewards. Ordinary people become easy targets of deception and extremism when they enter the political sphere (Adorno 1950; Lipset 1960). Elitists fear that extensive direct involvement of the masses will result in irrational government policies and even democratic breakdown because the public can be easily manipulated to act against the system. These dangers are especially acute when citizens lack education and experience with democratic governance.

The traditional-modern perspective argues that civic participation in societies dominated by traditional social structures and attachments will reduce political trust (Ekeh 1975; Kasfir 1976; Lipset 1959; Melson and Wolpe 1970).[12] Primordial publics feel alienated by modern bureaucratic

10. Most of the "conservative critics" focus on the system-level effects of participation. Although the individual-level mechanisms are typically not specified, they can often be inferred.

11. Thompson (1970, 22–26) singles out Lippman and Shumpeter as elitist scholars, and Pateman (1970, 2–21) discusses Mosca, Michels, and Schumpeter, although she also links the elitist approach to Berelson, Dahl, Sartori, and Eckstein. Walker (1966) references Beer, Berelson, Dahl, Hartz, Lipset, Key, Mayo, Milbrath, McClosky, Morris-Jones, Polsby, Schumpeter, and Truman in his discussion of the elitist theory of democracy. However, see Dahl 1966 for a rebuttal.

12. Distrust is one of the deleterious effects discussed in the literature critiquing the developmental perspective. The pessimistic critics (like the optimistic adherents of the developmental perspective) assume that trust is good and distrust is bad. I differ from these critics not only in my explanation for the cause of distrust but also in my assessment of the repercussions of distrust. Distrust can be beneficial for political development and for democracy.

systems that do not respond to personalized appeals or respect traditional hierarchies. This perspective also predicts that when communal identities (such as ethnicity and religion) form the basis for political action, participation will heighten conflict over resources, widen societal cleavages, foster intolerance, and harden divergent opinions. When citizens are motivated by primordial ties rather than cross-cutting affiliations, popular participation threatens system stability.

According to the instrumental perspective, citizens participate to capture state benefits, gain power, protect individual interests, and monitor government agents. If participants do not succeed, they will become alienated from the system.[13] Negative outcomes are especially likely in resource-scarce polities or times of economic crisis, when competition to secure wealth is particularly fierce (Berman 1997; Linz and Stepan 1978).

The last approach focuses on institutional capacity. Huntington (1968) argues that polities are vulnerable to instability and disorder when participation overwhelms institutional capacity. Social mobilization resulting from economic development prompts citizens to demand more from government. The anemic institutional structures in the Third World are insufficient to accommodate new demands and increases in participation. Participation spills out of legal and institutionalized channels into illegal, disruptive behavior. Frustrated citizens turn against the system. The overly active population threatens democratic stability.

Scholars from all four pessimistic perspectives tend to focus on how participation threatens the political system as a whole. However, like the optimists, the pessimists often assert or imply that the effects of participation at the system level (inefficiency, polarization, conflict, and democratic breakdown) result from changes at the individual level. Participants become misinformed, intolerant, frustrated, distrustful, extremist, and antidemocratic. These disenchanted citizens elect authoritarian leaders, disregard the law, become violent, fight their opponents, and surrender their democratic liberties in favor of security and prosperity.

In response to the anticipated dangers of mass involvement, leaders have sought to limit participation and insulate themselves from citizen influence. Kasfir (1976, 26–27) argues, "In subsaharan black Africa most leaders act as if they perceive participation—especially ethnic participation—as a distinct threat to the nation. They respond by introducing policies that cause many Africans to depart from the political arena." Leaders interested in protecting

---

13. For reviews of the instrumental perspective, see Bermeo 2003, 11–17; Finkel 2000; Salisbury 1975, 326–29; Scaff 1975.

their positions are not the only entities searching for mechanisms to restrict popular participation—aid organizations, foundations, and academics have expressed similar sentiments. In a recent study of mass publics, Bermeo (2003, 17) writes, "The desire to maintain and consolidate electoral democracy despite the citizenry's alleged inadequacies led many scholars to focus on questions of institutional design. What sorts of political institutions could best constrain the popular tendencies that worked against democracy?" Repressing activists and restricting suffrage are no longer considered legitimate policies, but other constraining mechanisms are widely advocated, including the creation of elite upper houses of Parliament, prohibitions on ethnicity-based parties, provisions for unelected or indirectly elected leaders, and laws insulating central banks, judges, and bureaucracies from popular influence. Such policies designed to constrain participation and limit citizen influence are at odds with those derived from the optimistic developmental perspective of participation.

Minimal, Mixed, and Contingent Effects of Participation

Between the optimistic and pessimistic schools of thought are four different perspectives that conclude that the effects of the mass public on democracy are minimal, mixed, or contingent on other factors.

The first perspective asserts that ordinary citizens have little influence on political fortunes, especially outside of advanced industrial democracies. The initial literature on democratization focused primarily on elites and ascribed little power to ordinary people (O'Donnell, Schmitter, and Whitehead 1986; more recently, see Bermeo 2003). This elite bias was motivated, at least in part, by the initial attention to the transition phase of democratization; elite decisions and actions are critical short-term stimuli for system breakdown and transition, while the influence of mass publics is more distant. The emphasis on elites was reinforced by the influential early cases of transition in Southern Europe and Latin America. The elite bias in the democratization literature began to erode as attention shifted to the consolidation phase of democratization, where mass attitudes and actions seem to play a larger role than in the transition phase. The general public also had a greater influence on the later cases of democratization in the former Soviet bloc and Africa than on the earlier cases in Southern Europe and Latin America (Bratton and van de Walle 1997; Bunce 2000). Today, most scholars acknowledge that ordinary citizens play at least some role in democratization, but attention to the influence of mass participation is relatively recent and still somewhat limited.

The second perspective also asserts that participatory programs are unlikely to affect democratic development but makes this argument for different reasons. These scholars acknowledge that mass political culture affects democratic outcomes but question participation's ability to bring about cultural change, especially in the short term. They assert that political culture is a function of long-term socialization and long-standing structural factors. Orientation and behavior are not subject to short-term manipulation (Almond and Verba 1963; Easton 1965).[14] Attempts to engineer cultural change through occasional acts of participation are unlikely to have a notable effect on the beliefs and behavior of citizens. While political culture is important, societies are typically stuck with what they have.

Scholars recently have questioned common assumptions of cultural stability. Based on statistical analysis of survey data, researchers assert that adult learning and experience play an important role in attitude formation.[15] In addition, studies of equilibriums and path dependence suggest that initial conditions can predict attitudes and behavior for generations to come, yet critical events—such as regime transitions—provide opportunities for democratic changes in political culture as well as in institutions.[16] Despite this recent literature, the assumption that political culture is fixed in the short term remains prominent in the field.

A third perspective argues that citizen activism is beneficial, but only in moderation. Almond and Verba (1963, 360) conclude from their five-nation study that the most conducive political culture for democracy includes a mixture of active and passive citizens. In a civic culture, "there is political activity, but not so much as to destroy government authority; there is involvement and commitment, but they are moderated; there is political cleavage, but it is held in check." Hirschman (1970, 31–32) echoes this sentiment when he argues that both voice and exit are necessary for system performance. Too much voice can overwhelm the system, but a "mixture of alert and inert citizens, or even an alternation of involvement and withdrawal, may serve democracy better then total, permanent activism or total apathy." The moderate-participation school does not give much indication of what level of participation is optimal, but adherents would probably take

---

14. For discussions of cultural stability and change, see Eckstein 1988; Finkel 2003; Mishler and Rose 1997.

15. For evidence of attitude change among adults, see Bratton, Mattes, and Gyimah-Boadi 2005; Brehm and Rahn 1997; Eckstein 1988; Finkel 2003; Gibson 1996; Mishler and Rose 1997.

16. See, for example, Bardhan 1997; Bates 1990; Calvert 1995; Hyden and Venter 2001; Nabli and Nugent 1989; Weingast 1997.

issue with the optimistic policy prescriptions to increase participation as much as possible as well as with pessimistic prescriptions for strict constraints on citizen involvement.

Finally, a growing number of scholars are realizing that the effects of participation are contingent on intervening variables. Participation is beneficial if citizens are well informed, involvement is meaningful, cleavages cut across one another, civil society is robust and pluralistic, institutions are trustworthy, the state is efficacious, electoral institutions are tailored to fit circumstances, and parties and other representative institutions are well developed. If these fortuitous conditions are absent, participation can be harmful for democracy. In response to mixed empirical findings and theoretical critiques, many contemporary scholars moderated the overly optimistic or pessimistic predictions of earlier theorists. As Radcliff and Wingenbach (2000, 984) note,

> Collectively, the recent literature argues for a more sophisticated and contextualized understanding of the conditions in which participation best fosters political skills, but it does not seriously call into question the existing consensus that participation does have developmental consequences.

Radcliff and Wingenbach also assert that the conditions under which participation produces developmental benefits are undertheorized and undertested. Many current scholars of participation would agree that context matters, but we do not yet understand how it matters.

Limitations of the Participation Debate

The theoretical debate about the consequences of participation is old and lively. However, it is not as illuminating as it could be. One problem is the failure to specify the causal mechanisms linking participation and democracy. Most theorists focus on the macro level without carefully considering the micro-level causes and effects.[17] Those who do focus on individual traits (that is, adherents of the developmental theory of participation) often theorize about participation in isolation from the context. Optimists argue that

---

17. Studies that examine the consequences of political participation at the system level of analysis typically test the effect of participation on (1) national economic growth and inequality; (2) political stability, responsiveness, and efficiency of the state; and (3) social cleavages and conflict between groups. See, for example, Bates 1981; Deutsch 1961; Hirschman 1970; Huntington 1968; Lipset 1959; Nelson 1987; Olson 1982; Przeworski and Limongi 1993; Putnam 1993; Schmitter and Karl 1996; Sen 1994; Shin 1994.

participation generates knowledge, democratic values, trust, and efficacy, but they do not consider how these individual traits interact with each other and with contextual factors to produce democratic deficits and strengths in a given country. Pessimists assume that participants who do not get what they want will turn against democracy without considering how individuals attribute blame to leaders, institutions, and systems. Both optimists and pessimists pay too little attention to the role of knowledge and expectations in attitude formation. They also tend to underestimate the durability of citizen attitudes, knowledge, and behavior and thus fail to consider the conditions necessary for participation to have an effect.

Second, empirical evidence on the consequences of participation (as opposed to the causes) is extremely thin, especially at the individual level of analysis. Finkel (1987, 442) laments that "developmental notions have largely been neglected in empirical literature. There has been little previous work done which investigates the individual-level effects of political participation or the ways in which various acts influence political attitudes or orientations." Given the large body of theoretical writing on the developmental effects of participation and the widespread implementation of policy programs based on the normative arguments, it is surprising that systematic empirical investigations are so few and far between. As long as the arguments on either side of the debate are based on theoretical conviction rather than empirical research, the debate will remain contentious and progress will be slow.

The limited empirical evidence that does exist is inconsistent, though optimistic predictions receive more overall support than do the pessimistic ones. For example, past research indicates that (1) workplace participation in the United States leads to feelings of harmony and competence;[18] (2) U.S. citizens feel more capable in states that facilitate direct participation through initiatives;[19] (3) voting in the United States increases external efficacy;[20] (4) campaigning fosters external efficacy[21] and democratic attitudes[22] in the United States and internal efficacy in West Germany;[23] (5) associational involvement heightens efficacy and skills in five nations[24]

18. See Pateman 1970.
19. See Bowler and Donovan 2002.
20. See Finkel 1985; Rahn, Brehm, and Carlson 1999.
21. See Finkel 1985.
22. See Muller, Seligson, and Turan 1987.
23. See Finkel 1987.
24. See Almond and Verba 1963.

as well as tolerance and civic-mindedness[25] and social trust in the United States;[26] and (6) civic education fosters tolerance, efficacy, social trust, civic behavior, and democratic attitudes.[27] However, the studies also present evidence that participation in elections and campaigns does not significantly alter efficacy and democratic attitudes.[28]

The evidence on institutional trust (and the similar concept of regime support) is the most limited and contradictory. Rahn, Brehm, and Carlson (1999) find that voting and campaigning have no effect on political trust in the United States. In a panel study of West Germany, Finkel (1987) establishes that voting leads to an increase in regime support, but campaigning has no effect and aggressive political participation has a negative effect. Finkel (2003) records a positive effect of civic education in South Africa and a negative effect in the Dominican Republic. Bratton and Alderfer (1999) observe the same negative influence of civic education in Zambia. Brehm and Rahn (1997) note that associational participation decreases citizen confidence in government in the United States. Considerably more empirical research is needed to augment and untangle these contradictory and complex results.

Third, an unhelpful disjuncture exists between the locations and types of participation that have been studied and the participatory programs that

---

25. See Verba, Schlozman, and Brady 1995.

26. See Brehm and Rahn 1997.

27. See Bratton and Alderfer 1999; Finkel 2003; Finkel, Sabatini, and Bevis 2000. While civic education is typically thought of as distinct from participation, research on the effects of civic education can offer insights into what we should expect from participation in Uganda's constitution-making activities as well as participatory programs in other states undergoing transition. Because citizens lack previous knowledge and experience with participation, all types of participation programs in fledgling democracies often include a civic-education component, such as voter education, leadership training, or rights education.

28. Jackman (1972) and Sullivan, Piereson, and Marcus (1982) conclude that there is no relationship between participation and the democratic attitudes of tolerance and support for freedom to oppose government once education was taken into account. Muller, Seligson, and Turan (1987) also find no relationship between campaigning and tolerance in their studies of Turkey and Costa Rica (though they do find a positive relationship for the United States). Clarke and Acock (1989) conclude that voting and campaigning in U.S. presidential and congressional elections does not affect internal or external efficacy; knowing that the preferred candidate won, rather than the act of participation, is associated with efficacy. Finkel's (1985) analysis of the United States shows no significant relationship between voting or campaigning and internal efficacy (though he finds a relationship with external efficacy). In his panel study of West Germany, Finkel (1987) finds that voting is not significantly related to internal efficacy (though voting is related to regime support) and that campaigning is not significantly related to regime support (though campaigning is related to internal efficacy). Finally, Rahn, Brehm, and Carlson (1999) show that campaign activity is not significantly related to external efficacy or political trust and that voting is not significantly related to political trust (though voting is related to external efficacy).

policymakers currently advocate. Although many participatory policy programs are directed at poor, transitioning countries, scholarship has focused largely on advanced industrial democracies. Academics have also overlooked the forms of participation that policymakers are most actively encouraging at present—attending local government meetings, contacting leaders, providing input on development projects, and constitution making. The studies reviewed previously illustrate the limited geographic distribution and scope of participatory venues receiving scholarly attention. Most studies have been conducted in the United States: one investigates participation in the workplace (Pateman 1970); several find effects of participation in associations (Brehm and Rahn 1997; Verba, Schlozman, and Brady 1995); and several more show the consequences of standard electoral participation (Clarke and Acock 1989; Finkel 1985; Jackman 1972; Muller, Seligson, and Turan 1987; Rahn, Brehm, and Carlson 1999; Sullivan, Piereson, and Marcus 1982). Five studies have been conducted outside the United States: one examines the effects of electoral and violent participation in West Germany (Finkel 1987); another analyzes the outcomes of campaigning in Costa Rica and Turkey (Muller, Seligson, and Turan 1987); another investigates the influence of associational participation in five nations (Almond and Verba 1963); and two research the effects of civic education in three developing countries (Bratton and Alderfer 1999; Finkel, Sabatini, and Bevis 2000). To my knowledge, no empirical studies have examined the individual-level consequences of local government meetings, contacting, and voting in transitioning states or new democracies, where it is important to recognize that the consequences may affect not just the quality of democracy but also its survival.

Fourth, the study of participation has to date remained separate from other important issues of democratization, such as elite negotiations, legal development, institution creation, and state performance. Yet public participation is fundamental to these topics. Scholars of democratization have recently recognized a need to expand their analyses of elite crafting to include the study of mass public reactions to elite-brokered arrangements (Bratton 1999; Bratton and van de Walle 1997; Diamond 1993; Di Palma 1990; Huntington 1991; Linz and Stepan 1996; O'Donnell, Schmitter, and Whitehead 1986). Similarly, scholars of law and development have moved from attempts to discover the best universal legal formulas to the study of how law functions in society and how to build support for the rule of law (Ghai 1996; Mattei 1999; Okoth-Ogendo 1991; Shivji 1991; Widner

2001). Institutional scholars have turned their attention toward the creation of informal institutions—such as political norms and culture—that support formal democratic structures (Calvert 1995; Granovetter 1973; Knight 1995; Laitin 1994; March and Olsen 1989; Nee 1998; North 1994; Ostrom 1990; Weingast 1997). Institutionalists now recognize that institutional trust and legitimacy are based on how individuals perceive government performance (Levi 1998; Pharr and Putnam 2000). The study of political participation should play a central role in each of these fields, yet it has so far remained isolated from these important topics.

This book seeks to respond to these deficiencies by analyzing the effects of citizen involvement in the Ugandan constitution-making process. Uganda is one of a number of countries that recently employed extensive popular participation in the process of crafting new constitutions. These countries—which historically have been plagued by conflict, instability, divisions, and authoritarian rule—sought to use participation to engineer norms and behaviors that would support the democratic institutions under construction. The move toward public participation in constitution making represents a dramatic change from the past, and not everyone has welcomed this change. The debates about the values and dangers of participatory constitution making reflect the more general debates about participation and democracy reviewed previously. As such, constitution making is a key arena that allows us to respond in a particularly illuminating way to questions about participation.

1.2. PARTICIPATORY CONSTITUTION MAKING: PANACEA OR POISON?

The current wave of political and economic liberalization has produced an explosion of constitution-making activity and a reevaluation of the best practices for constitutional reform. Several countries have adjusted the traditional elite-driven constitution-making model to provide for the direct inclusion of mass publics. Considerable disagreement about the virtues and vices of participatory constitution making has arisen, but little empirical data has been compiled to inform the debate. In particular, little is known about the effect of participatory constitution making on the political culture of ordinary people.

In recent decades, constitutional reform has reached unprecedented levels. More than half of the national constitutions in existence today have been changed or created anew in the past twenty-five years (Hart 2003,

2).[29] From 1990 to 2000 alone, seventeen African states, at least fourteen Latin American states, and nearly all the postcommunist states in Central Europe and the former Soviet Union drastically altered their constitutions or wrote new ones (Van Cott 2000). Authoritarian rulers are facing serious challenges in Africa, Central Asia, and the Middle East, indicating that constitution-building activities are likely to continue. In recognition of past weaknesses and current opportunities, many scholars and practitioners are actively championing the participatory constitution-making model as the best way to achieve a culture of democratic constitutionalism. Against this clamor of support, a much quieter but historically stronger voice questions the desirability of open participatory processes, favoring instead elite-negotiated settlements.

The Evolution of Constitution Making

Constitution making has traditionally been conceived as an elite affair that lies outside the realm of everyday democratic politics. Hart (2003, 3) summarizes the traditional view: "We used to think of a constitution as a contract, negotiated by appropriate representatives, concluded, signed, and observed." Hart points to the U.S. Constitutional Convention, a well-known model of traditional constitution making. In 1787, fifty-five chosen men deliberated in secret and emerged with a completed constitution, which was then ratified by state leaders (Hart 2003, 2; see also Skach 2005). More generally, during the period of colonial independence and up until the third wave of democratization, constitution making remained under the custody of politicians, constitutional lawyers, and scholars. Until recently, direct involvement of the general public in constitution-making processes was considered unnecessary and even dangerous. A constitution was judged democratic according to the nature of its provisions, not by how it was created (Hart 2003).

The traditional model of constitution making came into question when the liberal democratic constitutions adopted during the second wave of democratization failed to engender liberal democratic governance. Leaders often disregarded constitutional limits on their power, while citizens seldom looked to constitutions for guidance or protection (Ghai 1996; Okoth-Ogendo 1991). As such, the renewed attention to constitutionalism in the third wave has been concerned not only with the content of constitutions but also with the development of supportive values (Oloka-Onyango and

---

29. Widner (2005b, 503) reports that "between 1975 and 2003, nearly 200 new constitutions appeared in countries at risk of conflict as part of peace processes and the adoption of multiparty political systems." For regional distributions by decade, see Widner 2005b, 508.

Ihonvbere 1999; Shivji 1991; Weingast 1997). Some observers argue that the general public's minimal knowledge about government rules and citizens' weak attachment to constitutional principles constitute major impediments to democratic development (Barya 1993; Ghai 1996; Hyden and Venter 2001; Klug 1996; Odoki 2005; Selassie 1999; Waliggo 1995; Weingast 1997).

Many current academics, activists, and policymakers concerned with fostering constitutionalism now focus less on the content of constitutions and more on the process of constitution making.[30] They assert that the nature of the constitution-making process has important implications for political culture as well as for the provisions and power arrangements embodied in the final document. Scholars and practitioners in search of a new model that would build legitimacy and create more durable institutions have focused on public participation. The initial cases of participatory constitution making devised by innovative reformers in Uganda and elsewhere sparked a new understanding of constitution making and a global change in policy practices:

> Clearly, there is an emerging trend toward providing for more direct and far-reaching popular participation in the constitution-making process, not only through the election of a constituent assembly or voting in a referendum on the proposed constitutional text, but also in the form of civic education and popular consultation in the development of the constitution. Some scholars refer to this as "new constitutionalism." Aspects of this approach have been employed around the world in recent years, including in Europe, Africa, Latin America, and Asia. (U.S. Institute of Peace 2005, 7)

Participatory programs vary in the activities employed, the scope of inclusion, the perceived legitimacy of the process, and the ultimate effect on

---

30. Studies of the process of constitution making are fairly recent. Elster (1993, 174) writes that "the comparative study of constitution-making is virtually non-existent. Comparative constitutional law is, needless to say, an established discipline. The comparative study of ordinary law making is a central field of political science. The comparative study of revolutions has a long history. But to my knowledge there is not a single book or even article discussing the process of constitution-making in a general comparative perspective. The gap is puzzling but it appears to be undeniable." Since Elster made that statement, a small but growing number of scholars have conducted case studies and comparative studies of constitution making; see, for example, Elster 1997, 1998; Gloppen 1997; Hart 2003; A. Howard 1993; Hyden and Venter 2001; Klug 1996; Lal 1997; Selassie 1998; Skach 2005; U.S. Institute of Peace 2005; Waliggo 1995; Widner 2005b.

the system, but they share the common characteristic of soliciting active citizen participation rather than relying on appointed representatives or expert deliberations.[31] Table 1.1 presents eight constitution-making programs that included considerable popular participation.[32]

The policy innovations displayed in table 1.1 were not developed in isolation; constitution makers typically consult international experts, read about other cases, and visit other new and old democracies in search of useful ideas.[33] Reformers today actively champion participatory programs for countries undergoing transition (Citizen's Forum for Constitutional Reform 1999; Commonwealth Human Rights Initiative 1999; Daruwala 2001; Hatchard 2001; Hyden and Venter 2001; Kuria 1996; Majome 1999; Wapakhabulo 2001). There are numerous calls for programs modeled off the successful cases in table 1.1. The United Nations Electoral Assistance Division and the Commonwealth Secretariat recommended the Fiji process as a model for countries undertaking constitutional review (Lal 2002).[34] The Commonwealth Human Rights Initiative (1999) developed a guide for best practices in constitution making that focused on "a process that constructively engages the largest majority of the population." In a letter to the chief justice of India, the initiative's director recommended that the country adopt a participatory constitutional review process modeled on the processes in South Africa, Eritrea, and Uganda (Daruwala 2001). A coalition of Nigerian civil society

---

31. McWhinney (1981, 27–33) outlines five methods of constitutional reform: the constituent assembly, parliamentary enactment, an expert commission, executive diplomacy, and the popular initiative via petition and referendum. He argues that constituent assemblies are most conducive to public participation. I dispute his claim. The cases described in table 1.1 employed combinations of all five methods while accommodating extensive public participation. Furthermore, the same methods can be used without allowing for participation. Hyden and Venter (2001, 216) argue that national conferences are less inclusive. See also Elster 1997 for a typology of different modes of constitution making.

32. Other programs also incorporated some degree of participation. However, the scope of inclusion, the type of activities, and the organizers' intentions distinguish these efforts as more participatory than most. Benomar (2004) asserts that the processes in Namibia, Colombia, and Brazil also included considerable public participation, as does the recent process in Kenya. East Timor also included significant public consultation, but like Brazil, the outcomes of the consultative phase were not sufficiently considered during the drafting phase (Kritz 2003). See Widner (2005b, 515) for data on the distribution of public consultation procedures by region.

33. For example, the Eritrean Commission organized an international symposium that included constitution-making experts from Ethiopia, Uganda, South Africa, Namibia, and Ghana. Fiji's commissioners visited South Africa, Malaysia, and Mauritius and solicited papers from international experts.

34. As another example, I attended a conference on constitutionalism in Africa sponsored by the Ford Foundation and the Faculty of Law at Makerere University and held at the International Conference Center in Kampala, Uganda, October 5–8, 1999. The heads of the Ugandan and Eritrean Constitutional Commissions presented papers on their experiences in a session on "The Way Ahead." Their descriptions launched a discussion of the best practices for the future.

TABLE 1.1. Selected Cases of Participatory Constitution Making

Trinidad and Tobago: 1971–73 Constitutional Commission
- Invitation of 35 organizations to private meetings (only 24 attended)
- Distribution of approximately 80,000 copies of booklet prepared by commission
- 39 public meetings in important centers throughout the country
- Receipt of 100 memoranda followed up by 24 meetings
- A miniconvention in Tobago and a national convention in Trinidad

Nicaragua: 1985–87 National Constituent Assembly and Consitutional Commissions
- 24 political, religious, labor, and professional associations meet with commission
- 150,000 copies of the first draft distributed and debated
- 12 televised public deliberations among representatives of opposing parties
- 73 *cabildos abiertos* (town meetings) throughout country involving 100,000 citizens
- 2,500 oral presentations and 1,800 written comments submitted

Uganda: 1988–95 Constitutional Commission (UCC) and Constituent Assembly (CA)
- UCC held 86 district and institutional seminars to sensitize public and elicit views
- Development and distribution of educational materials throughout country
- Commissioners participated in 83 radio programs and 20 television programs
- 2,763 newspaper articles on constitutional issues during UCC
- Commissioners twice attended seminars in all 813 subcounties, first to educate citizens and then to collect views
- 25,547 memoranda from individuals and groups collected, recorded, and analyzed
- CA Candidates Meetings in every parish, with nearly 45% of adult population attending
- 1994 election for CA, with participation by approximately 74% of all eligible voters
- Distribution of 100,000 abridged draft constitutions in six vernacular languages
- Drama troupes performed play about constitution in 170 locations
- Extensive citizen lobbying and media coverage during 16 months of CA debate, including weekly radio program by NGO group

South Africa: 1994–95 Constitutional Assembly (CA)
- 1994 election for Parliament (which also served as CA), with participation by approximately 81% of all eligible voters
- Consultations with the public at the village level by each of the parties
- Assembly published newspaper with a circulation of 160,000
- Educational campaign through media, billboards, and Internet reached 73% of population
- Publication of all debates within the CA
- Collection of nearly 2,000,000 submissions from public during the comment period

Fiji: 1995–96 Constitution Review Commission (Reeves Commission)[a]
- Public hearings throughout Fiji
- Collection, publication, and review of 852 oral and written submissions
- Commissioning of research papers
- Broadcasting of debates and citizen memoranda on the constitution

Eritrea: 1995–97 Constitutional Commission
- Seminars and public discussions throughout the country
- Civic educational campaign that reached 557,000 of 3,000,000 citizens
- Radio programs, dramas, and poetry competitions to teach illiterate population
- Village-based debates on constitutional proposals

Albania: 1997–98 Constitutional Commission
- Establishment of independent body, Administrative Center for the Coordination of Assistance and Public Participation, to promote public involvement
- Symposia and NGO discussions produced recommendations and identified issues

TABLE 1.1—Continued

- Three-part television series summarizing constitutional debates
- Broad-based review of the draft constitution, including public hearings
- Civic-education campaigns, including television and radio call-in shows, newspaper serials, essay contests, and dissemination of pamphlets and issue papers

Rwanda: 2000–3 Constitutional Commission
- Six months spent on local programs and debates
- Referendum with 90% turnout and 93% of voters approving the constitution
- US$7 million budget for participatory constitution-making activities

[a]The Reeves Commission was Fiji's third experience with participatory constitution making. In 1987 the Falvey Committee collected 800 written and 161 oral submissions, visited centers outside Suva, and included comments from the council of chiefs. The Manueli committee organized 32 hearings in 14 rural and urban centers in 1988 and collected submissions between November 1988 and May 1989. The Reeves Commission began in a participatory manner, but the later decision-making stage of the process was largely isolated from public input (Benomar 2004, 90; Lal 1997, 2002).

organizations, the Citizen's Forum for Constitutional Reform (1999), drew on experiences in other African countries to argue that the "participatory approach to constitution making is probably one of the best panaceas to instability, public cynicism, and alienation from government, coups, and counter coups." The U.S. Institute of Peace (USIP) and the UNDP conducted a study of eighteen countries[35] and concluded that "participatory constitution making is today a fact of constitutional life as well as good in itself" (Hart 2003, 2) as well as that "emerging norms call for broad participation by civil society and the public" and that "constitutions produced without transparency and adequate public participation will lack legitimacy" (Benomar 2004, 88, 89). These are just some of the many calls to extend the participatory model to new places.

Faith in the new participatory model is so strong that policymakers and scholars encourage mass participation even where conditions seem prohibitive, such as in Iraq. The Coalition Provisional Authority in Iraq originally intended to appoint an elite constitution-making body according to the traditional model. However, leaders inside Iraq and advisers from abroad argued that mass involvement was necessary if the process was to be viewed

---

35. This extensive study examines how constitution-making processes impact conflict resolution and peace building in eighteen countries: Albania, Bosnia and Herzegovina, Brazil, Cambodia, Colombia, East Timor, Eritrea, Ethiopia, Fiji, Hungary, Namibia, Nicaragua, Poland, South Africa, Spain, Uganda, Venezuela, and Zimbabwe. This comparative case-study analysis is extremely useful in providing lessons about the consequences of different constitution-making practices. However, the case studies remain at the macro level of analysis and do not systematically examine the individual-level consequences of the programs; they rely on expert assessments of how participatory programs affected mass attitudes and knowledge without explicitly testing the accuracy of those claims.

as legitimate; they pressured the authority to open up the process and include the mass public (Arato 2004; Benomar 2004; Diamond 2005; Kritz 2003; USIP 2005).[36] Despite severe security concerns, the Coalition Provisional Authority consented to hold elections for the National Assembly (the body responsible for drafting the constitution). In addition, Article 60 of the Law of Administration for the State of Iraq for the Transitional Period (TAL) specified that the Iraqi National Assembly focus its constitution-making energies "in part by encouraging debate on the constitution through regular general public meetings in all parts of Iraq and through the media, and receiving proposals from the citizens of Iraq" (quoted in USIP 2005, 3). According to USIP, "Iraq's new National Assembly should embrace a model of robust public participation in the constitution-making process." USIP (2005, 10, 3) recommended that the period of public education and consultation be extended to allow for widespread public involvement. Diamond (2005, 21) concurred:

> The process of constitution-making must be democratic and broadly participatory, not merely through election of a constituent assembly or a constitutional referendum (or ideally, both), but through the involvement of the widest possible range of stakeholders in the substantive discussions and procedural planning, and through the organization of an extensive national dialogue on constitutional issues and principles.

In sum, participatory constitution making has become the favored solution to the most challenging cases of democratization.

Arguments for and against Participatory Constitution Making

Supporters of the participatory method argue that public engagement in the creation of new constitutions educates citizens and empowers them to defend their constitutional rights. Some observers even argue that public participation is essential in modern-day constitution making if the process and the product are to be considered legitimate (Hart 2003; Mattei 1999; Oloka-Onyango and Ihonvbere 1999; Van Cott 2000). In addition to ensuring constitutional legitimacy and knowledge, participatory constitution making is said to capitalize on public excitement about regime change to strengthen democratic attitudes, encourage public consensus, facilitate cit-

---

36. The constitution-making process that Kritz (2003), director of the Rule of Law Program at the USIP, recommended for Iraq in his testimony to the U.S. Senate is nearly identical to Uganda's, although with a shorter time frame.

izen engagement, and build support for state institutions. Rather than quickly erecting formal institutions and hoping for subsequent changes in attitudes and behavior to fit the new institutions, advocates of the new model claim that the participation creates democratic, engaged, trusting, and rule-abiding citizens who feel attached to the constitutional principles even before the new system is enacted.[37]

The new model, however, also has staunch critics, who assert that the substantial resources devoted to participatory activities are unwarranted, ineffective, and even counterproductive.[38] Most notably, the critics argue that the lengthy period required to foster mass participation prolongs the phase of transitional rule, distracts attention from other important democratization and development issues, and legitimizes the entrenchment of the regime overseeing the process. Some scholars, lawyers, and judges argue that constitutions created by multiple agents are prone to being cumbersome, inconsistent, and difficult to interpret.[39] Critics also claim that political leaders have more difficulty making concessions and striking political bargains when negotiations are open to public scrutiny than when negotiations are done in secret (Elster 1993, 181; Gloppen 1997, 256; Skach 2005, 161–63, 166).[40]

Some critics also argue that participation in constitution making is more likely than is everyday politics to foster conflict, polarize populations, and overrun minorities—in part because the stakes are extraordinarily high and the mechanisms for mediating conflict and protecting minorities are not

---

37. My summary is based on arguments about the benefits of participatory constitution making in Arato 2004; Benomar 2004; Carlson 1999; Citizen's Forum for Constitutional Reform 1999; Daruwala 2001; Diamond 2005; Ebrahim 1998; Furley and Katalikawe 1997; Hart 2003; Hatchard 2001; Hyden and Venter 2001; Klug 1996; Kritz 2003; Lal 1997; Odoki 1999; Selassie 1999; U.S. Institute of Peace 2005; Waliggo 1995; Wapakhabulo 2001; Widner 2005a, 2005b, as well as on the following interviews: Maitum 1999; Matembe 2001; Odoki 2001; Oneka 1999; Ssempebwa 2001; and Waliggo 1999.

38. The monetary costs of participatory programs are high, especially compared to spending on basic services. The estimated costs of the constitution-making programs in U.S. dollars are: $30 million ($0.67 per capita) for South Africa; $10 million ($0.55 per capita) for Uganda; $6 million ($0.15 per capita) for Ethiopia; and $4.5 million ($1.50 per capita) for Eritrea (Hyden and Venter 2001, 203. The estimate for Uganda is less than half the amount estimated by other sources: Mukholi 1995, 42, 99; United Nations Development Programme 1994, 12–13). The low figure in Ethiopia reflects the relatively low level of government-organized public participation in the process. There are also high human-capital opportunity costs, given the large number of highly trained individuals involved in these processes over extended periods.

39. See Riker 1995; Rosenn 1990, although agreement on fundamental principles prior to participation can facilitate coherence (Benomar 2004).

40. For reviews of critiques of the Ugandan process, see Barya 2000; Furley and Katalikawe 1997; Hansen and Twaddle 1995; Makara and Tukahebwa 1996; Mujaju 1999; Oloka-Onyango 1996, 2000.

yet in place.[41] Arato (2004, 3) notes that "populist democratic constitution-making" alarms some groups "because populist democracy entails unbound assembly (representing the 'constituent power'), restrained by no prior rules, nor by any separation of powers." Others argue that ordinary people have little grasp of constitutional issues and can easily be frustrated or manipulated by leaders. Finally, some critics fear that by bringing constitutional issues into the public realm to be debated and fought over, the constitution will lose its force as a higher and immutable law of the land.[42] Hart (2003, 3) summarizes the critiques:

> The idea [of the right to participate in making a constitution] is hotly contested by those who argue that only elites in modern societies possess the moderation, technical expertise, negotiating skills, ability to maintain confidentiality, and above all rational incentives to compromise so as to maintain power that make for effective constitution making.

The participatory model of constitution making unquestionably requires more time and resources than do traditional models, which are usually limited to parliamentary debate, a constitutional conference, or closed-door expert deliberations. However, it remains an empirical question whether the benefits touted by model supporters actually exist or whether the grave warnings of the critics are warranted. What effect does participatory constitution making have on democratic constitutionalism? Does participation induce citizens to support their new constitution, government, and democracy, or does it leave them feeling confused, alienated, and divided?

Limitations of the Constitution-Making Debate

A casual observation of the cases in table 1.1 indicates that participatory constitution making is no panacea for democracy and stability. For example,

---

41. For example, critics argue that the leadership in Uganda used the participatory process to enshrine constitutional limitations on the democratic right to organize by claiming merely to be responding to public demands for the continuation of the movement system. Critics argue that the freedom to organize, like all basic human rights, should not be subject to majority opinion or popular mobilization (Barya 2000; Oloka-Onyango 2000).

42. Skach (2005, 116) highlights the dangers when political parties organize themselves around procedural rules rather than substantive issues: "In several post-communist countries, for example, similar anti-system political parties sprang up in the early years of democratization. These parties were often based on an 'opposed to reform' versus 'supporting reform' cleavage. As a consequence, a strange political competition stabilized itself around the axis concerning, essentially, the legitimacy of the regime rather than substantive debates over policy."

seven years after the constitution-making process ended, Eritrea has still not put its new constitution into effect and remains one of the least democratic and most oppressive countries in the world.[43] Similarly, three separate episodes of public consultation have not prevented the flaring of ethnic tensions, coups, and political instability in Fiji. However, those countries that are least predisposed to stable and peaceful democratic governance are the most likely to adopt the participatory model in hopes of ameliorating their deficiencies (Hart 2003, 10). Countries may fail to achieve democratic stability despite employing the participatory model, not because of it. In addition, some countries that included extensive participation in constitution making, such as South Africa, are doing better than expected.

More systematic analysis is needed to evaluate the effectiveness of the model. As Skach (2005, 161) reminds us, however, such systematic analysis is very limited: "There is simply no comparative evidence that a polyarchic constitution-making process necessarily leads more directly to polyarchy, or that a hegemonic constitution-making process produces hegemony." Much of the academic work makes hopeful predictions based on participatory theory rather than on investigating empirical outcomes of past programs. The existing empirical work on the topic remains at the system level of analysis; a number of scholars have used case studies to investigate how participatory processes affect conflict, stability, government effectiveness, rule of law, constitutional provisions, and expert assessments of constitutional legitimacy.[44] USIP and UNDP are currently conducting a comparative case study of eighteen conflict-prone countries that employed a variety of participatory and nonparticipatory constitution-making practices.[45] This research is extremely valuable, but it does not adequately evaluate the benefits or drawbacks of the participatory model. The primary rationale for participatory constitution making is its hypothesized influence on the political culture of citizens rather than its supposed influence on constitutional content. A thorough investigation of the process must thus examine the individual-level outcomes. The key question remains how participation in constitution making influences individual citizens' attitudes, knowledge, and behavior.

---

43. In 2005, Freedom House ranked Eritrea last in political rights and second-to-last in civil rights (Freedom House 2005).

44. For examples of case studies of participatory constitution making in Africa, see Barya 1993; Ebrahim 1998; Furley and Katalikawe 1997; Gloppen 1997; Hansen and Twaddle 1995; Hart 2003; A. Howard 1993; Hyden and Venter 2001; Klug 1996; Mattei 1999; Odoki 1992; Oloka-Onyango 1996; Regan 1995; Selassie 1999.

45. Other comparative case studies of constitution making include Elster 1997, 1998; Skach 2005.

1.3. PARTICIPATION, INFORMATION, AND EVALUATION

This book takes on the twin debates about participation and participatory constitution making by examining how the Ugandan constitution-making process shaped participants' political culture. The remaining chapters argue that participants in the Ugandan process were likely to be more democratic in their attitudes, more distrustful of state institutions, more knowledgeable about government and the constitution, and more concerned about the fairness of the constitution-making process. However, participants did not tend to feel more politically capable or to judge the constitution more favorably than did nonparticipants. Those outcomes belie the predictions of both the optimistic developmental theorists and their pessimistic critics. The optimists would expect the increases in democratic attitudes and knowledge but not the decline in trust. The pessimists would expect the decline in trust but nothing else. Neither side can account for the lack of a direct effect on efficacy and constitutional legitimacy. How, then, can we explain these findings? Why might participation produce distrusting democrats? The remainder of this chapter develops a theoretical approach to answering these questions.

New Institutionalist Perspective on Trust

For clues to help solve the puzzle of how participation led to a greater number of distrusting democrats, I look to the burgeoning social science literature on trust. The new institutionalist school of thought maintains that trust is granted or withheld as a rational response of individuals to their institutional context. Levi (1998, 78) writes, "Trust is relational. The initial grant of trust depends on one person's evaluation that another will be trustworthy. Its maintenance requires confirmation of that trustworthiness, or else trust will be withdrawn." Trust is not merely a function of the socialized beliefs of the citizens; it is also a function of the incentives that government agents face and citizens' knowledge of government trustworthiness (Hardin 1998, 12). According to Putnam, Pharr, and Dalton (2000), trust depends on three factors: (1) the trustworthiness of the agent; (2) the information that the principal receives about agent trustworthiness; and (3) the principal's evaluation of the available information.[46]

---

46. Putnam, Pharr, and Dalton (2000, 23) argue, "Public satisfaction with representative institutions is a function of the information to which citizens are exposed, the criteria by which the public evaluates government and politics, and the actual performance of those institutions." I draw on their theoretical model explaining institutional trust (22–27). My contribution is the inclusion of participation within an expanded model of trust.

So far, most new institutionalists have focused on the first factor (Norris 1999; Putnam, Pharr, and Dalton 2000, 25). Scholars assert that the largest influence on agent trustworthiness (and thus on trust) comes from institutional performance.[47] Far less attention has been paid to the remaining two factors—citizen access to information about the government and their evaluation of available information.[48] But I argue that these two factors are important for explaining the variation in trust between participants and nonparticipants in Uganda. The institutional performance variable (the trustworthiness of the agent) is important for explaining why the consequences of participation in Uganda differ from the effects predicted by theories based primarily on the United States.

Participation in Context

My theoretical approach states that participation induces two important changes in the active citizen, (1) heightening the attainment of political information and (2) altering the criteria used to evaluate that information. First, participants learn about the polity through their involvement. They experience firsthand government procedures, norms, and activities, and they come into contact with government officials. They also develop an interest in the target of their activity. Second, participants become concerned with the fairness of government practices, the effectiveness of public involvement, and the degree to which collective decisions are implemented. They come to judge government less by its immediate effect on personal well-being and more by the way in which decisions are made and business is conducted.

Participation is thus likely to induce gradual attitude change through the two factors mentioned previously; yet the content of the information messages influences the direction of attitude change. In some cases, participants will receive positive messages about the well-being of the polity, while in others the message will be more critical. Institutional contexts and

---

47. Levi (1998, 88) concentrates on the micro-level evaluations of agent performance: "The major sources of distrust in government are promise breaking, incompetence, and the antagonism of government actors toward those they are supposed to serve. Citizens are likely to trust government only to the extent that they believe that it will act in their interest, that its procedures are fair, and that their trust of the state and of others is reciprocated." Finkel, Sabatini, and Bevis (2000, 1854) focus on macro-level indicators of institutional performance: "Clearly, the dominant influences on trust are the regime's political and economic performance."

48. A few notable studies of trust focus on citizen information and criteria of evaluation in advanced democracies. Jennings (1998) investigates the different expectations and criteria that U.S. citizens use to evaluate local and national governments. Bianco (1998) examines how citizen perceptions of common interest affect trust in legislators. A number of chapters in Pharr and Putnam 2000 examine the impact on trust of television, postmaterialist values, social activism, and party dealignment.

information sources condition the messages that participants receive as a result of their participation.

Participation and Institutional Trust

According to this theoretical approach, participation is likely to affect institutional trust by (1) increasing the participant's knowledge about actual institutional performance and (2) building attachment to democratic principles, thus altering the participant's expectations about how institutions should perform. The direction of the effect of participation on trust depends on the actual performance of government institutions (the content of the information messages). In polities where the government behaves democratically (relative to expectations), participation will bring "good news" and heighten trust in institutions. Where democratic performance is lower than expected, participation will make citizens more skeptical of government by providing "bad news" about institutional performance. Thus, the level of democratic institutionalization plays a crucial role in understanding participation's effect on institutional trust.

This theoretical model explains why participants in the Ugandan constitution-making process were likely to be more democratic and more knowledgeable yet more distrusting than were nonparticipants. In Uganda, as is to be expected in transitioning polities, institutional performance is poor. By participating, citizens learned that a large gap exists between actual government performance and the democratic ideals that they have come to value. This gap probably widened over time as government democratic performance increasingly fell short of participants' democratic expectations. This approach also reconciles the difference between the predictions in the literature on the developmental effects of participation (participation increases trust) and the finding that participation decreased trust in Uganda. The developmental theory of participation assumes that governments are performing democratically and that institutions are functioning well—or at least in accordance with the population's expectations. In such contexts, my theory also predicts that participation will increase trust. In the context of government performance that falls short of expectations, my theory predicts the opposite effect, accounting for the apparent decrease in trust in the Ugandan case.[49]

---

49. The estimated effects of participation in Uganda are consistent with the estimated effects of education, media exposure, and urban residence on attitudes in Uganda and elsewhere in Africa. Bratton, Mattes, and Gyimah-Boadi (2005, 206) found that formal education is associated with higher preferences for democracy and more critical attitudes toward the government in the twelve African countries that

Participation and Support for the Constitution

This book offers additional insights into how participation affects citizens' attitudes about government. It asks whether participation makes citizens distrustful of government institutions because they become disenchanted with the fundamental rules and structures of government or because they simply are dissatisfied with how the rules are being implemented. To answer this question, I examine the effect of participation on support for the constitution.

Again, the influence of participation on attitude change (in this case, constitutional support) is not as predicted by developmental theory or its critics. Citizens who participated in the constitution-making program were no more supportive of the constitution than were those who did not participate. However, there are three reasons to believe that participation indirectly bolstered support for the constitution. First, average support for the constitution was much higher in Uganda than in other African countries. Second, those who participated in constitution-making activities were better able to offer opinions about the constitution (most of which were supportive). Third, citizens who were active in the process tended to evaluate the constitution based on the legitimacy of the process, while those who were less active were concerned with their current circumstances. Support based on procedural legitimacy is thought to be more enduring than support based on current personal benefits.

The same theoretical approach that explains why participants were more likely to distrust government institutions also explains the patterns regarding participation and constitutional legitimacy in Uganda. Participation in constitution making (1) heightens citizen interest in and access to information about the constitution and (2) changes the criteria participants use to evaluate the constitution by raising the salience of procedural concerns and deemphasizing current personal benefits. In most hybrid or new democracies, constitutionalism is an unfamiliar concept. Participation teaches citizens about the constitution, thus increasing their ability to form opinions and their willingness to share those opinions. In addition, participants become concerned with the fairness of the constitution-making process when they invest time and energy in it. Participants will evaluate the fairness of the process according to what they learn. The messages to which participants

they surveyed: "Education apparently sharpens critical faculties, which leads to a sense of dissatisfaction with the way democracy actually works and to recognition that fully functioning liberal democracies are rarely being realized in African countries." Media exposure and urban residence are associated with similar attitudes (32).

are exposed ultimately determine whether they deem the constitution legitimate or illegitimate.

In Uganda, where leaders actively sought to influence public opinion regarding the constitution and where alternative sources of information were limited, elites were highly influential in shaping how citizens viewed the constitution-making process and by extension the constitution. While most participants were in close proximity to police, courts, elections, and local governments (and thus could judge institutional trustworthiness for themselves), they depended on elites for information to evaluate their constitution, a more remote institution. Where elites were happy with the outcome, citizens learned that the process was fair and the constitution legitimate (to the extent that they learned anything at all). Where elites were unhappy, citizens learned that the process was unfair and the constitution flawed. The large majority of Ugandan citizens heard positive messages, thus explaining the relatively high level of support for the constitution.

In sum, my theoretical perspective highlights the critical role that context plays in conditioning the influence of participation on citizen attitudes. The Ugandan case demonstrates that institutional performance and information environments matter because they influence the messages to which participants are exposed. In contrast to the optimistic developmental theory of participation, these messages will seldom be completely positive. However, the pessimists are equally incorrect in assuming that in poor, transitioning states, the messages will be totally negative. The effect of participation lies between the two extremes. The remaining chapters further illuminate my theoretical approach with reference to the Ugandan case.

CHAPTER 2

Ugandan History and the Constitution-Making Process

> The current constitution-making exercise is a significant achievement by the N[ational] R[esistance] M[ovement] Government in its efforts to democratize power by allowing the people to freely participate in the determination of important national issues that affect their lives. This is a fundamental departure in the politics of Uganda. The fact that the people have taken full advantage of the opportunity augurs well for the formulation of a popular and durable constitution and for the future of democracy in Uganda. The major challenge that faces the constitution-making process is to evolve a democratic constitution based on the national consensus of all the people of Uganda. (Odoki 1992, 1)

Justice Benjamin Odoki, the chair of the Uganda Constitutional Commission (UCC), portrayed his country's constitution-making process as a radical break from the political past, which had been characterized by constitutional manipulations, violence, instability, and the demobilization of the public. Although the Ugandan constitution-making process developed as a reaction to the tumultuous past, it was deeply shaped by historical conflicts. This chapter reviews Uganda's constitutional and political history. It also describes the recent constitution-making exercises in detail, paying close attention to how public participation in the process expanded over time. In short, this chapter shows how Ugandan history led to the development of a participatory program and generated the controversies that emerged during the process.

The chapter also sets the stage for the analysis of participatory constitution making in the rest of the book. The way the process was implemented influenced who participated and the effects of participation on democratic attitudes, civic skills, and institutional trust (chapter 3). Uganda's mixed democratic and authoritarian political environment—both during and after the constitution-making process—fundamentally conditioned the effects of participation on attitudes about government institutions (chapter 4). Finally, elite debates and opinions about the fairness of the constitution-making process shaped mass support for the constitution (chapter 5). This book contends that the consequences of participation are shaped by the context in which the participation takes place; this chapter provides information on the Ugandan process and context.

2.1 HISTORICAL BACKGROUND: NINE GOVERNMENTS, THREE CONSTITUTIONS, AND ONE FAULTY ELECTION

Ugandan history has been fraught with widespread instability, sectarian politics, gross human rights abuses, political assassinations, coups, rebel activity, lawlessness, corruption, and economic decline.[1] Prior to the current 1995 constitution, Uganda had three others that leaders abrogated, ignored, or suspended with impunity. Nine different governments have come to power through extralegal means since independence in 1962 (Kasozi 1999, 59). Before the Constituent Assembly (CA) election in 1994, there had been only one national election in postindependent Uganda, and that election was allegedly rigged. Between 1964 and 1985, more than a million Ugandans were killed in politically motivated violence, and hundreds of thousands of others were forced to flee their homes.[2] This turbulent, undemocratic, and violent past left the population with little or no knowledge of or attachment to democratic constitutional principles. Upon taking power, Yoweri Museveni's National Resistance Movement (NRM) government had only a narrow base of support, formal structures of governance had withered away, and the new government's only claims to legitimacy were its promises to restore democracy, economic growth, and the rule of law. This section examines Uganda's turbulent history from precolonial times through the early years of the NRM government.

Past Constitutions, Governments, and Transitions

The boundaries of Uganda, like most in Africa, were determined by colonial powers. The state boundaries include a variety of groups with different social, political, and economic structures.[3] Prior to colonial intervention, the area

---

1. For more in-depth reviews of Ugandan political and constitutional history, see Kanyeihamba 1975; Karugire 1980; Kasfir 1976; Kasozi 1999.
2. Kasozi (1999, 4) shows that the political violence steadily escalated over time: "It is estimated that the number of people slain for political motives during the first Obote administration (1962–71) ranged between 400 and 1,000. The number of people killed during the Amin regime (1971–79) was not less than 50,000 and could have been as high as 300,000. In the second Obote period (1980–85), the estimated number of those killed ranged between 300,000 and 1 million."
3. The independence constitution listed fifty ethnic groups (Uganda Constitutional Commission 1992a, 72).

contained a small number of highly centralized kingdoms (such as Nkore, Buganda, Bunyoro, and Tooro) and far more decentralized segmentary societies (such as the Bakiga, Bagisu, Bamba, Bankonjo, Iteso, and Lugbara) (Karugire 1980, 17–48; Kasozi 1999, 17–18; Mukholi 1995, 1). In their initial attempts to gain control, the British focused their efforts on the centralized kingdom of Buganda. Through a system of indirect rule, they recruited primarily Baganda (people of Buganda) to administer territories, developing infrastructures and educational systems there while leaving other areas, particularly the north, undeveloped. The British recruited residents of the economically disadvantaged north and east to serve in the Ugandan army in a deliberate attempt to balance the power of the Baganda (Human Rights Watch 1999, 29; Kasozi 1999, 6; Mukholi 1995, 3). The ethnic and regional inequalities that developed under colonial rule still plague Uganda. In addition, support for the government and the constitution remains regionally concentrated (Human Rights Watch 1999, 30; Kasozi 1999, 29).

The political and constitutional arrangements that emerged in the prelude to independence exacerbated sectarian tensions. Fearing a loss of autonomy within the proposed unitary Uganda, Buganda boycotted the first general election for the Legislative Council in 1958, the Wild Constitutional Committee, and the 1961 election. The two strongest political parties that emerged in the initial elections were associated with different religious groups: the Uganda People's Congress (UPC) with the Protestant Church, and the Democratic Party (DP) with the Catholic Church. Thus, ethnic tensions around the "Buganda question" were compounded by religious tensions (Kasozi 1999, 59–68; Mukholi 1995, 8–9; Oloka-Onyango 1995, 157).

The independence constitution of 1962 represented "a balancing act aimed at satisfying the competing political interests and aspirations of diverse groupings in Uganda" (Okoth 1996, 50; see also UCC 1992a, 50–51).[4] It contained a "quasi-federal" arrangement that granted Buganda a special federal status with sizable powers, while the other kingdoms—

---

4. To bolster the legitimacy of the current constitution and regime, the NRM government has actively promoted the idea that none of the previous constitution-making programs involved Ugandans' participation. However, the independence constitution was developed out of consultations with the public and then vetted by a constitutional conference (Oloka-Onyango 1995, 157). After Buganda rejected the Wild Constitutional Committee report, the colonial government established the Munster Commission to create a democratic constitutional framework for an independent Uganda that accommodated the traditional rulers (Mukholi 1995, 9). The Munster Commission held consultations with different interest groups and categories of people in Uganda. Its report served as the template for the London Constitutional Conference, attended by the colonial government and representatives of the kingdoms, political parties, and other important interest groups (Mukholi 1995, 9–10; Oloka-Onyango 1995, 157).

Ankole, Tooro, Bunyoro, and Busoga—received semifederal status with fewer powers. The remaining areas were to be governed on a unitary basis by the national government. Important issues, such as the relationship between the states and the center, the powers of the president and executive prime minister, and the status of the "lost counties" territory, were left unresolved (Mukholi 1995, 13–15; Oloka-Onyango 1995, 158). At independence in 1962, the British left Uganda with an ostensibly democratic government embodied in a Westminster-style constitution as well as with a history of colonial rule based on concentrated power, exclusion of the general population, sectarian politics, and militarized coercion (Oloka-Onyango 1998, 5–6).

The Bugandan leadership pushed for new elections just prior to independence and hurriedly created its own party, Kabaka Yekka (KY), which formed a strategic alliance with the UPC to shut out the DP and take power (Kasozi 1999, 68). The UPC's Milton Obote became the first prime minister of independent Uganda, and in 1963 Sir Edward Mutesa, the *kabaka* (king of Buganda), became president (Karugire 1980, 183–87).

Cracks soon developed in the UPC-KY alliance as Obote and the *kabaka* vied for power. Because the constitution was vague about the distribution of power, it did not help to resolve these conflicts. In 1966, just four years after independence, Obote suspended the constitution, deposed Mutesa, abolished the kingdoms, arrested cabinet members, promoted Idi Amin to army chief of staff, and declared himself executive president of Uganda (Karugire 1980, 196; Kasozi 1999, 73–85; Mukholi 1995, 15–16). These actions enraged the Baganda and ended Uganda's brief period of democratic rule.

> The abrogation of the 1962 constitution marked the beginning of political instability in the country. Obote demonstrated that the basic law of the land could be disregarded with impunity. The use of force to abolish the constitution became a dangerous precedent. It meant that any individual or group of individuals could seize power and flout the existing constitutional arrangements. (Mukholi 1995, 17)

Soon after suspending the independence constitution, Obote forced through the interim constitution of 1966. He arrived at Parliament with heavily armed troops, informed members that they were thus constituted into a constitutional assembly, outlined the major features of the interim constitution (which members were told could be found in their pigeonholes), and called for a motion of adoption. The motion was passed without debate after a number of members walked out in protest (Kasozi 1999, 84; Oloka-Onyango 1995, 158). The "pigeonhole constitution," as it was dubbed, abolished the federal arrangements, transferred the kingdoms' properties to the state, and concentrated power in the position of the executive president. When the Buganda *lukiiko* (legislative council) refused to recognize Obote's government or his constitution, army troops stormed the palace, and Kabaka Mutesa escaped into exile in Britain (Kasozi 1999, 85–87; Mukholi 1995, 16–18).

In 1967, Obote introduced a new constitution to the National Assembly, which had again transformed itself into a constitutional assembly. The assembly lacked legitimacy, as the members were mostly UPC supporters who had already stayed past their elected terms. The 1967 constitution went even further than the pigeonhole constitution in concentrating power at the center. According to Mukholi (1995, 18), political turmoil increased following these constitutional upheavals:

> Insecurity, wanton killings and oppression of anti-establishment elements increased. The government adopted coercive means to contain opposition using security forces and the Preventative Detention Act. In 1966 a state of emergency was declared in Buganda and extended to the rest of the country three years later. The suppression of dissenting views and criticism against the government culminated in the banning of opposition parties in 1969. Uganda became a one party state.

In 1971, Idi Amin seized power in a military coup. Amin initially gained support by promising a return to civilian rule through democratic elections (Kasozi 1999, 103; Okoth 1996, 52). However, it soon became apparent that he intended to hold onto power by authoritarian means. He declared himself president for life and used executive degrees and terror to enforce his will (Kasozi 1999, 104–27). These decrees made the constitution irrelevant, and his use of terror made a mockery of the rule of law (Human Rights Watch 1999, 32). Estimates indicate that between fifty thousand and five hundred thousand Ugandans were killed or simply disappeared during Amin's rule (Human Rights Watch 1999, 32; Kasozi 1999).

On April 10, 1979, under the umbrella of the Uganda National Liberation Army, the combined forces of twenty-two groups toppled Amin's government with the help of the Tanzanian military. Next, a series of unstable civilian and military governments ruled Uganda, ostensibly under the control of the National Consultative Council, an organ of the National Liberation

Army (Kasozi 1999, 128–36). In 1980, Uganda held its first postindependence general election. Four parties contested the election: the UPC, led by Obote; the DP, headed by Paul Ssemogerere; the Uganda Patriotic Movement, recently formed by Museveni; and the Conservative Party of Baganda traditionalists. The UPC was declared the winner, but international observers and opposition candidates argued that gross malpractice had occurred (Kasozi 1999, 136–43).[5]

The period that followed the contentious 1980 election is dubbed Obote II, and many observers consider it the most brutal time since independence (Human Rights Watch 1999, 34–35; Kasozi 1999, 145). Rebel groups became active throughout the country, and government troops responded with massive abuse and killing. Museveni's Popular Resistance Army, which later became the National Resistance Army, was among the guerrilla movements that formed in opposition to the Obote government (Kasozi 1999, 165). The movement was militarily most active in the central Buganda region known as the Luwero triangle. Many of the Baganda who aided the NRM in their struggle did so in the hope that removing Obote would allow for the restoration of their former kingdom and federal status (Mulondo 2001).

Museveni claims that he "went to the bush" to wage guerrilla war in response to the rigged election, government corruption, political manipulation of sectarian interests, and gross human rights abuses (Human Rights Watch 1999, 34; Mukholi 1995, 24; Museveni 1997, 123). The NRM's political philosophy was enshrined in the "Ten-Point Programme," the first point of which was the restoration of democracy. This democratic rhetoric was accompanied by generally democratic behavior during the insurgency (Kasfir 2005). Museveni maintained strict control over the use of violence by his soldiers against civilians. In areas "liberated" by the NRM, the Resistance Council (RC)[6] system of elected local officials was established (Kasfir 2005; Okoth 1996, 58).

Obote's reliance on the military to maintain power eventually led to his downfall. As rebel activity against the government intensified, ethnic cleavages deepened between the Langi and the Acholi, two ethnic groups from the north that dominated the military. In July 1985, Obote (a Langi) was once again removed from power in a military coup, this time led by Brigadier Bazillo Okello and General Tito Okello, two Acholi officers (Ka-

---

5. It is widely believed that DP would have won if the election had been free and fair. Museveni's Uganda Patriotic Movement won only one seat.

6. The name *resistance councils* was later changed to *local councils*. I use the two terms interchangeably depending on the time period.

sozi 1999, 171–74). Museveni's NRM made great progress in its guerrilla war and continued to fight the Okello government until the NRM captured Kampala and the Ugandan government on January 26, 1986 (Human Rights Watch 1999, 35–36; Mukholi 1995, 24).

From the colonial period through 1986, Ugandan leaders ruled by force, not by law. The constitutions became increasingly vacuous as leaders adapted the documents to suit their needs or simply ignored constitutional constraints. The country was plagued by violence, instability, sectarian divisions, and economic decline. Many older Ugandans associated the failure of 1962 and 1967 constitutions with violent political crises, even if they did not know the details of those documents or of the principles of constitutional rule. Many younger Ugandans had not heard of a constitution until after Museveni came to power. Regardless of age, most people were eager for change, and many were hopeful that Museveni's government would be the handmaiden of democratic reform and a return of stability.

Museveni and the NRM Government: The Early Years

Like nearly all his predecessors, Museveni captured the presidency through the use of force (Mujaju 1999, 14). The political environment was chaotic, and the NRM government initially enjoyed only a small base of support (Besigye 2001; Kasfir 2000, 62; UCC 1992a, 54). While many people adopted a wait-and-see attitude, others were openly hostile to Museveni's rule, especially people in the north and supporters of the UPC. Like his predecessors, Museveni accepted the authority of the 1967 constitution but suspended some parts of it to legalize his rule. Legal Notice No. 1 of 1986 stipulated that the unelected National Resistance Council (NRC) would rule for a four-year interim period (Besigye 2001; Human Rights Watch 1999, 36; UCC 1992a, 54). The measure also suspended political party activity during the interim period. Museveni and the NRM government argued that political parties had exacerbated ethnic and religious sectarian tensions and created conflict, disunity, and violence in Uganda; curtailing party activity, they argued, was therefore necessary to calm tensions and produce a climate of reconciliation and consensus (Mukholi 1995, 25; Museveni 1997, 187–89, 195).[7] Instead, candidates were to compete for office on individual merit under a system that became known as the no-party or

---

7. Museveni's rhetoric on the need for banning political party activity has since changed from his initial emphasis on the need for a period of transition and reconciliation to an argument that parties are unfit for an agrarian society where politics is based on economic class rather than sectarian affiliation (Kasfir 2000).

movement system. Parties were allowed to exist and operate national head-quarters, hold meetings of national executives, and organize seminars or workshops but were not permitted to open or operate branch offices, hold delegates' conferences and public rallies, or sponsor candidates for office (Kasfir 1999; Mujaju 1999, 14). According to most observers, these restrictions violate the basic democratic principle of freedom of association.

Despite these seemingly undemocratic beginnings, the NRM government instituted a number of reforms that Ugandans welcomed, thus expanding the government's initial support base. In his first main speech after taking power, Museveni promised "not a mere change of the guards" but a "fundamental change" modeled on the Ten-Point Programme and called for a return to constitutional democracy as a primary goal (Besigye 2001; Furley and Katalikawe 1997; Mwesige 2004; Oloka-Onyango 1995, 159). Museveni constructed a broad-based government that included members of opposition groups (Human Rights Watch 1999, 36). In addition, the NRM allowed far greater freedom of the press and speech than had previous regimes and appointed several oversight committees such as the inspector-general of government and the Human Rights Commission (Oloka-Onyango 1995, 159).

Fundamental to the NRM political reforms was an attempt to acquire legitimacy and support by encouraging popular participation in governance (Golooba-Mutebi 2004; Kasfir 2000, 2005). Museveni wrote in his autobiography (1997, 176) that in addition to security and economic reconstruction, participation was his chief concern upon taking power in 1986, because "we owed it to the people of Uganda to restore to them some level of democratic participation, of which they had been deprived since the early 1960s." The RC system was extended to the whole country to encourage popular participation in local affairs and to increase support for the movement system (Karlstrom 1996; Kasfir 2000; Museveni 1997, 189–90; Mwesige 2004). In 1989, direct elections were held throughout the country for representatives to village-level councils (RC-1), and indirect elections were held for higher-level councils (RC-2–RC-5) and the NRC (Okoth 1996, 58–59).[8] The leadership also instituted or encouraged other venues for involving (or controlling) citizens, such as women's councils and *chaka-mchaka*.[9] Furthermore,

---

8. There are five levels of RCs. Citizens directly elect the representatives of their village council (RC-1). Each council then elects the council one level higher from among the previously elected representatives.

9. *Chaka-mchaka* were politicization education programs ostensibly created to empower the population by teaching them political and human rights as well as military training. However, evidence suggests that these compulsory programs were used largely to assert political control, to demonize opposition parties, and to indoctrinate civil servants and students in movement ideology (Human Rights Watch 1999, 65–69; Mwesige 2004, 55–58).

voluntary associations and nongovernmental organizations (NGOs) prolifer-
ated during this period and provided citizens with new opportunities to participate in professional and economic associations, cultural institutions,
women's organizations, and human rights groups. The NRM government
has been far more accommodating of NGOs than were previous regimes, although regulations at times have been strategically enforced to serve government interests and to silence opposition (Human Rights Watch 1999, 103–
11; Mwesige 2004, 55–61; Tripp 2000, 61–63).

Considerable variation has existed in the degree to which these ostensibly
participatory institutions allowed for voluntary action aimed at influencing
the government, on the one hand, or coerced attendance for the purpose of
controlling or manipulating citizens, on the other hand.[10] Considerable variation has also occurred in who was encouraged or able to participate in political activities.[11] Nonetheless, the NRM clearly sought to build legitimacy
in the eyes of the Ugandan public and donors abroad by increasing popular
involvement in politics. Furthermore, they largely succeeded, both in mobilizing activity and in garnering political support for doing so—at least initially.[12] The constitution-making process was part of this larger impetus toward encouraging popular participation.

In addition to political reforms, Museveni's government ushered in economic changes that turned economic decline into respectable levels of
growth. Uganda experienced a 2.2 percent decline in per capita gross domestic product in 1984, a 5.2 percent decline in 1985, and a 1.9 percent decline in 1986. Following Museveni's takeover, Uganda saw 1.3 percent
growth in per capita gross domestic product in 1987, 5.2 percent growth
in 1988, and 3.0 percent growth in 1989. From 1997 until 2000, Uganda

---

10. On average, civil society activities tended to have more voluntary upward-oriented participation,
while many argue that *chaka-mchaka* fall at the other end of the spectrum, with attendance coerced for
the purpose of political indoctrination. RC and council involvement along with constitution-making
activities fall in between but are closer to the voluntary end of the spectrum (Barya 2000; Kasfir 2000;
Mwesige 2004; Okoth 1996; Oloka-Onyango 2000; Tripp 2005; Tripp and Kwesiga 2002). In my
open-ended interviews, only a handful of respondents reported that they were required to attend RC or
constitution-making activities. Debate is ongoing about whether RCs and constitution-making activities transmitted influence and opinions primarily from the bottom up or from the top down.

11. Location of residence, gender, education, resources, and other traits affected whether people were
restricted or free to participate. See section 3.3 for information about the influences on participation in
the constitution-making process.

12. Golooba-Mutebi (2004) argues that the initially high levels of excitement about and participation
in the RC system were unsustainable and have declined considerably over time. Nonetheless, survey evidence from twelve African countries shows that Uganda is among the most participatory societies in
Africa and that high levels of political participation and engagement have been sustained or even increased over time (Bratton, Lambright, and Sentamu 2000; Logan et al. 2003).

had an average 3.3 percent per capita gross domestic product growth rate (World Bank 2002).[13] Museveni's government also received a large amount of external aid and assistance as well as international praise for its health, education, and economic reforms.

Finally, Museveni's government brought a level of peace and security to much of the country that had been seriously lacking during the previous period. The NRM established far greater discipline in the army and police than had previous governments and reined in much of the banditry that had plagued the country. When I asked Ugandans about their opinions of Museveni, the current government, or the 1995 constitution, by far the most common answer I heard was, "Things are much better. Now I can sleep in my house." This statement is a powerful reference to a time when people had to sleep "in the bush" to avoid the soldiers, police, rebels, and thieves who attacked houses at night. The improvement in security was most marked in the central area of the Luwero triangle, which had been primary fighting ground of the NRM insurgency.[14]

While the onset of Museveni's rule was accompanied by marked increases in prosperity and security in much of the country, these benefits have not touched citizens in every region. In the north and parts of the east and west, violent conflicts between rebel groups and government forces continue to endanger citizens, undermine the rule of law, devastate economic activity, and prohibit infrastructure development. Rebel armies—most notably the Lord's Resistance Army—have committed massive human rights abuses, including thousands of child abductions, attacks, rapes, and mutilations of civilians. The rebel armies have been particularly culpable, but government forces are also accused of large-scale abuses, forced displacement, limitations on movement, and other violations against citizens in the troubled areas (Human Rights Watch 1999, 120–30). The ongoing violence exacerbated the historical political, religious, and ethnic animosities that many citizens in these regions held against the current government when it took over.[15]

---

13. This is compared to an average for the same time period of −0.35 percent for sub-Saharan Africa and 1.4 percent for the world (World Bank 2002).

14. Despite improvements in much of Uganda, conflict, violence, and internal political instability remained key concerns well into the period of NRM rule. The continuing instability in some parts of the country was certainly a concern for people living in those areas, but residents of other areas also seemed to fear a return to the insecurity under previous regimes. When people were asked about their main concerns in a 2000 Afrobarometer survey, "political insecurity" was the most frequent response. However, in 2002 this response dropped to the fifth-most-frequent after development concerns (Logan et al. 2003, 29–35).

15. See Logan et al. 2003 for evidence and analysis of the stark differences in political attitudes between "insiders" and "outsiders" in Uganda; see also Human Rights Watch 1999, 120–29.

The deteriorating economic and security conditions in such places stand in stark contrast the dramatic improvements witnessed by most Ugandan citizens in the first decade of NRM rule.

In the next chapters, I present evidence that overall trust for government institutions is very high in most of Uganda. This high level of support can be understood only in relation to the gross human rights abuses, violence, instability, and economic decline under previous regimes. The much higher levels of security, freedom, public participation, and prosperity under Museveni and the NRM are both noticed and appreciated by the majority of the population; the relative difference in past and present government performance probably accounts for the overall high levels of trust in government institutions. While Ugandans generally supported the government, they lacked knowledge of and attachment to democratic constitutional principles. Furthermore, compliance with government rules, regulations, and institutions had withered along with the government organs. Transforming the public's initial enthusiasm for peace, participation, and prosperity into enduring legitimacy and compliance with the government was a major NRM goal during its first decade.

2.2. THE UGANDAN CONSTITUTION-MAKING PROCESS, 1988–1995

The constitution-making process, which is the focus of this book, represents a major change ushered in by the NRM government in its early years. Early in its history, the NRM identified the importance of creating a democratic constitutional framework. However, the participatory model of constitution making developed only gradually, over time. The planned program of constitution making was altered several times; with each change, it grew to encompass more citizens in new activities. What was initially to be accomplished during an interim period of four years ended up lasting until 1995, nine years after the NRM took power. During this time (1) the UCC's tenure was extended, (2) the legal notice stipulating that the existing NRC would ratify the constitution was altered to provide for a separate universally elected CA, (3) the CA ran twenty-one months beyond what was initially mandated, and (4) the NRM government twice extended its interim tenure, ostensibly to accommodate the constitution-making process (Barya 2000, 28; Furley and Katalikawe 1997, 252; Museveni 1997, 192–93). In the end, the program included a large percentage of the population in a wide variety of activities over an extensive period.

There are competing interpretations of leaders' motivations for the participatory program. A generous interpretation is that the leaders genuinely believed in democracy; they recognized the need to build attachment to the constitution and strengthen democratic political culture while creating democratic structures and rules. Less charitably, some argue that the NRM government was eager to capitalize on initially high levels of public trust to build a lasting support base, increase its national and international legitimacy through seemingly democratic programs, weaken the opposition, obtain favored institutional rules, and secure the NRM's hold on power before being forced to engage in competitive politics. While Museveni chose the commissioners and intervened at critical moments to secure his favored provisions, it is also the case that no single actor decided to engage in an eight-year-long participatory constitution-making program. Rather, many actors, from the president and high government officials to average citizens, influenced the design of the program, which evolved piece by piece over time to become one of the most participatory constitution-building exercises to date.[16] Those involved had different motivations, and the same policy choice often served both the expedient interests of those in power and the benevolent interests of those who wanted to build a stable democratic system. In short, Ugandan constitution making was an evolving process, not a preplanned event. This section describes how the process developed until the promulgation of the constitution in 1995.

In 1981, during the beginning of the guerrilla struggle for power, the NRM first wrote about a democratic constitution-making process: "As part of laying the groundwork for returning Uganda to democratic government, the Interim Administration shall see to it that a new constitution based on popular will is drafted and promulgated by a Constituent Assembly elected by the people themselves" (quoted in Odoki 1999, 5; see also Furley and Katalikawe 1997, 245). Soon after coming to power in 1986, the NRM established the Ministry for Constitutional Affairs to oversee a process of constitutional reform. The type and process of reform were contentious issues. Some who wanted to see the restoration of the kingdoms and federalism favored the reinstatement of the 1962 constitution, while many Obote supporters and multipartyists favored the 1967 constitution. Some government officials suggested that the existing NRC could perform necessary ratifications and reforms, while others recommended a national conference to pre-

---

16. South Africa's process reached a slightly higher proportion of the population than did Uganda's process but was much shorter and involved fewer participatory activities. South Africa's effort was also among the most expensive constitution-making exercises in Africa (Hyden and Venter 2001, 203).

pare an entirely new constitutional instrument. Museveni, in consultation with the minister of state for constitutional affairs, opted for a commission of experts to draft the constitution, with ratification by another body. This plan resembled the processes that took place in most anglophone countries, including Nigeria, Ghana, Zambia, and Tanzania (Odoki 1999, 4–6).

The UCC

Not until several years after the NRM assumed power were the first concrete actions taken to initiate the constitution-making process. Despite Museveni's rhetorical emphasis on the restoration of democratic constitutionalism, he paid little attention to the administrative requirements of making a constitution, and the process got off to a somewhat chaotic and slow start (Furley and Katalikawe 1997; Njuba 2001; Odoki 2001; Oneka 1999; Waliggo 1999). The process began when the minister of constitutional affairs submitted a bill to establish the UCC, and after three weeks of debate, the NRC passed Statute No. 5 of 1988. The statute held that the president, in consultation with the minister, would appoint a twenty-one-member commission of experts. The commission was to prepare a draft constitution for presentation to the minister within two years, although an allowance was made for an extension (NRC 1988). To prepare the constitution, the commission members were instructed to "seek the views of the general public through the holding of public meetings and debates, seminars, workshops and any other form of collecting views" and to "stimulate public discussion and awareness of constitutional issues" (NRC 1988). The statute clearly mandated public consultation, but given the two years initially allocated for the UCC to complete the entire consultation and drafting exercise, it is fair to say that the government envisioned participation involving mainly elites, interest groups, and representatives of different sectors of society, not the average citizen.

The first commissioners were appointed in February 1989, and Justice Benjamin Odoki was named as the chair.[17] The appointment process was haphazard, and the president and minister for constitutional affairs did not consult widely with other leaders or even the commissioners themselves before announcing appointments (Furley and Katalikawe 1997, 247, 51; Matembe and Dorsey 2002; Odoki 2005, 1). Although the commissioners came from the different regions, religions, and sectors of Ugandan society and included some individuals with past affiliations to political parties, the method of appointment fueled speculation that the commissioners were

---

17. The UCC is popularly known as the Odoki Commission.

aligned with and beholden to the president. The UCC was also hindered by a shortage of funding, work space, and staff. The commission had to utilize resources, offices, and personnel at the ministry, which made it harder for commission members to establish their independence from government. Finally, the enabling statute was vague about the procedures for promulgating the constitution except to say that the UCC was to present an advisory draft constitution to the ministry for consideration, further fueling speculation that the NRM would determine the content of the final constitution. This poorly planned beginning made it more difficult for the commissioners to establish their seriousness, credibility, and independence (Furley and Katalikawe 1997; Njuba 2001; Odoki 2001, 2005; Ogwal 2001; Ssemogerere 2001; Ssempebwa 2001; Waliggo 1999).

The UCC started work in March 1989 by drawing up a plan of action that dramatically expanded the concept of consultation to encourage every citizen to participate. Although the initial UCC plan was extensive, it expanded even further as the commission received feedback from the population during the process (UCC 1989). According to the UCC report (1992a, 25),

> The people demanded to be enlightened on constitutional issues; they organized their own seminars and discussion. They requested the Commission to give them more time to write their views which they wanted collected from them directly by the Commission in order to ensure they were properly recorded. The people continued to request that they be fully informed at every stage what the Commission was doing with their views. They demanded to be given the Commission's Report directly so that no other power could interfere with their views. They asked to be fully represented in the processes of debate and adoption of the draft constitution, and especially in the proposed CA, to enable them to defend the views they had submitted to the Commission. The entire exercise, therefore, has been highly influenced by people's understanding of participatory democracy.

With agreement of the NRM's leaders, who were quite willing to prolong the period before they had to face elections, the transition period was extended to accommodate the expanded program of public education and participation.

The UCC activities can be broken down into six phases:

1. planning, publicity, and internal seminars;
2. education of the people and discussion of constitutional issues;

3. collection of the people's views;
4. analysis and study of the views;
5. review of the constitution and comparative study of constitutions; and
6. preparation of the final report and draft constitution. (Odoki 1999, 8)

In the first phase, the UCC took two months to plan its program, hold internal seminars, and prepare materials for educating Ugandans about constitutional issues. The second phase, aimed at educating the public, was the most extensive and time-consuming part of the process (UCC 1992a, 30–34). It began on August 7, 1989, with the district constitutional seminars. Teams of commissioners attended two-day seminars in each district. These seminars were attended by a total of 10,037 people, including (1) members of the NRC, (2) district administrators and their senior officials, (3) RC-5 and RC-3 executive members, (4) mass mobilizers, (5) county and subcounty chiefs, (6) community elders and heads of religious organizations and schools, and (7) other important persons (Odoki 1992, 5; UCC 1992a, 30).

Based on feedback obtained during the district seminars, the UCC prepared additional educational booklets and reprints of the 1962 and 1967 constitutions, *Guidelines on Constitutional Issues*, *Guiding Questions on Constitutional Issues*, and a *Brochure on Preparation of Memoranda*. These materials were distributed at all seminars and workshops as well as to local government councils (RCs) and civil society groups as a way of facilitating constitutional discussions (UCC 1992a, 32; Odoki 1992, 5).

Also based on suggestions given at the district seminars, the UCC organized and attended seminars in 813 subcounties.[18] The commissioners opened these seminars by explaining the purpose and the central attributes of democratic constitutions, Uganda's constitutional history, the importance of a new constitution, and the key constitutional issues at stake, including gender issues (Matembe and Dorsey 2002, 127). They then solicited views from the public and instructed citizens about how the constitution-making process would proceed (UCC 1991a; Waliggo 1995, 27). Odoki (1999, 9) explains,

These [subcounty seminars] formed the core of the entire exercise of educating and sensitizing the people from the grassroots. . . . We found the

18. The commission held seminars in each subcounty, except in Kumi and Soroti Districts, where the commission held seminars in each county with free transportation provided to citizens who wanted to attend (UCC 1992b, vii, 33).

exercise though tiresome and hazardous was worthwhile. It confirmed our belief that the ordinary Ugandan has an idea of what he wants and how he wants to be governed. We were encouraged by the tremendous response we received from the people at the grassroots.

During this second phase, the UCC also conducted two-day seminars for government employees such as the police, army, and prison officials as well as civil society groups such as institutions of higher learning, youth groups, women's organizations, professional associations, and political parties. Civic organizations organized their own seminars, workshops, and conferences and invited the commissioners to speak (Odoki 1999, 9; UCC 1992a, 31–32). Commissioners broadcast forty radio programs in Luganda, twenty in Runyankore, five in Lusoga, four in Luo, four in Ateso, and ten in English. They participated in twenty television programs and held more than fifteen press conferences (Kizito 1992, 121). The second phase took longer than what had initially been mandated for the entire UCC exercise. In the middle of this second phase of extensive public education, the minister of constitutional affairs extended the UCC's term so that it could complete its work (Mukholi 1995, xi).

The third phase, collecting people's views, began in May 1991. During the subcounty seminars in the previous phase, RCs had been instructed to organize meetings at each level and to prepare memoranda based on the *Guiding Questions on Constitutional Issues.* The RC-1s were encouraged to involve all the people of the village or cell in their meetings. RC chairs were to educate citizens about constitutional issues, solicit everyone's views, and prepare memoranda for submission to the UCC. The RC-2s then prepared memoranda based on the views expressed by the RC-1s, and so on up the chain. The UCC members traveled again (sometimes more than once) to all subcounties to collect the RCs' memoranda. In addition, reports of all the previous educational seminars were compiled to record the views expressed at those events (Odoki 1992, 7; Odoki 1999, 10; UCC 1992b, vii–ix, 35).

During the third phase, the UCC also collected memoranda from interested Ugandans in the country and abroad as well as from civil society groups.[19] The commission accepted position papers and compiled newspaper articles expressing opinions on constitutional issues. Finally, commission members organized an essay contest for students from primary school

---

19. The UPC refused to participate and did not send a party memorandum.

TABLE 2.1. Submissions to the
Uganda Constitutional Commission

District seminar reports	33
Institutional seminar reports	53
Subcounty seminar reports	813
Individuals' memoranda	2,553
Group memoranda	839
RC-5 memoranda	36
RC-4 memoranda	13
RC-3 memoranda	564
RC-2 memoranda	2,225
RC-1 memoranda	9,521
Essay competition	5,844
Newspaper articles	2,763
Position papers	290
Total	25,547

Source: Adapted from Uganda Constitutional
Commission 1992b, 323.

through university level (Odoki 1992, 7; Odoki 1999, 9–10; UCC 1992b,
vii–ix, 35).

The volume of submissions sent to the commission, indicated in table
2.1, attests to the extensive participation that the UCC encouraged. These
figures are impressive, especially if one considers that most of the submissions came from groups of people rather than from individuals.

While the extent of participation was unprecedented, the Odoki Commission still involved only a minority of Ugandan citizens. In my random
sample survey of citizens, 4.9 percent stated that they had participated in
a seminar where a commissioner was present; 11.7 percent reported sending
memoranda, either as an individual or as part of a group; and 13.6 percent
said that they attended a local council meeting where memoranda were discussed.[20] My examination of the UCC archives and my open-ended interviews with local council officials and citizens show considerable deviation
from the intended model, where every RC was to hold meetings attended
by all citizens in the area. In only a few areas I visited did citizens report
being required to attend RC-1 meetings on the constitution. In some areas,
respondents reported high attendance at the RC-1 meetings by individuals
who had been mobilized to attend by local council officials or civil society
organizations. In other areas, few if any regular citizens attended the RC-1

---

20. These are self-reports of attendance at events that occurred nearly a decade prior to the time when
I conducted the survey.

meetings, and in some places no meetings were held. Involvement in the creation of a RC-1 memorandum ranged from the council chair drafting it on his own to participation by the entire village. In general, it seems that only council members and a few opinion leaders attended meetings of the higher-level RCs (RC-2 to RC-5).[21] There was a great deal of confusion about how council leaders were to organize activities in their areas and about what happened to their submissions after they were sent to higher levels.[22]

The fourth phase of the UCC program required analysis of the views collected. The memo submissions had to be translated into English, summarized, and grouped by topic (Odoki 1992, 8; UCC 1992a, 37–39).[23] The commission identified issues on which consensus existed and those that were controversial (see section 2.3). On controversial and sensitive issues, the UCC conducted a statistical analysis of basic frequencies across submission type and region (UCC 1992b, 343–401). The commission then interpreted the people's views. The work in this fourth phase was done not only to decide what should be included in the draft constitution but also to document how all such decisions were made. Odoki (1999, 11) notes,

> This elaborate system of analyzing people's views was put in place to allay the fears and suspicions of the public that their views would be ignored or rigged. The list of all persons and organizations that submitted views to the Commission and the statistical analysis were published in one volume of the Commission's Final Report entitled Index of Sources of Peoples Views. This proved that the Commission had been transparent in its analysis of all the views submitted to it.

The fifth phase of the process consisted of a comparative study of constitutions. Commissioners went on study tours to the United States, the United Kingdom, the Federal Republic of Germany, India, Sweden, Denmark, and Iceland, with visits sponsored by those countries. Commission

---

21. Most of the memoranda to the UCC contain lists and signatures of participants. However, these lists do not always represent who was present at the meetings preparing the memoranda. Sometimes only officials signed even though other people were in attendance. Sometimes even people who did not attend were asked to sign documents. In the areas where the survey was conducted, I asked local officials about attendance at the meetings and about the accuracy of the list of names for their location.

22. In some cases, higher-level RCs failed to forward the lower-level submissions after receiving them. Bushenyi District was the most well organized of the districts that I visited, but even there two women claimed with much distress that they later received a list of the submissions and that their village's memoranda had been "edited out" (interview, Bushenyi District, March 2001).

23. The commissioners were from different areas and ethnic groups and thus spoke different languages. Translations were required to enable each commissioner to read the memoranda from all areas.

members also visited Namibia, Botswana, Zimbabwe, Ghana, Nigeria, and Ethiopia. In addition, the UCC studied Uganda's political and constitutional history as well as the country's current social, economic, and political conditions and needs (Odoki 1999, 10–13). In the final phase, the commissioners prepared the draft constitution and a 750-page final report, which they presented to President Museveni on December 31, 1992 (UCC 1992a).

The Constituent Assembly Campaigns and Elections

Museveni initially wanted the NRC and the National Army Council to debate the draft constitution and prepare the final version (Odoki 1999, 16). In the December 1991 *Interim Report on the Adoption Process,* the UCC members argued that many Ugandans expressed concern with the initial plan for ratification.[24] They felt that the plan for the NRC to transform itself into a constitutional assembly was reminiscent of the 1967 constitution-making process and lacked legitimacy. The NRC (like the 1967 Parliament) had extended itself beyond its initial four-year term without elections. Many members were presidential appointees or historical affiliates of the National Resistance Army who had never been elected; others had been elected only indirectly through the RC colleges (Mukholi 1995, 35). The UCC recommended the creation of a separate body from the NRC with the sole purpose of debating and promulgating the constitution as a means of legitimating the constitution. The commissioners suggested that most CA delegates should be elected by universal adult suffrage, with the others elected by special interest groups (Odoki 1999, 16; UCC 1991b). By most accounts, the president and members of the NRC only reluctantly agreed to a separately elected CA as a result of public pressure (Furley and Katalikawe 1997, 251–52; Odoki 2005, 253–65; Tripp 2005, 13).

On February 18, 1993, the minister of state for constitutional affairs introduced a bill for the creation of the CA. A total of 240 NRC members spoke in the heated debate of the bill, with most controversy centered on the composition of the CA. Only after Museveni presided over a daylong closed session did the NRC pass the Statute No. 6 of 1993, which specified that 214 CA delegates would be directly elected by secret ballot and universal suffrage. The bill also called for additional members to represent special groups: (1) thirty-nine women's representatives elected, one per district, by electoral colleges made up of RC-3 officials and women's councils; (2) ten

---

24. Discussion of the ratification procedures was a recurring theme in the memoranda to the UCC. The majority of the memoranda I reviewed expressed a preference for a directly elected body to ratify the constitution.

TABLE 2.2. Number of Constituent Assembly Delegates by Category

Directly elected delegates from electoral areas	214
Women delegates, one from each district	39
National Resistance Army	10
National Organization of Trade Unions	2
National Youth Council	4
National Union of Disabled Persons of Uganda	1
Two members of each party: Conservative Party, Democratic Party (Uganda Patriotic Movement and Uganda People's Congress did not send delegates)	4
Presidential appointees	10
Total	284

Source: Adapted from Odoki 1999, 17.

representatives of the National Resistance Army; (3) two representatives from the National Organization of Trade Unions; (4) four representatives from the National Youth Council; (5) one representative from the National Union of Disabled Persons; (6) two representatives from each of the four political parties that participated in the 1980 election; and (7) ten presidential appointees. Thus, more than a quarter of the proposed 288 CA delegates were to be special representatives. The UPC refused to participate, and the Uganda Patriotic Movement (Museveni's party beginning in 1980) did not send delegates, so the number of party representatives was four instead of eight. This arrangement favored the NRM because the special group representatives were, on balance, expected to support the government. Table 2.2 shows the distribution of CA delegates.[25]

The CA statute also stipulated the rules for campaigning, which centered on joint CA candidates' meetings: "Reacting to the violence and divisiveness of previous campaigns, the CA Statute called for meetings of the candidates with the public in controlled circumstances with rules and procedures to avoid adhominem attacks, and a Presiding Officer overseeing the event" (United Nations Development Programme 1994, 26). All candidates in a given electoral area appeared together at the candidates' meetings held in each parish (RC-2).[26] After the presiding officer introduced the draft constitution and the constitution-making process, each candidate received a set amount of time (at least twenty minutes) to speak to the audience about constitutional issues. The audience then had time to ask questions of the candidates. The candidates' meetings were accessible to most citizens, were

25. For a full list of representatives' names, see Mukholi 1995, 93–99.
26. In some cases, CA candidates' meetings were held between contiguous parishes.

well attended, and "provided entertainment, diversion and civic education for the nation for over two months" (United Nations Development Programme 1994, 26). In my survey, 43.6 percent of respondents reported attending at least one candidates' meeting.

Outside of the confines of the candidates' meetings, the law severely restricted campaigning. The CA statute (NRC 1993) stipulated that "public rallies and any form of public demonstration in support of or against any candidate shall not be permitted." The statute also constrained party activity during the campaigns and election:

1. Elections for delegates shall be nonpartisan and every candidate for election as a delegate within an Electoral Area shall stand and be voted for by voters upon personal merit.
2. Any person who uses or attempts to use any political party, tribal or religious affiliations or any other sectarian ground as the basis for such person's candidature for election as a delegate commits an offence and shall, upon the satisfaction of the Commissioner of that fact, be disqualified from standing as a candidate for election as a delegate.

Despite these official restrictions, candidates used posters, the media, and "consultations" with small groups, and (although against the spirit of the law) many spoke at social gatherings and other forums to promote their election (Oloka-Onyango 2000, 51; Tripp 2005, 15; Tukahebwa 1996, 69). Government officials in particular violated campaign restrictions with impunity and illegally used government resources and work appearances to campaign (Makara 1996, 85; Makara and Tukahebwa 1996, 13; Mujaju 1999, 24; Oloka-Onyango 1995, 170; Tukahebwa 1996, 75). In addition, widespread bribing of voters occurred. According to evidence from my interviews and the observations of others, both government and opposition candidates engaged in bribery (Kasfir 1995; Makara and Tukahebwa 1996, 11–15; Odoki 1999, 18; Oloka-Onyango 1995, 171). One woman told me, "Candidates on both sides were giving money for votes. Someone was giving us soap to vote for him. Each promised something. Someone even gave a bull" (interview, Mpigi District, January 2001).

In addition to events involving candidates themselves, the campaign period generated other related activities and sources of information about constitutional issues. The Civic Education and Training Task Force of the CA Commission utilized the media to announce simple themes and hold more elaborate discussions. It also produced posters in English and sixteen vernacular languages; more than one hundred thousand abridged draft constitutions in English and six vernacular languages; and a large number of booklets, brochures, pamphlets, and flyers. Just before the election, the task force sent out drama troupes to perform a play on the constitution, *The Shield,* at more than 170 locations as well as on radio and television (United Nations Development Programme 1994, 21–31). In addition, a group of officially recognized NGOs conducted voter and civic education efforts as well as election monitoring throughout the country under the umbrella of the Civic Education Joint Coordination Unit.[27]

The CA elections took place on March 28, 1994,[28] generating the highest rate of participation in the constitution-making process as well as high levels of contestation, turnover,[29] and legitimacy. An estimated 85 percent of eligible voters, or 7,186,514 Ugandans, registered to vote, and 87.5 percent of registered voters turned out (Mukholi 1995, 37).[30] Turnout rates were slightly higher in areas suffering from civil conflict and where the NRM was weakest—such as in north and east—than in the more stable and progovernment central and western areas (Kasfir 1995). Although party competition for seats was outlawed, a fair amount of competition between individuals took place. Elections were contested in 211 of 214 constituencies, with an average of five candidates contesting each seat (Kasfir 1995). Notably, incumbency proved to be slightly more of a liability than an advantage: of the 140 incumbent NRC county representatives who ran for the CA, 69 won seats in the CA, and 71 lost. Incumbents were penalized the most in the north and east, where only 33 and 40 percent, respectively, won seats in the CA. Finally, most winners garnered a sizable percentage of the vote (an average of 48.5 percent), indicating that they had a sufficient mandate (Kasfir 1995).

The electoral context, rules, and practices seem to have favored the NRM government. An estimated two-thirds of those elected were said to be pro-

27. Two of the main partners in the Civic Education Joint Coordination Unit were the Uganda Joint Christian Council and the National Organization of Civic Education and Monitoring.

28. The elections had originally been scheduled for December 1993 but were postponed as a result of logistical problems. The interest-group election of CA representatives was held in April 1994 (Mukholi 1995, 39).

29. By turnover, I mean the defeat of incumbent NRC members who chose to run for seats in the CA. While it is not exactly correct to talk of turnover because the NRC and the CA ran concurrently, the CA was widely recognized as a prelude to the next parliamentary elections, with about 85 percent of incumbent county NRC members running for the CA (Furley and Katalikawe 1997; Geist 1995, 104–5; Kasfir 1995, 169; Odoki 2005; Tripp 2005, 14).

30. In my survey, 59.9 percent of respondents reported voting for a CA delegate.

movement.[31] Although the electoral playing field was certainly uneven, it is difficult to determine the degree to which it was improperly tilted in favor of the NRM. Opposition candidates have argued that they were unfairly disadvantaged in the campaigns and elections as a result of (1) the legal restrictions on freedom of political association and organizing; (2) the legal restrictions on campaigning outside of the joint candidates meetings; (3) the organizing of the NRM as a party in violation of the law; (4) the NRM's use of official venues and state resources for campaigning; (5) the bribery of voters; (6) the difficulties of campaigning in opposition strongholds due to civil war and instability; (7) the intimidation and harassment of opposition candidates and supporters; (8) ballot rigging; and (9) the president's targeted policy actions such as the reinstatement of monarchies to garner support for favored candidates.[32] However, Geist (1995) argues that the restrictive campaigning rules and ban on partisan activity may have helped the poorly organized parties avoid internal squabbles and compete with the NRM on a better footing than if the restrictions had not been in place. The fact that more sitting NRC members were defeated than victorious is telling because one would expect these members of government to benefit most from such alleged advantages. While some important democratic shortcomings undoubtedly existed, most internal and external observers believed that it was "a transparent and open election that was perceived as a legitimate expression of the will of the people by Ugandans and the international community" (United Nations Development Programme 1994, 32).

In my interviews, respondents indicated that campaign and election activities fostered considerable excitement and discussion of constitutional issues—and typically did so more than the UCC activities. For Ugandans, the import of the CA campaigns and election was much greater than I initially expected based on literature regarding elections in established democracies. However, the heightened importance of the event for most Ugandans is understandable. The CA election was only the second national election in

---

31. The exact partisan composition of the CA is unknown since candidates were required by law to run on individual merit rather than on party affiliation, but the NRM clearly had the upper hand. The affiliations and policy positions of most candidates were well known from past experience and from the campaigns. In total contradiction to his own no-party movement system, Museveni declared "We have won!" following the CA election (Tripp 2005, 15). Furthermore, the voting records and caucus membership clearly indicate that the NRM obtained the votes necessary to secure all its favored provisions.
32. For discussions of the freeness and fairness of the CA campaigns and elections, see Barya 2000; Furley and Katalikawe 1997; Hansen and Twaddle 1995; Kasfir 1995, 2000; Makara and Tukahebwa 1996; Mujaju 1999; Okeny 1995; Oloka-Onyango 2000; Regan 1995; Tripp 2005. I also relied on Ogwal 2001; Olet 2001; Ssemogerere 2001; Walubiri 2001.

Uganda since independence (the other being the controversial 1980 parliamentary election) and the first since the NRM had come to power. Many of my respondents referred to the CA election as the founding event for their new political dispensation.

The CA Debate

The CA delegates were sworn in on May 12 and 13, 1994, and they elected James Wapakhabulo as chair and Victoria Mwaka as deputy chair. The CA statute stipulated a term of four months; however, the CA chose not to act as a rubber stamp on the draft constitution as seems to have been envisioned. Instead, it debated every section of the draft. The debates became very heated, with the delegates polarized on certain key issues (described subsequently). In response, a number of caucuses developed in the CA. The National Caucus for Democracy grouped together delegates advocating multiparty politics. On the other side, the Movement Caucus brought together supporters of the movement or no-party system (also generally members or supporters of the government). The Women's Caucus was very active in promoting the interests of women and other marginalized groups (Tamale 1999; Tripp 2000; Tripp and Kwesiga 2002). Finally, there were caucuses based on region or ethnicity, the most active and prominent of which was the Buganda Caucus (Wapakhabulo 2001, 11). The sizable majority of candidates affiliated with the Movement Caucus meant that the government often pushed through its desired policies without accommodating the interests of opponents such as the multipartyists, Muslims, northerners, and Buganda loyalists.

Citizen participation in the constitution-making process continued during the CA debates. In my survey, 21.1 percent of respondents reported following the CA debates in some way. Some of these activities were initiated by state actors and some by citizens. For example, the CA Commission was charged with disseminating information about the debates to the public. In addition, CA delegates were instructed to consult with their constituents on contentious issues.[33] CA delegates often held consultations on their own accord, though this practice varied greatly from delegate to delegate. A few Ugandans told me in interviews that they contacted their delegates about constitutional issues or traveled to the capital, Kampala, to witness the debates in person.

---

33. In the event that an issue could not be resolved on the first vote (that is, that a proposal received at least half but not two-thirds of the votes), the rules required a recess of at least one week for delegates to consult their constituents. This happened only on one occasion.

The CA received several time extensions from the NRC and ultimately promulgated the constitution after seventeen months, on October 8, 1995, in the presence of the president and the NRC (Mukholi 1995, 43). In the end, an estimated 80 percent of the draft constitution was retained (Odoki 1999, 20). The 1995 Uganda constitution is one of the longest in the world, and the creation process lasted eight years and cost tens of millions of dollars (Hyden and Venter 2001, 203; Mukholi 1995, 42, 99; United Nations Development Programme 1994, 12–13).

Constitution-Making Programs Organized by Civil Society Groups

Alongside the activities organized by government agents, civil society groups developed their own events to mobilize public participation and to influence the constitution. The media, NGOs, professional associations, interest groups, and cultural and religious associations became very active, mobilizing not only group members but all citizens to take part in the process. Just as the government process developed over time, so did the constitutional programs of civil society. One NGO leader, Florence Nekyon (2001), reported, "For the activist groups, by the time we got organized it was partway through—it was already the CA." Not until the latter part of the process did many groups implement their programs.

The press was active even during the UCC process, as evidenced by the 2,763 newspaper articles on constitutional issues indexed in the UCC report. Kizito (1992, 121) notes,

> On their own volition, newspapers launched their own campaign to educate the people on the constitutional process. Many of them serialized the 1962 and 1967 constitutions. Regular contributors were given center spread to comment on any constitutional issue. . . . Letters to the editor pages were often used by people to forward their views or reply to writers' views on the constitutional process. Several pressure and interest groups utilized the media to push their ideas to the people.

In addition, the media carefully tracked the UCC activities, the CA campaigns and debates, and the adoption of the constitution in 1995. The UCC secretary, John M. Waliggo, also commented on the press's interest in the constitution-making process: "Everywhere we went, the TV, radio and print media followed us. Each seminar was widely reported on. For five years the media and people were never tired of the constitutional process. It remained very popular throughout" (quoted in Matembe and Dorsey 2002, 147–48).[34]

Some of the most active civil society groups were women's organizations, which feared that women would be left out of the government programs because of cultural norms discouraging women's involvement in public life. A coalition of women's NGOs—including Action for Development, Uganda Women Lawyers, and the University Women Association—worked with the Ministry of Women in Development to organize a parallel educational and consultation program during the time of the UCC. These groups designed a program to educate women and collect their views, which were also submitted to the UCC in a summary report (Matembe and Dorsey 2002, 132–36). In addition, almost half of the memoranda submitted to the UCC came from women or women's groups (Matembe and Dorsey 2002, 130). The National Association of Women Organisations in Uganda developed a radio program on constitutional issues called *Brain Trust* that aired weekly during the CA tenure.[35] The association conducted civic education on women's constitutional issues in ten districts and provided support for women CA delegates and representatives of other disadvantaged groups. Finally, the National Association of Women Organisations arranged for rural women to communicate their views to their CA delegates (Nekyon 2001). As a result of their mobilization and hard work, women's organizations won favorable constitutional provisions that altered their political involvement thereafter (Matembe and Dorsey 2002; Tamale 1999; Tripp 2000; Tripp and Kwesiga 2002).

Action for Development also directed their efforts toward educating the entire public (not just women) on constitutional issues (Akwi 2001; Matembe and Dorsey 2002; M. Mugisha 1999). The National Organisation for Civic Education and Monitoring, a coalition of fourteen different organizations, and the Uganda Joint Christian Council, representing the Church of Uganda, the Roman Catholic Church, and the Orthodox Church, were most active in civic education (Nekyon 2001; Onegi-Obel 2001; Oneka 1999). The Uganda Association of Women Lawyers and the Foundation for Human Rights Initiative organized events to educate the public on legal is-

---

34. In addition to his work on the UCC, Waliggo wrote a weekly column on constitutional issues and CA debates that appeared in the largest circulating newspaper from 1994 until the promulgation of the 1995 constitution (Matembe and Dorsey 2002, 156).

35. National Association of Women Organisations in Uganda is a coalition of women's NGOs and community-based organizations that formed in 1992 in large part to coordinate efforts to mobilize women in the constitution-making process.

sues and lobbied the UCC and the CA for human rights and other provisions (Akwi 2001; Odida 2001; Ssewanyana 2001). The Buganda kingdom was active during the process in support of a number of issues related to traditional leaders and Buganda (Englebert 2002; Mulondo 2001). Relations between the government and the NGOs were not always smooth, and government officials occasionally took actions to limit the influence of organizations perceived as hostile,[36] but the constitution-making activities of public and private groups generally were mutually supportive.

I mention only a few of the many civil society groups that mobilized citizen participation during the constitution-making process. I include citizen participation in civil-society-run programs in my exploration of the effects of participatory constitution making on citizens more generally. The effect of the participatory process on the organizations themselves is an important topic—my sources indicate that it had a major effect—but it is beyond the scope of this book.

In total, the Ugandan constitution-making process involved a range of participatory activities, including (1) attending educational seminars; (2) discussing issues at local governmental and associational meetings; (3) contributing views in oral and written forms; (4) campaigning; (5) public debates; (6) elections; (7) attention to media; (8) contacting leaders; and (9) lobbying elected CA delegates. These activities were initiated and organized by a variety of different individuals and groups: (1) the UCC; (2) the five levels of RCs; (3) CA candidates and supporters; (4) the CA Commission; (5) civic educators; (6) the media; (7) schools and other institutions; (8) NRM officials; (9) political parties; and (10) a plethora of NGOs and civic associations. So although the types of activities in which citizens engaged were standard forms of participation found in most democracies, the groups and actors mobilizing citizens to participate were somewhat unusual. Actors such as the commissioners were interested in including all citizens, not merely those already politically active and likely to vote. The citizens themselves were relatively new to democratic participation and had yet to establish regular patterns of political behavior and affiliation. As I show in chapter 3, citizens participated in the program primarily because they were

---

36. The most notable example of conflict is that of the National Organisation for Civic Education and Monitoring. Although the newly formed group was nonpartisan and included individuals from different political backgrounds, Museveni publicly accused it of being a partisan organization. The CA commission then withdrew the organization's accreditation, and some of its workers were harassed. The government appears to have overreacted to the bad behavior of a few individuals who were poorly screened by the organization. The government later allowed the organization to operate (Onegi-Obel 2001; Tripp 2000, 62–63).

pulled into the process by mobilizing elites and were not solely self-selected based on socioeconomic status, knowledge, and initial attitudes. Thus, the Ugandan program was unique in terms of who participated rather than of the kinds of participation in which they engaged.

2.3. CONSENSUS AND CONTENTIOUS ISSUES

Understanding Uganda's constitution-making process, its participants, and its consequences requires some knowledge of the issues at stake. The vast majority of constitutional issues were easily settled in a manner acceptable to all: a few contentious issues received the majority of attention. The issues amenable to national consensus included (1) the supremacy of a democratic constitution; (2) a liberal bill of rights that also specified rights for disadvantaged groups; (3) a directly elected president; (4) a system of checks and balances among legislative, executive, and judicial branches of government; (5) the devolution of power from national to local governments; (6) a professional army subordinate to civilian rule; and (7) English as the official language (UCC 1992a, 10). Five issues elicited strong disagreement at all stages of the process: (1) the position of the kingdoms and traditional rulers; (2) a federal or unitary form of government; (3) the national language; (4) the land tenure system; and (5) the movement or multiparty political system. This section describes the debates on each contentious issue as well as the outcome as reflected in the 1995 constitution. These contentious issues shaped whom leaders mobilized to participate (chapter 3) and the effect of participation on citizen views about the constitution (chapter 5).

The role of the kingdoms and traditional rulers was more contentious during the UCC than during the CA. The monarchists, led by Baganda, argued for the restoration of traditional rulers on the grounds that traditional rule is a cultural right illegally abolished by Obote. Some monarchists argued for a complete restoration of political power to the traditional leaders as well as the restoration of their cultural positions and material possessions. In opposition, the republicans argued that traditional leaders were archaic and that the relationship between cultural leaders and elected leaders was potentially destabilizing. They pointed to the conflict between the *kabaka* and Obote that preceded the 1966 constitutional crisis as a warning of what would happen if traditional leaders were restored (Englebert 2002; Odoki 1999, 15).

The UCC recommended that traditional leaders be restored where the people wanted such leaders but that their role be restricted to culture and development. Just prior to the CA election, the NRC passed the Restoration of Traditional Rulers Statute of 1993, arguably as a way to gain votes from the Baganda. Buganda and some of the other kingdoms were restored, along with their property, thus preempting the constitution-making process.[37] While the restoration at first pleased monarchists, many ultimately remained dissatisfied because the constitution failed to grant traditional leaders political power and taxation rights (Englebert 2002; Kingdom of Buganda 2001; Mukholi 1995, 33, 49–50; Odoki 1999, 15).

The issue of federal or unitary system is intimately linked to the former issue regarding traditional rulers.

> The monarchists considered [federalism] part and parcel of (*ebyafee*) "returning our things" as it was in the 1963 constitution with Kingdoms existing as federal states. Those who opposed this arrangement feared that the 1962 scenario would be recreated whereby some areas would enjoy this "privilege" while others had only unitary status. (Odoki 1999, 15)

The issue of form of government in Uganda is more about the restoration of a strong kingdom than about federalism as most political scientists conceive of it. The widespread use of the term *federo* in all the debates about the form of government, even by elites speaking in English, indicates the importance of Ugandan history in the debate.[38]

The draft constitution and the 1995 constitution provide for decentralization, with some government functions devolved to the district level. The UCC and the CA thus endorsed the system that had been in effect since 1986. Although the UCC, the majority of CA delegates, and the government tried to portray decentralization as a compromise position between federal and unitary systems, the Baganda traditionalists remain unsatisfied and continue to lobby for a constitutional amendment restoring federalism (Byarugaba and Makara 1996, 138; Englebert 2002; Kingdom of Buganda 2001; Mukholi 1995, 48–52).

---

37. Many Ugandans believe that this government action was motivated by the desire to obtain Buganda's support for the government's favored candidates in the CA election. The politically strategic nature of the restoration is evident from the contrast in the president's support for the restoration of the *kabaka* in Buganda, which was likely to win the NRM votes, and his opposition to it in his home territory of Ankole, where the restoration was unpopular with the majority of voters (Englebert 2002; Furley and Katalikawe 1997).

38. Byarugaba and Makara (1996, 140) define the term as follows: "'*Federo*' is a local connotation of undiluted form of federalism. It also connotes restoring Buganda's glory as it was in the past, perhaps 30 or 40 years ago. Literally, '*federo*' is understood by a local Muganda [person of Baganda ethnicity] to mean the latter."

Ugandans also had strong feelings about the adoption of a national language. Most Baganda favored their language, Luganda. Most citizens from other regions preferred Swahili, while some favored a combination of the two or another language altogether (UCC 1992b, 362–63). The UCC recommended English as the official language without a specified national language (Odoki 1999, 15). In the CA, a proposal for Swahili won a majority of votes but did not achieve the necessary two-thirds. Delegates were required to consult with their constituents, and the proposal was defeated when it came up for a second vote. The 1995 constitution stipulates English as the official language but gives Parliament the power to prescribe the use of another (unspecified) language for education, legislation, administration, and judicial functions (Wapakhabulo 2001, 9).

Selecting a land tenure system was contentious, especially in the CA. During colonial times, British administrators awarded land to collaborating chiefs, thus creating landless squatters.[39] Land tenure remained an unresolved issue throughout the postindependence period. In the CA, divisions emerged between advocates of the landless peasants and supporters of the landlords (Wilson 2001). The debate also had an ethnic component, with Baganda, in the central region, being more supportive of the landlords' position (UCC 1992b, 396, 398). Unable to find a system acceptable to a supermajority, the CA left the matter to be settled by the Parliament within two years of its first sitting (Wapakhabulo 2001, 9).

The type of political system was (and still is) the most contentious constitutional issue in Uganda (Furley and Katalikawe 1997, 250; Makara and Tukahebwa 1996, 4; Mukholi 1995, 33; Oloka-Onyango 1998, 25; UCC 1992a, 11). As discussed in section 2.1, Museveni implemented the "movement system of government" (also known as no-party politics) after coming to power in 1986. During the constitution-making process, conflict arose over whether to extend the movement system or return to a multiparty system. The multipartyists (those supporting an immediate return to a multiparty system) argued that freedom of association is a fundamental right that cannot be restricted in a democracy. The movementists (those favoring the continuation of the movement system of government) maintained that political parties bore responsibility for Uganda's past political problems and thus needed to be suspended for some time to allow for national reconciliation and development (Odoki 1999, 15; UCC 1992a, 11). This debate is

---

39. The struggle about what to do with territories of this kind in Bunyoro, the "lost counties," aggravated tensions between the *kabaka* and President Obote and precipitated the 1966 constitutional crisis.

highly polarized and acrimonious, and the available data do not clearly demonstrate which system Ugandans in general preferred (Mukholi 1995, 33–34, 52–56; UCC 1992b, 351).[40]

In its report, the UCC (1992a, 217) recognized that the "people of Uganda have important values they cherish in both systems and they have serious elements they fear in both." It recommended that the constitution include both systems and that the people decide periodically, through referenda, which system they prefer. The report proposed that the movement system be maintained for five years (including the constraints on party activity) after the promulgation of the constitution and that a referendum be held on the subject in the fourth year (UCC 1992a, 213–31).

The issue of political system was a major issue during the CA campaigns, with the multipartyists winning an estimated 64 of the 214 directly elected seats (Mujaju 1999, 27).[41] Once in the CA, delegates organized themselves into rival caucuses on the issue. Sixty delegates walked out of the CA proceedings in protest when an amendment to delete the movement system from the constitution was defeated by a vote of 199–68 (Mukholi

---

40. The president and other political leaders argue that the majority of Ugandans expressed preference for the movement system of government, so the restrictions on party activity are thus a result of rather than an infringement on participatory democracy (Odoki 1999, 15–16; Wapakhabulo 2001, 10). Critics sharply disagree. In the absence of survey data conducted at the time of the constitution-making process, it is impossible to say for certain what proportion of the public supported the restrictions. The memoranda submitted to the Constitutional Commission, the 1994 CA election, the 2000 referendum on the political system, and a 2000 public opinion survey all seem to indicate majority public support for the movement system, which in practice restricted multiparty activity (Bratton and Lambright 2001; UCC 1992b). However, this evidence is far from conclusive. Of the memoranda that mentioned a preference for political system, 58 percent preferred the movement system, 25 percent preferred a multiparty system, 12 percent preferred some combination of the two, and 4 percent preferred some other system. The memoranda are not statistically representative of the general population, and the proportions vary considerably by category, with individuals and village-level local councils submitting the majority of pro-movement statements. During the CA elections, the issue of what political system was preferred was central, and more candidates known to prefer the movement system were elected than those with stated preferences for multiparty systems, although many other factors also influenced the vote. In the 2000 referendum where citizens were asked to choose between the continuation of the movement system and the introduction of multiparty politics, 91 percent of the valid votes were cast in favor of the movement system, with just 9 percent supporting a multiparty system. However, Bratton and Lambright (2001) point to the low turnout rate (52 percent of registered voters), campaign inequalities favoring the movement, and confusion regarding the purpose of the referendum, arguing that the referendum did not properly reflect the public will. Nonetheless, in the 2000 Afrobarometer survey, 78 percent of those who responded cited a preference for the movement system (2001, 439). Finally, it is also not clear that support for the movement is synonymous with support for restrictions on parties (though it is hard to see how the movement system could be maintained without some restrictions).

41. A total of 68 (64 plus the 4 party representatives) of 286 CA delegates supported multiparty politics.

1995, 52–57).[42] A number of multiparty CA delegates ultimately refused to sign the 1995 constitution.

The constitution provides for both systems of government by name in Article 69 and gives the people of Uganda the right to choose through referendum, much as the UCC recommended in the draft constitution. However, the most controversial part of the 1995 constitution is Transitional Provision Article 269, which states that from the commencement of the constitution until Parliament makes a law regulating political organizations, parties are prohibited from operating branch offices, holding delegates' conferences and public rallies, sponsoring or campaigning for or against a candidate, and engaging in activities that interfere with the movement political system.

Each of these issues had potential winners and losers. As the constitution-making process progressed, the rhetoric of the opposing forces became more acrimonious and their behavior more unscrupulous. While many Ugandans were satisfied with the way these contentious issues were resolved, some were highly critical of both the process and the constitution. The majority (which benefited from government assistance) ultimately pushed through its preferences in the CA without making sufficient compromises to appease opponents. The next section reviews existing analysis of the process and offers an additional approach for evaluating the participatory constitution-making model.

2.4. PRAISE, CRITICISM, INTENTIONS, AND OUTCOMES: EVALUATING PARTICIPATORY CONSTITUTION MAKING

The Ugandan constitution-making process has received widespread praise, both from the international community and from Ugandans themselves (Commonwealth Human Rights Initiative 1999; Hyden and Venter 2001; Matembe 2001; Mukholi 1995; Nekyon 2001; Odoki 2001, 2005; UCC 1992a; United Nations Development Programme 1994; Waliggo 1995; Wapakhabulo 2001). Indications are that most Ugandans think the methodology employed was in the interest of society as a whole and that the process was conducted in a free and fair manner. At a minimum, the development of the constitution generated excitement and interest among citizens eager to have their views heard. This is evidenced by the high atten-

---

42. The delegates who walked out included Paul Ssemogerere, Cecilia Ogwal, Dan Nabudere, and Senteza Kajubi. My survey and open-ended interviews included respondents from the electoral areas of these CA delegates.

dance at conferences, seminars, and workshops organized by the UCC, the large number of memoranda sent to the commission, the even greater numbers of citizens who attended the CA candidates' meetings, the high turnout in the CA election, and the attention paid to the CA debates.

Furthermore, in a survey of organized civil society groups conducted in 1990 by the Center for Basic Research in Uganda, 90 percent of the responding groups agreed that the process was a positive development, 80 percent agreed that the exercise was necessary and appropriate at that time, and 59 percent felt that the necessary preconditions existed to ensure its success (Oloka-Onyango and Tindifa 1991, 7).[43] In another study that asked citizens about the CA campaigns and election, more than 80 percent of those surveyed in Jonam Constituency, Nebbi District, said that the election was free and fair, while more than 70 percent surveyed in Fort Portal Municipality, Kabarole District, agreed (Gingyera-Pinycwa 1996, 43; Mujaju 1996, 60).[44] The same project included seven case studies covering the entire campaign and election period. The seven investigators concluded that the campaign and election exercise was valid, free, and fair (Byarugaba and Makara 1996, 140).

> All the researchers concluded that this particular election raised a lot of enthusiasm amongst voters and the majority of the voters and candidates were confident that the electoral process was properly managed. These perceptions accounted for the large number of people who turned up to vote and the few petitions that were filed by candidates with the High Court over election malpractices. (Mukwaya 1996, 125)

In the in-depth interviews I conducted with citizens throughout the country, the majority of respondents echoed the sentiments of one woman: "The process didn't need improving. There is no better thing than to get

---

43. On the flip side, 41 percent reported that the "political atmosphere was not conducive enough to enable broad and democratic debate on the constitutional process, because it was not adequately preceded by the requisite conditions that would ensure success" (Oloka-Onyango and Tindifa 1991, 7). The survey found that 2.2 percent of the organizations argued that the exercise was wholly unnecessary, and 32 percent reported that the UCC was not adequately publicizing the major issues concerning Uganda's future constitutional framework. The survey was conducted in 1990, partway through the UCC's term, and was designed to obtain the views of the "most organized sector of society" on the key constitutional issues being debated as well as on the process itself (2). The forty organizations that responded (of seventy that received the survey) included trade unions, professional associations, NGOs, religious organizations, the press, political parties, academic associations, student groups, and cooperative unions (37–39).

44. These results cannot be assumed to represent the entire Ugandan population since neither the locations nor the citizens surveyed were randomly sampled.

down to the layman" (interview, Luwero District, January 2001). Most Ugandans felt the constitution-making process was legitimate.

Although most Ugandans were pleased, a vocal minority argued that the process was tainted, illegitimate, unfair, and wasteful.[45] Opposition politicians, opinion leaders, and scholars have actively expressed concerns in the media, at seminars and conferences, and in discussions with fellow citizens and foreign diplomats.[46] The more common critiques of the process include allegations that (1) civil war hindered participation in areas where support for the NRM was low; (2) political party activity was banned throughout the process, and freedom of association was severely restricted; (3) Museveni appointed constitutional commissioners who favored the NRM and used his authority to pressure them to alter the draft in his favor; (4) the commissioners biased the memoranda submissions by using misleading wording in the *Guiding Questions* and collecting views through the pro-NRM local government council system; (5) the consultation exercises were used more to teach about the movement system and to indoctrinate citizens than to collect their views; (6) Museveni preempted the constitution-making process by reinstating the kingdoms just prior to the CA elections as a means of ensuring that NRM candidates were elected; (7) NRM candidates violated campaigning regulations with impunity and used state resources to heighten their electoral chances; (8) the NRM behaved like a political party during the CA campaigns and elections, in violation of the movement's doctrine and the law; (9) the provisions for presidential appointees and special interest delegates stacked the CA with progovernment forces; (10) Museveni pressured the CA delegates through promises of ministerial appointments, threats of censure, private sessions with members, and involvement in the Movement Caucus; (11) the process was excessively long and complex, allowing the movement to entrench itself in power and diverting scarce funds and human resources from more important tasks.[47] Government manipulations of the process increased over time and seemed

---

45. Little criticism of the process arose from international sources at the time.

46. The UPC party led formal protest actions against the process on a number of occasions: (1) the UPC and many of its followers boycotted the UCC seminars and did not send memoranda; (2) the UPC also boycotted the CA and refused to send its allotted two delegates; (3) the UPC filed a petition against the CA election rules; (4) sixty-four delegates walked out of the CA proceedings in protest when the political system was discussed; and (5) a small number of CA delegates boycotted the promulgation of the 1995 constitution. Some prominent UPC members, such as Celia Ogwal, defied the orders of Obote and other top UPC leaders and contested in electoral areas for some of the 214 directly elected seats, causing a rift in the party (Ogwal 2001).

47. Critics of the process at both the elite level and the mass level repeated the items on this list.

to be most blatant during the CA debates. The most outspoken critics argue that what emerged was a partisan or NRM constitution. For example, Mujaju (1999, 2) argues that "the lengthy process of making Uganda's constitution was a device to silence the opposition and design what is clearly a movement constitution."

An important body of literature and commentary describes the Ugandan constitution-making process and evaluates the competing claims about its freeness and fairness.[48] Opinions on this topic vary considerably. Nonetheless, the dominant academic perspective recognizes that notable deviations from the democratic ideal occurred but also asserts that public involvement was impressive and that the process prior to 1995 was relatively free and fair.

My objective in this book is different from most previous works on the topic, which evaluate the fairness of the process. Instead, I seek to determine how individuals responded to the process, whether or not it was completely free. Even though the playing field was not level, the vast majority of citizens and leaders continued to play the game. What effect did the game have on the country's political culture? At the end of the game, did the players have a different perspective than those who watched from the sidelines?

In addition to the arguments about the fairness of the process, a related debate concerns the motivations of the leaders who oversaw the constitution-making process. Supporters of the process argue that Museveni's involvement in constitution making was motivated by his belief in participatory democracy; the ten-point plan developed during the guerrilla struggle; his previous experiences with undemocratic, sectarian, and violent governments; and his concern for the Ugandan people (Mukholi 1995, 9; Odoki 1992; Waliggo 1995; Wapakhabulo 2001). Critics argue that he is first and foremost motivated by the desire to legitimize and entrench NRM rule and to maintain power at all costs (Barya 2000; Furley and Katalikawe 1997; Kasfir 2000; Mujaju 1999; Ogwal 2001; Oloka-Onyango 2000). Similar arguments are made about the constitutional commissioners, the CA delegates, government ministers, and other key actors. Supporters contend that these leaders acted out of conviction and desire for a peaceful and democratic Uganda. Critics counter that they were motivated by their interest in material enrichment, securing power now and in the future, and pleasing Museveni in hopes of being appointed to coveted ministerial, administrative, or judicial posts. Some analysts acknowledge that a large number of actors

---

48. Some of the most notable writings on this issue include Barya 1993; Furley and Katalikawe 1997; Hansen and Twaddle 1995; Justus and Oloka-Onyango 2000; Makara, Tukahebwa, and Byarugaba 1996; Odoki 2005; Oloka-Onyango 1995; Oloka-Onyango and Tindifa 1991; Regan 1995; Tripp 2005.

with different interests influenced the process and that policy choices often served multiple goals simultaneously (see, for example, Furley and Kata-likawe 1997; Geist 1995).

Again, my goal here differs somewhat from that of the previous literature that debates the altruistic or self-serving intentions of the leaders. I seek to determine the outcomes—intended or unintended—of the process. On the one hand, if we assume that Museveni and others were motivated entirely by altruistic desires to build a democratic and stable Uganda, whether they were successful remains an open and important question. On the other hand, if we assume that Museveni and his ministers, the Uganda constitutional commissioners, and the CA delegates were motivated entirely by their self-interested search for power and enrichment and did not care at all about citizen attitudes, participatory theory still suggests that the methods they chose involving mass public participation would have unintended consequences for the participants. My goal is to identify benefits and drawbacks to the participatory process that took place rather than to assign praise or blame to specific leaders.

Although not my primary focus, the debates among Ugandan elites about the fairness of the process and the motivation of the leaders are still relevant to this study. In chapter 4 I argue that officials' increasingly undemocratic and unfair behavior led participants to distrust government institutions. While most people seem to be reacting to increasingly undemocratic government actions after the promulgation of the constitution in 1995, a few also noted pre-1995 constitution-making activities. Furthermore, chapter 5 asserts that citizen evaluations of the process were profoundly influenced by elite opinions and arguments on the subject. I show that the extent to which the elites declared that the process was fair and genuine affected the degree to which the general public viewed the constitution as legitimate. The feeling among some opposition elites that the NRM had unfairly manipulated the process translated into negative assessments of the constitution among certain sections of the population.

2.5. UGANDA AS A TEST CASE

The Ugandan constitution-making process allows us to probe the consequences of participation in a particularly illuminating way. The effects of participation tend to be small and endogenous and thus difficult to substantiate with certainty. However, the effects of participation in the Ugandan case are expected to be more pronounced than in other participatory venues for a number of reasons. First, the development of a new constitution is a particularly salient issue, and the effects of participation are likely to be more dramatic when the stakes are high. Second, the constitution-making process was among the first opportunities for citizen participation after the regime change. The timing of the process also heightened the salience for the participants; founding elections are more influential than those that follow. Furthermore, the messages that participation conveyed were not redundant for the participants. Most Ugandan citizens were socialized under an authoritarian system; they were less likely to get cues about how to think, feel, and act democratically from their families, schools, media, and other institutions than would be their counterparts in developed democracies. Attitudes about the constitution were not yet formed, citizens possessed little political knowledge, and most had no prior experience with political participation. The messages Ugandans received by participating in constitution making may have been the first or only messages they got about democracy, their constitution, and their new government.

Third, to evaluate analytically the results of participation, the observed outcome variables must exhibit variation. In the Ugandan case, the outcome variables of interest—democratic attitudes, civic competence, institutional trust, political knowledge, and constitutional legitimacy—range across the entire spectrum of possibilities. The variation in democratic culture among Ugandan citizens warrants an explanation and provides predictive power for determining the causal importance of participation. Fourth, elite mobilization, more than individual initiative, determined who participated in the constitution-making process.[49] Previous Ugandan regimes locked most citizens out of the political arena, so leaders played a crucial role during the constitution-making process by pulling people into the public sphere. Individual characteristics and attitudes were less important motivators for participation than is typically the case. This phenomenon makes it easier to separate the effect of participation on attitudes from the effect of attitudes on participation.

Fifth, enhancing democratic culture was a deliberate focus of at least some of the designers and implementers of the Ugandan constitution-making process. A participatory program that is specifically designed to increase knowledge, build supportive attitudes, and enhance democratic behavior is

49. Chapter 3 demonstrates that mobilization factors (such as the respondent's relationship to the government, the local community, and civil society as well as the probability that the respondent received and accepted the messages from the program organizers) significantly predict participation in Uganda.

more likely to produce these changes.[50] Sixth, compared with other cases of participatory constitution making, Uganda's process was among the most extensive in the types of participation employed, the scope of inclusion, and the time allowed for public participation; many citizens participated in a variety of activities over an eight-year period. In sum, if participation does affect participants' attitudes, knowledge, and behavior, then we should see this phenomenon in the case of Ugandan constitution making. If we do not see it here, then claims that we will see it in other cases are suspect.

The Ugandan case is valuable because the effects of participation in constitution making are likely to be larger than the effects of most programs of public participation. However, the difference between participation in the Ugandan process and participation in other programs is a difference in magnitude, not a difference in kind. Ugandans engaged in standard activities that are part of the democratic repertoire. As part of the constitution-making process, they attended local government meetings, contacted government officials, wrote editorials, called radio talk-show programs, planned activities with their local associations, campaigned for their favorite candidates, attended rallies, voted, and lobbied government officials. The underlying mechanisms of change in other cases of participation are expected to be the same as those deduced from the Ugandan case. Thus, while the consequences of participation are magnified in the Ugandan case, the analysis is relevant to other participatory programs in different contexts.

2.6. AFTER THE ADOPTION OF THE 1995 CONSTITUTION

Understanding the constellation of attitudes that I found during my field research in 1999, 2000, and 2001 requires some knowledge about the government's political performance following the promulgation of the constitution. Rather than ushering a more democratic dispensation, as people had hoped, observers note that the promulgation of the constitution in 1995 heralded a period of troubling democratic performance:

> Since the constitution was adopted in 1995, Uganda has slid precipitously backward in terms of civil and political liberties. There have been increasing restrictions on the freedom of association, harassment and intimidation of opposition members and media workers, efforts to ram through undemo-

---

50. Participation programs are often designed primarily to elicit information from participants, make decisions, choose leaders, and display support rather than to produce change in participants' political culture.

cratic legislation in parliament without a quorum, and the narrowing of political control from what once was a broad based government to a much
smaller circle of individuals. (Tripp 2005, 1)

Observers hold different opinions about the causes, trends, and depth of the
democratic deficit in Uganda while nonetheless agreeing that important
authoritarian tendencies remain at play.[51]

Some of the most egregious and well-known violations in the half decade
following the adoption of the constitution include the following:

1. government forces arrested members of Parliament and violently
   broke up seminars and workshops organized by NGOs and parties (Human Rights Watch 1999, 4–5; U.S. Department of
   State 2002);
2. despite the constitution's guarantee of freedom of the press, on
   a number of occasions, the government ordered the arrest of
   journalists and the temporary shutdown of newspapers under
   the draconian Press and Journalism Law of 1995 (Human
   Rights Watch 1999, 111–12; U.S. Department of State 2002);
3. Ugandan army soldiers are accused of harassment, looting, large-
   scale forced detention, and other human rights abuses, primarily
   in areas experiencing civil war, and the civil war still rages in the
   north, with devastating consequences (Human Rights Watch
   1999, 120–29; U.S. Department of State 2002);
4. the United Nations Security Council charged the Ugandan army
   with violating human rights and international law in the Democratic Republic of the Congo, including torture and the plun-
   der of natural resources (Africa Confidential 2003, 3; United
   Nations Security Council 2001);
5. police allegedly have abused prisoners, committed torture, coerced confessions, and engaged in extralegal killings (Human
   Rights Watch 1999, 130–43; Tripp 2005);
6. the 2001 presidential and parliamentary elections were plagued
   by rigging, intimidation, violence, bribery, and other irregular-
   ities, and Museveni reacted to political challengers with intolerance and threats and relied heavily on the armed forces to silence

---

51. Freedom House (2005) records a slight improvement in political and civil rights between 1994 and
1998, followed by a return to previous levels by 2000. Following the period of this research, slight improvements were again registered from 2003 through 2005.

critics (Carbone 2003, 498; A. Mugisha 2004, 141; Tripp 2005, 23; U.S. Department of State 2002)—for example by calling Besigye and his wife "traitors" and declaring that he would "crush" the opposition and "blow them up" (Africa Confidential 2001, 2);

7. upon taking power in 1986, Museveni constructed a "broad-based government" by offering posts to people of different social backgrounds and political affiliations, but following the adoption of the constitution, there was a narrowing of the political base and a purging of those who were critical of the president so that by 1996, nearly everyone in government shared Museveni's beliefs, despite the fact that the movement was supposed to be all-inclusive (Carbone 2003, 498; Mugisha 2004; Tripp 2005, 22);

8. freedom of political association has been severely constrained, as Parliament first "deliberately" failed to pass a political organizations bill, leaving in place the very stringent Article 269 that was intended for the transitional period and thus shackling political parties (Human Rights Watch 1999, 89), and then passed legislation that further limited the political space and centralized power, ignoring parliamentary rules such as one requiring a quorum and using other heavy-handed techniques (Tripp 2005, 23);

9. Parliament passed a number of controversial amendments to the constitution, most notably the Constitution (Amendment) Act No. 13 of 2000, which changed the constitution to "legalize" some government actions that the Supreme and Constitutional Courts had previously ruled unconstitutional (Nsambu 2001);

10. the government dragged its feet and obstructed the passing of enabling legislation for constitutional provisions: the Domestic Relations Bill, for example, languished in Parliament and provisions for an Equal Opportunities Commission were ignored despite concerted efforts on the part of women's groups (Tripp 2005, 27);

11. corruption has increased considerably, especially among the top echelon of government officials, and, following the 2001 presidential elections but preceding the parliamentary elections, Museveni publicly announced that he would fill political posts and distribute resources according to regional political support (Africa Confidential 2001, 2).

All of these actions took place prior to or during my field research, and various respondents mentioned these events when asked about the government.

However, most Ugandan citizens seem not to have been especially disturbed by these political events. Despite violations of human rights and democratic constitutionalism, the government and the political system still enjoyed considerable support among the population (Africa Confidential 2001; Bratton, Lambright, and Sentamu 2000; Logan et al. 2003). In June 2000 (less than a year before I conducted my survey) the Afrobarometer survey indicated that 93 percent of Ugandans were at least somewhat satisfied with the president's performance, 52 percent were satisfied with their members of Parliament, and 72 percent were satisfied with the way democracy actually worked in Uganda. Furthermore, the Afrobarometer survey evidence indicates that political trust remained very high at that time, as 82 percent of respondents said that they trusted the NRM (in sharp contrast to the 32 percent who trusted political parties), 76 percent trusted the Electoral Commission, 63 percent trusted the courts of law, and 53 percent trusted the police (Bratton, Lambright, and Sentamu 2000).

While foreign observers assert that Uganda was not a democracy because it did not allow freedom of association or allow for party competition, most Ugandans thought otherwise. Only 7 percent of Afrobarometer respondents said that Uganda was not a democracy, while 32 percent said that it was a democracy with major problems, 32 percent said it was a democracy with minor problems, and a surprising 25 percent reported that Uganda was a full democracy. These high levels of satisfaction, support, and trust (which are also evident in my survey data) are well above the average sentiments expressed by citizens living in the eleven other African countries surveyed by Afrobarometer at that time. While these figures declined notably by the time of the second Afrobarometer survey (August and September 2002), Ugandans still tended to rate their democracy, government, and leaders higher than did their counterparts in other African countries.[52] In addition,

---

52. Logan et al. (2003, 9) reported "a substantial shift among respondents from reporting that the country is fully democratic (25 percent in 2000, just 11 percent in 2002) to reporting that it is a democracy with minor problems (32 percent in 2000, 43 percent now)." They continue, "Still greater concern may be aroused by a substantial decrease in the level of satisfaction with Uganda's democratic system. In 2000, fully 72 percent of Ugandans expressed some degree of satisfaction with the way democracy actually works in practice in their country, a level that was surpassed only by an early post-transition Nigeria (84 percent) among other Afrobarometer countries (12-country Round 1 mean of 58 percent). But the number who report being somewhat or very satisfied has dropped to 60 percent in 2002, while the number expressing dissatisfaction has doubled to one-third of all respondents (33 percent). (Note that again the question was not asked of all respondents in 2000, so the figures are not exactly comparable.) Nonetheless, Uganda still compares relatively well with other Round 2 countries surveyed to date.

most Ugandans say that their civil and political liberties improved following the enactment of the 1995 constitution. When asked in 2002 to compare their present system of government with the former system of government under the old constitution (that is, before 1995), Ugandans reported that things were better or much better now with respect to freedom to say what they think (85 percent); freedom to vote as they choose (79 percent); freedom from unjust arrest (67 percent); freedom of political affiliation (62 percent); ability to influence government (56 percent); and equality of treatment (51 percent) (Logan et al. 2003, 19).

While most Ugandans seem to have tended to overlook or accept their government's many democratic deficits, the evidence in later chapters indicates that those who participated in the constitution-making process were especially uneasy about their government's poor democratic performance. This is not to say that participation is the only factor that affected Ugandans' political assessments. For example, support for the government and regime is regionally concentrated: it is highest in the west and lowest in the north.[53] Regional differences are based on political affiliations and historical legacies as well as on the performance of the current government in each area. Individuals who felt close to the NRM were more positive about their leaders and institutions than those who felt close to political parties.[54] Although regional and partisan differences in institutional trust existed, those who participated in the constitution-making process felt differently about their government institutions than did other citizens within their own regions or those who shared their partisan biases. In short, participants reacted more negatively than did nonparticipants to democratic violations, regardless of their locations of residence or their political affiliations.

It is surpassed by Namibia (78 percent), but is now trailed by Nigeria (57 percent), as well as Ghana (46 percent), South Africa (44 percent) and Cape Verde (33 percent)" (10).

53. For example, analysis of the first-round Afrobarometer survey in Uganda revealed wide variation in perceived extent of democracy in 2000: "Hefty regional differences were observed on this question. Whereas northerners were most likely to say that Uganda was 'not a democracy' (24 percent), easterners and westerners were most inclined to hold the opinion that Uganda had attained 'full democracy' (33 and 30 percent respectively)" (Bratton, Lambright, and Sentamu 2000, 8). Bratton and Lambright (2001) also recorded regional variation in turnout and voting in 2000. Finally, Logan et al. (2003) argued that the regional differences in political support, trust, satisfaction, and perceived extent of democracy persisted or increased between 2000 and 2002.

54. Based on the second-round Afrobarometer surveys in 2002, Logan et al. (2003, 10, 11) wrote that "opposition partisans are also much more critical of the political system: a mere 28 percent rate it as relatively democratic, while more than one out of five (22 percent) contend that Uganda is not a democracy at all. In contrast, 72 percent of Movement backers consider the country fairly democratic, and just 2 percent do not consider it a democracy." They also note that "76 percent of Movement partisans are satisfied with the country's democracy in practice, compared to just 32 percent of those affiliated with the opposition."

2.7. CONCLUSION

This chapter began with a review of Ugandan political and constitutional history. The country's often brutal history generated its profound need to develop a new democratic political culture, strengthen government legitimacy, and foster a spirit of constitutionalism. The participatory constitution-making process seemed to offer a means of achieving these goals. The process deviated in several ways from the democratic ideal, and the government exhibited significant authoritarian tendencies during and after the constitution-making process. Nonetheless, I argue that Uganda provides a critical test case for the participatory model of constitutional reform. States that employed the participatory model in the past—and many that are likely to do so in the future—were troubled by political instability, repression, lawlessness, and civil conflict.[55] The model is attractive precisely because it promises a remedy to these ills. The relevant empirical question is not whether an ideal program in a consolidated democracy strengthens democratic citizenship but rather whether participatory constitution making holds promise for transitioning states that lack a democratic culture. While by no means perfect, the Ugandan process was generally more balanced, transparent, and inclusive than other participatory programs to date. Furthermore, the majority of respondents felt positively about the process and Uganda's democratic performance at the time. The Ugandan constitution-making process represents a relatively optimistic scenario of what we can expect from participatory programs in troubled states undergoing transition.

The UCC report (1992a, 36) boldly states that the process had many benefits for Ugandan participants:

> The methodology employed has yielded tremendous results. People have become politically aware. They are eager to assert and defend their rights. They are convinced of their right to participate in their own governance. Never again will they allow major decisions which concern them to be decided upon without their being consulted. Participatory democracy and a search for a consensus have gradually become a new culture in Uganda. The ordinary citizens have found the exercise most reassuring. Their views on

---

55. Widner (2005b, 515) found that broad-based consultation was least common in Europe and most common in Africa, the Americas, and the Pacific Islands. Furthermore, the countries that had adopted the most participatory constitution-making processes in the past (such as Albania, Brazil, Columbia, Eritrea, Fiji, Kenya, Namibia, Nicaragua, Rwanda, South Africa, Trinidad and Tobago, and Uganda) had recent histories of authoritarian rule, severe social or economic inequalities, human rights abuses, and violence.

the new constitution did not appear to be much different from those of the elites. They can now confidently participate in all other national exercises, fully convinced that their views will carry weight. The exercise has taught people tolerance of views that differ from their own.

The remaining chapters of the book evaluate these claims. Chapter 3 evaluates the consequences of participation for the development of democratic attitudes, self-confidence in civic skills, and support for government institutions. Chapter 4 evaluates the influence of participation on constitutional and political knowledge. Chapter 5 evaluates the effect of participation on support for the constitution. Chapter 6, the conclusion, returns to the question of the net value of the participatory model based on a greater understanding of actual costs and benefits.

CHAPTER 3

Changing Attitudes

This chapter seeks to establish whether participation in Ugandan constitution-making activities influenced participants' political attitudes and thereby to answer three questions. (1) Does involving citizens in the making of a democratic constitution inculcate democratic attitudes, or does it harden conflicting identities and foster intolerance? (2) Does participating in a unique program cause citizens to feel more competent with regard to subsequent political activity, or are nonhabitual activities ineffectual in building civic skills? (3) Are active citizens more likely to support the state institutions that they took part in creating or to criticize the actual performance of those institutions? In short, how did participation affect democratic values, subjective political capabilities, and institutional trust?

In answering these questions, I explicitly account for the possibility of reciprocal relationships between participation and the attitude variables. I first analyze the factors that predict participation; this model serves as the basis for the subsequent analysis of the effects of participation. I seek not merely to record the correlation between participation and attitudes but rather to probe the causal effect of participation on attitude change to the fullest degree possible given the limits of cross-sectional survey data. Qualitative analysis of in-depth interviews provides additional insights about the direction and nature of causal connections.

Section 3.1 reviews the related theoretical and empirical literature about the consequences of participation on democratic attitudes, civic competence, and institutional trust and develops the three hypotheses to be evaluated. Section 3.2 introduces the empirical data and the methodology used to evaluate the hypotheses. Section 3.3 presents a model predicting participation. Sections 3.4, 3.5, and 3.6 specify the multiple equation models used to estimate the consequences of participation and present the results for each of the three systems. The chapter concludes with a summary of the key findings and their implications.

3.1. LITERATURE ON CONSEQUENCES OF PARTICIPATION

Chapter 1 discussed the different perspectives on participation and the general influences that participation is thought to have on the individual. This chapter specifically focuses on the relationships between (1) democratic attitudes and participation, (2) subjective political capabilities and participation, and (3) institutional trust and participation. For each relationship, I discuss the expressed goals of the Ugandan leaders most involved in the process and review the pertinent arguments of the optimistic participatory theory, the perspective that is most prevalent today. Based on existing literature, I develop the three hypotheses that are evaluated later in the chapter.

Democratic Attitudes and Participation

> We are happy to observe that the constitutional debate in all types of fora
> has been conducted in a mature way with due respect to pluralistic views
> and with a sense of mutual acceptance of one another. This augurs well for
> the creation of a democratic culture of tolerance, compromise, give and
> take, acceptance of majority views while respecting interests of the minor-
> ity, and resolution of conflicts through peaceful means, which is absolutely
> essential for sustaining democracy. (Odoki 1992, 13)

The designers of the Ugandan constitution-making process—among them Benjamin J. Odoki, chair of the Uganda Constitutional Commission (UCC)—felt strongly about the need to build democratic norms to support the new institutions being developed and used participation as a means to bring about the desired changes in attitude. They believed that participatory constitution making would inculcate democratic attitudes in two ways. First, as this quotation indicates, citizens could experience democracy throughout the process and thus internalize democratic habits and norms. Second, participatory constitution making provided an opportunity to disseminate information and educate citizens about democracy and rights. Another commissioner, Frederick E. Ssempebwa (2001), conveyed this perspective:

> Many people had got accustomed to being treated illegally and wouldn't
> complain. They thought, for example, it was the order of the day to be ar-
> rested by police. You were detained for two–three days and you thanked

God. You said, "That's all right. At least I haven't been assaulted or killed." You know? So that's what had come to be known in Uganda, a system that did not observe the rule of law, and people were accepting that. So we went all out to convince people that, "Look, under the new constitutional regime, you will have definite rights, and you can insist on them because they will be insured in the constitution."

Participatory constitution making provided opportunities for practice in and education about democracy.

The vision of the Ugandan policymakers mirrors the ideas of classical scholars of democracy and more recent participatory theorists. These optimistic theorists hold that participation increases citizen attachment to key principles of democracy: citizen rights and duties, tolerance, public involvement in decision making, equality, autonomy, freedom, resistance to hierarchy, and respect for the rule of law. They posit that participation leads to an increase in democratic attitudes in several ways. Citizens who participate learn about the democratic process, institutional structures, governmental procedures, national norms, and citizen rights and duties. When citizens become familiar with workings of a democratic government and its advantages, they are more likely to become attached to the foundational principles of democracy (Nelson 1987; Salisbury 1975; Thompson 1970). Participation enables citizens to understand and evaluate the long-term costs and benefits of adhering to democratic norms (Nie, Junn, and Stehlik-Barry 1996, 6). Individuals also become more tolerant when, through participation, they are exposed to the wide variety of interests and opinions in the polity and the democratic mechanisms for resolving conflict (Almond and Verba 1963; Mill 1948; Rousseau 1968; Salisbury 1975). Citizens who invest time and resources in participation want to feel that their action was efficacious and proper. Therefore, participants will eagerly embrace the democratic norms of civic duty and popular influence on government (Clarke and Acock 1989, 553; Verba, Schlozman, and Brady 1995).[1]

Drawing on the motivations expressed by the designers of Uganda's constitution-making process and on the writings of scholars, I hypothesize that participation has a positive effect on democratic attitudes, ceteris paribus.

---

1. Of the four reviewed methods by which participation builds democratic attitudes, the first three are consistent with the precepts of rational choice. Radcliff and Wingenbach (2000) argue that rational egoistic individuals learn through participation that their goals are best served by adhering to democratic norms in the same way that rational agents in computer simulations learn that nice strategies are most effective. The last explanation is derived from psychological models of cognition whereby individuals resist dissonant information and beliefs (Clarke and Acock 1989).

Political Capabilities and Participation

> We aimed at getting women to talk. Women are not encouraged to speak in public, so we tried to encourage them to speak. It depended on who was facilitating the program as to whether or not we succeeded. (M. Mugisha 1999)

Another objective of the constitutional commissioners was to develop feelings of civic competence within the general population. Previous regimes did not allow much public participation. The commissioners worried that under the new constitution, citizens would fail to become involved even if given the chance because they lacked the necessary skills. Building political capabilities was also a central goal of a number of nongovernmental organizations (NGOs) active in the process, particularly those representing traditionally disadvantaged groups, such as Action for Development. As Maude Mugisha, the group's executive director at the time of the constitution-making process, explained to me, the organization's constitution-making activities sought not only to gather women's views but also to empower women to participate in politics in the future. This meant teaching women about government, encouraging them to speak in public, and helping them develop the civic skills needed to advocate for their interests.

Rather than organizing standard civic education exercises to teach people about government, the various government institutions and NGOs facilitated participation in constitution-making activities (such as soliciting opinions on what should be included in the constitution, mobilizing around the Constituent Assembly [CA] election campaigns, and lobbying the CA delegates). Supporters of this approach argued that the best way for citizens to learn the skills needed to participate in politics and to feel confident in their ability to do so was by practicing politics.

The idea that participation builds political capabilities is prominent in classical theorizing on democracy. For example, in his well-known study of America, Tocqueville (1945, vol. 1, chapter 14) wrote,

> The humblest individual who co-operates in the government of society acquires a certain degree of self-respect; and as he possesses authority, he can command the services of minds more enlightened than his own. He is canvassed by a multitude of applicants, and in seeking to deceive him in a thousand ways, they really enlighten him. He takes a part in political undertakings which he did not originate, but which give him a taste for undertakings of the kind.

Mill (1948, chapter 5) also stressed that citizens learn politics by practicing politics, as did many contemporary participatory theorists (Barber 1984; Mansbridge 1995; Pateman 1970; Thompson 1970). Given these views, I hypothesize that participation has a positive effect on subjective political capabilities, ceteris paribus.

Institutional Trust and Participation

> We held these mass meetings at the subcounties. We invited everyone to come and give us his or her opinion. In the past there was a lot of mistrust of the government. This was a bad thing. We needed to change this. . . . We explained to the people that the constitution is not just a piece of paper. It explains how power is to be shared. It explains about what powers are, who holds them, and who looks over the power holders. We wanted them to feel that the constitution was going to liberate us. That there would be equality for each person's views—the old illiterate woman would have the same weight as the educated official. There would be checks on the leaders. Then we told how the people were to participate, how to collect opinions and such. . . . We explained that after the people created the new constitution, the government would work for the people. (Waliggo 1999)

Waliggo's words reflect the desire to overcome the distrust and apathy that characterized previous regimes in Uganda. According to Van Cott (2000), the central purpose of constitutional reform is often to legitimize the regime overseeing the changes. Ugandan leaders felt a need for renewed legitimacy to govern effectively, and they turned to constitutional reform as a means of erasing past government transgressions and starting afresh with a new social contract. They hoped that using public participation as the basis for this reform would grant additional legitimacy to the process, the newly created political system, and its leaders. A volume on the constitution-making processes in Eritrea, Ethiopia, South Africa, and Uganda concludes (Hyden and Venter 2001, 209),

> Ignoring the "rules of the game" and how they are constituted has proved increasingly costly to political leaders in Africa. By paying attention to these issues, however, political leaders can . . . use constitution-making to jump-start politics by giving it and its principal actors a fresh legitimacy.

In short, participatory constitution making is thought to increase legitimacy and build trust in government.

One of the major functions of participation, discussed in classical writings on democracy, is to enhance government trust and legitimacy. In a review of the theoretical literature on participation, Salisbury (1975, 326) argues,

> Political participation is regarded as a legitimizing act. Insofar as the citizens participate in governmental affairs, through voting and whatever other means exist, they give their consent to decisions and so legitimize those decisions and the regime that makes them. This perspective is, of course central to much discussion of democracy and its requirements from Locke to Schumpeter.

At the individual level, Salisbury adds (1975, 328), the increase in legitimacy is reflected in higher political trust.

Later scholars picked up the idea that participation builds trust in government and elaborated on the causal mechanisms at work. Participation leads to political trust through (1) creating citizen perceptions that the processes for selecting leaders and making decisions are fair; (2) increasing the likelihood that citizens will agree with government output (either because they feel the output is a product of their interests or because they altered their original interests to reflect the interests of others); and (3) building attachment to the political community (Almond and Verba 1963; Bowler and Donovan 2002; Clarke and Acock 1989; Pateman 1970; Tyler 1998).

The third main hypothesis in this chapter is based on this classical view of the influence of participation on political trust: participation has a positive effect on trust in government institutions, ceteris paribus.

In sum, Ugandan policymakers and academic scholars lead us to expect that participation is associated with higher democratic attitudes, subjective political capabilities, and institutional trust. The following section describes how the three hypothesized relationships are modeled and evaluated.

3.2. DATA AND MODEL DESIGN

As discussed in previous chapters, the Ugandan constitution-making process involved a range of participatory activities between 1988 and 1995: attending educational seminars, discussing issues in local government and associational meetings, contributing views in oral and written forms, campaigning, public debates, elections, and the lobbying of elected CA delegates. The random sample survey included questions to operationalize the endogenous variables: participation, democratic attitudes, political capabilities, and institutional trust. It also recorded respondents' demographic characteristics, socioeconomic status, wealth, ethnic and religious background, attitudes, behavior, and location of residence. Before delving deeper into variable descriptions and the exact specification of the equations, I describe the basic structure of the models and the estimation technique to be used.

Simultaneous-Equation Models with Reciprocal Causation

The ideal research design for evaluating the effects of participation would be to measure the qualities and attitudes of an individual before and after the treatment of participation was introduced. Since this type of panel study was not possible, given the extensive time over which the participatory constitution-making process took place and the resources available,[2] I had to rely on cross-sectional data: each respondent was interviewed only one time, after the participation took place. Thus, I have chosen to compare citizens who reported having participated with those who did not—or, more accurately, to compare citizens who reported differing levels of participation.

The comparison is made somewhat more complicated by the fact that individuals were not randomly assigned into a treatment group (those who participated) and a control group (those who did not) as in a controlled experiment. Because Ugandan citizens self-selected into the different categories, those who did and those who did not participate are likely to differ from each other in relevant ways from the outset. Therefore, I include a series of exogenous control variables. (For an in-depth treatment of natural experiments and statistical analysis, see Achen 1986.)

In addition, the direction of causation must be considered. The theories presented in this book argue that participation causes attitude change, but scholarship also holds that participation is caused by the political attitudes in question. In other words, the hypothesized causal relationships are reciprocal. Many Ugandan citizens may have participated precisely because they were democrats, felt politically competent, and trusted the government institutions to ensure that their participation would be meaningful.[3]

---

2. The lack of identification papers and methods for tracking the location of individuals makes panel studies extremely difficult to carry out in developing countries. When the hypothesized treatment takes years or even decades to produce effects (as with participation), the tracking requirements of a panel study become almost impossible to satisfy.

3. Many studies demonstrate that democratic attitudes, civic competence, and institutional trust are important predictors of participation in other contexts; see, for example, Bratton 1999; Brehm and Rahn 1997; Verba, Burns, and Schlozman 1997.

To properly evaluate the effect of participation, the reciprocal relationship between participation and attitude change must be accounted for. Therefore, I explicitly model the reciprocal relationships in simultaneous-equation nonrecursive systems, which estimate the influence of participation on the attitudes while allowing for the possibility that the attitudes affect participation.[4] I estimate the simultaneous-equation models using a two-stage least squares (2SLS) procedure.[5] In the first stage, the endogenous variables (attitude and participation) are separately regressed on all the exogenous variables in the model. The predicted values from the first stage (which have been cleansed of any association with the error term) are then used in the second-stage equations.[6]

Because theories of participation posit a reciprocal relationship between individual characteristics and participation, I explicitly model the influence of attitudes and knowledge on participation as well as the reverse. However, there is reason to believe that the effects of individual traits on participation are attenuated in the current data as a result of the nature of the government-initiated program of participatory constitution making. Based on my qualitative and archival research, I expected that citizens participated in the program primarily because they were pulled into the process by mobilizing elites and were not solely self-selected based on socioeconomic status, knowledge, and initial attitudes. Rosenstone and Hansen (1993) argue that elite mobilization can at times counteract the predisposition for wealthy, educated, engaged, and democratic citizens to participate more than others. Based on his study of Zambia, Bratton (1999, 550) argues that elite mobilization and institutional linkages are more crucial for predicting participation in new democracies than in established democracies. Likewise, based on his research into civic education programs in South Africa and the Dominican Republic, Finkel (2000, 34) writes, "At least in the short-term, [democratic] orientations themselves do not necessarily appear to be powerful predictors of individual participation." I expected that individuals par-

---

4. The systems are identified. The instruments (variables excluded from one equation in the system but included in the other) were deliberately incorporated into the survey questionnaire for this purpose.

5. I refrain from using three-stage least squares estimates because of the potential to spread specification error throughout the system (Cragg 1983).

6. For ease of interpretation and comparability, this book presents the standard 2SLS procedure using linear regression estimators. However, the variables measuring participation are ordered rather than continuous variables. The participation activities index has fifteen values, and the respondent-identified participation measure has four. Therefore, I also ran all the models with a 2SLS procedure using an ordered probit estimator when relevant. The results are statistically and substantively very similar, especially for the participation activities index. The text reports the ordered probit results only when a notable difference exists in statistical significance between the two specifications.

ticipated in the Ugandan constitution-making process because they had a personal connection with a government leader, were members of associations or certain ethnic groups, and were located in regions that had easy access to the sites of political activity. Initial attitudinal and knowledge traits should be less important influences on participation than is typically the case for routine participation in established democracies.

3.3. THE PATHWAYS TO PARTICIPATION

To specify the reciprocal models, I must first describe how I measure participation and then examine the factors that contributed to participation.[7] I draw on the rich academic literature on political participation for my analysis of what constitutes participation and what helped or hindered Ugandan citizens in becoming involved. However, I adapt my measures and model to better suit the Ugandan case based on my in-depth interviews, archival research, and news analysis as well as others' accounts of the process.

Measuring Participation: Participation Activities Index and Respondent-Identified Participation

The measures of participation rely on the respondent's self-report of his or her participation in constitution-making activities prior to the promulgation of the constitution. I use two different measures of participation to check that the findings are robust to question wording. The primary measure of participation, the *participation activities index,* is an index variable created from the sum of six separate survey questions. Each question asks whether the respondent participated in a specific constitution-making activity: (1) attending a seminar where a member of the UCC was present; (2) submitting a memorandum to the UCC either as an individual or as part of a group; (3) attending a meeting where people discussed questions about the constitution; (4) attending a CA delegates' meeting (a campaign rally); (5) voting to elect a delegate to the CA; and (6) obtaining information about debates in the CA.[8] The reported level of participation was moderate. The

---

7. Appendix B includes the question wording and descriptors for all the variables used in the book.

8. The Cronbach's alpha for the participation activities index is 0.73, indicating a single underlying concept, and the factors are almost equally weighted (0.43, 0.61, 0.68, 0.65, 0.57, and 0.55). There does not appear to be a clear hierarchical ordering to the activities whereby those who participated in costly activities also participated in easier activities. For example, it is not the case that those individuals who attended a seminar where a member of the UCC was present (the least frequent and most demanding activity) also engaged in all other activities; two-thirds did not. Conversely, the most frequent activity was voting, but 21 percent of those who engaged in only one activity, did something other than voting.

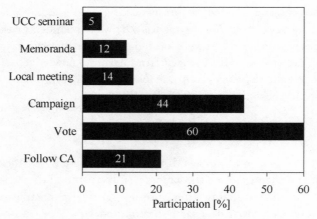

Fig. 3.1. Participation rates in constitution-making activities. (Data from author.)

average citizen participated in 1.5 activities: 35 percent of the sample participated in 0 activities (answered no to all six questions), while only 13 percent participated in three or more. Figure 3.1 shows the self-reported participation rate in each of the six activities.

The alternative measure of participation, *respondent-identified participation,* comes from a different question that was asked earlier in the survey: "Between 1988 and 1995, how did you participate in the constitution-making process?" Up to three activities mentioned by the respondent were recorded as open-ended answers and then postcoded.[9] The variable consists of the sum of the total number of activities reported; it ranges from 0, meaning no reported participation, to 3, meaning three participatory acts reported. Because this alternative measure of participation relied on respondent recall, the reported participation is even lower than the main measure. Furthermore, in the open-ended question, most citizens did not identify voting as a participatory act. Thus, only 6 percent of the sample recalled participating in two or more activities, and 70 percent reported not participating at all.

I use the two different measures of participation to verify that the fram-

Nonetheless, I tested two different weighted index variables using the same questions as the participation activities index. First, I weighted activities more if they were more exacting in time (for both travel and attendance) and/or effort required. Second, I weighted the activities by the proportion of the population that did not participate. The main findings of the book remain with these alternative constructions. I use the unweighted simple sum of participation activities index in this paper for ease of interpretation.

9. If a respondent gave just one or two answers, the interviewer prompted, "Any other ways?"

ing of the question does not unduly bias the results.[10] Both measures are subject to some measurement error, and alternating between the two allows an assessment of potential bias.[11] I expect the bias of the first measure, the participation activities index, to be less pronounced, so I report the findings using this measure and note where the results of the two measures diverge.

Influences on Participation

What led Ugandan citizens to participate in Ugandan constitution-making activities? Based on existing literature, I hypothesize that participation is based on (1) resources from demographic and socioeconomic status; (2) orientations that would induce citizens to become involved in politics; and (3) factors that would facilitate the recruitment or mobilization of citizens. The model contains variables for each of these three categories.

First, the model has a series of demographic and socioeconomic status variables that measure individual-level resources. The demographic variables are: a dummy variable for gender (*male*), a dummy variable for *urban residence,* and a continuous measure of *age.* Given the traditional dominance of older men in Ugandan public life, it is reasonable to expect that participation is positively associated with being a man and being older, whereas the relationship with urban residence is uncertain.[12] Scholars of politics in

10. The participation activities index asks about specific activities; in contrast, the respondent-identified participation measure is open ended. With the participation activities index, the burden of recall and interpretation is less difficult. It also produces a more nuanced scale because it records six rather than three activities. Finally, the types of participation measured are standardized across respondents. However, this measure records participation only in activities that the researcher found important, not in those the respondent could identify, and the yes/no response makes inaccurate reporting more likely. The respondent-identified participation variable counters these biases of the main measure.

11. Both measures are self-reported participation. The activities happened some time ago; it is possible that some respondents forgot that they participated. However, in open-ended interviews, most respondents noted that these were important activities given the nature of the topic (the constitution) and the timing of the activities (early in the transition). To assess the difference between actual and reported participation, I conducted open-ended interviews with subjects selected from lists of participants (memoranda, meeting attendance sheets, seminar attendance sheets). I also matched survey respondents with names on the lists of participants and checked their answers. Some discrepancies arose as a result either of memory loss or of inaccuracies in the lists of participants, but by and large, reported participation accorded with recorded participation.

12. Most empirical research from advanced industrial democracies, along with modernization theory, would lead us to expect that urbanites are more participatory than rural residents. However, several studies of developing countries produce the opposite conclusion. In Verba et al.'s 1978 study of seven countries, rural residents were somewhat more participatory than urban residents; Nelson (1987) concluded that rural residents in developing countries are more participatory in community activities. Based on Afrobarometer survey results from Africa, Bratton (2006) found that rural residents were significantly more likely to vote, attend community meetings, and contact informal leaders (controlling for poverty, gender, age, employed, and education).

both developed and developing countries find that socioeconomic status exerts a strong influence on participation (Brehm and Rahn 1997; Nelson 1987; Rosenstone and Hansen 1993; Verba, Burns, and Schlozman 1997; Verba, Nie, and Kim 1978; Verba, Schlozman, and Brady 1995). The model has a dummy variable for education, *primary school education*,[13] and a measure of wealth captured in an index variable summing the respondents' *access to basic needs*—food, medicine, fuel, and cash income.[14] Higher socioeconomic status typically facilitates greater participation, so I expected positive coefficients for primary school education and access to basic needs.

Second, the model controls for *interest* in politics, a commonly used measure of "psychological orientation" (Bratton 1999; Rosenstone and Hansen 1993; Salisbury 1975; Verba, Burns, and Schlozman 1997; Verba, Schlozman, and Brady 1995). Bratton (1999; 553) notes, "In comparative research, interest in politics has been shown to be positively related to political participation and to constitute a foundation on which other, more sophisticated political attitudes are built." On the whole, Ugandans have a high level of political interest: 66 percent of respondents agreed strongly with the statement, "I care about national politics."

Third, the model includes a series of variables reflecting the context in

---

13. Completing primary school education is the most substantial predictor of participation. Including measures of higher levels of education such as completing secondary school or above were not significant, did nothing to improve the predictive power of the model, and introduced problems of high multicollinearity with the other variables in the model. Thus, I opted to use only the measure for primary school education in the equations predicting participation.

14. The measure of access to basic needs is based on the question: "In the last twelve months, how often have you or your family gone without: a) enough food to eat, b) medicine or medical treatment that you needed, c) enough fuel, and a d) cash income? Never, rarely, sometimes, or often?" Due to the difficulty of obtaining accurate income figures from respondents working primarily in the informal economy, I tested several different measures of wealth. Only the one that measured the lower range of wealth (access to basic needs) was significant in predicting participation. A weighted scale of the number of durable consumer goods owned by the respondents' households (own consumer goods) was insignificant and the coefficient was virtually zero (standardized coefficient = 0.01, p = 0.79), nor did it improve the predictive power of the model. Another commonly used measure of socioeconomic status, employment, was found not to influence participation in constitution-making (standardized coefficient = 0.03, p = 0.35). The correlation between the measure of basic needs and the measure of consumer goods is 0.37, while the correlation between the measure of basic needs and the measure of employment is only 0.09, reflecting the high level of self provisioning in Africa. Bratton (2006) conducted a more in-depth study of poverty and wealth in Africa based on the Afrobarometer surveys. He notes that in response to the open-ended question "In your opinion, what does it mean to be 'poor'?" 46 percent mentioned lack of food and 36 percent mentioned lack of money. I find the measure of basic needs to be the most valid and reliable indication of the type of wealth that matters for political participation, and so I use this measure for the following analysis. Therefore, the results should be interpreted as distinguishing between those who are impoverished and those who more often have their basic needs met, and not for distinguishing between middle- and upper-class Ugandans.

which the participatory constitution-making process was organized and how citizens were mobilized to participate. As described in chapter 2, local government Resistance Councils organized many of the constitution-making activities, especially during the UCC's tenure. Therefore, members of the councils and those close to them were likely to be particularly active (Oneka 1999).[15] The variable *local council position* measures the level and position a respondent held in the local government councils, and another dummy variable, *close to high official,* marks respondents who had personal relationships with higher-level government officials. The local community was the main site of participation and mobilization, so individuals who were well integrated into their communities may have had higher participation rates. The model has a measure of *community integration.*[16]

Many associations deliberately tried to increase their members' participation by encouraging them to participate in activities organized by the government and by sponsoring activities (M. Mugisha 1999). Associations representing traditionally disadvantaged populations (such as women, the disabled, and workers) were particularly active in mobilizing members and in lobbying to have protective provisions and concessions included in the constitution. I expected a positive relationship between my index of *associational affiliations* and participation.[17] The model also contains a dummy variable for *Baganda ethnicity.* Chapter 2 showed that many of the contentious constitutional issues in Uganda, such as federalism, the status of traditional leaders, national language, and land tenure, involved the Baganda. Baganda leaders actively mobilized their members to take part in the constitution-making process as a way of winning provisions favored by the ethnic elite (Mulondo 2001). Other ethnic groups were less well organized and effective at mobilizing members.[18]

---

15. Members of higher-level councils were typically called on to attend lower-level as well as higher-level meetings. Also, the higher a person's position on the council, the more likely he or she was to participate. The chair, vice chair, and secretary almost always attended meetings.

16. Other scholars use this measure of community integration (see, for example, Brehm and Rahn 1997, 1006). The results do not change significantly if I exclude this measure from the equations.

17. A number of scholars show a positive relationship between associational membership and political participation (Bratton 1999; Finkel 2000, 9–10; Kuenzi and Lambright 2005; Nelson 1987, 125–26; Putnam 1993).

18. In a review of literature on participation, Nelson (1987, 126) found that ethnicity was commonly used to predict participation. I checked for missing-variable bias by including in the model (one at a time and all together) dummy variables for the other ethnic groups. Only the Bagisu were significantly more likely to participate, but they were only marginally so and only when the variable was included on its own. Since I have no theoretical explanation for this finding, I have chosen not to include the dummy variable for the Bagisu in the model. Members of Nilotic ethnic groups were not significantly less likely

Finally, individuals who were exposed to the process organizers' messages were more likely to participate. In addition to working through the local government councils and associations, the organizers relied heavily on the media to pass on information about opportunities for participation and cues about the importance of participation (Kizito 1992). The model has three variables measuring frequency of *exposure to news through radio, newspapers, and meetings*. The model also incorporates measures of the difficulty of the road conditions leading up to the respondent's house and the total distance from the respondent's house to the site of the election rallies and parish meetings. These measures record both organizers' difficulty in conveying their message to potential participants and the burden that participation placed on citizens who had to travel to the locations. I expected the measures of *road difficulties* and *distance to headquarters* to be negatively associated with participation.

Therefore, the equation predicting who participated is specified as follows.

$$
\begin{aligned}
\text{participation} = {} & \beta_0 + \beta_1 \text{ male} + \beta_2 \text{ urban residence} + \beta_3 \text{ age} \\
& + \beta_4 \text{ primary school education} \\
& + \beta_5 \text{ access to basic needs} + \beta_6 \text{ interest} \\
& + \beta_7 \text{ local council position} \\
& + \beta_8 \text{ close to high official} \\
& + \beta_9 \text{ community integration} \\
& + \beta_{10} \text{ associational affiliations} \\
& + \beta_{11} \text{ Baganda ethnicity} \\
& + \beta_{12} \text{ exposure to news on radio} \\
& + \beta_{13} \text{ exposure to newspapers} \\
& + \beta_{14} \text{ exposure to news in meetings} \\
& + \beta_{15} \text{ road difficulties} \\
& + \beta_{16} \text{ distance to headquarters} + \mu_i
\end{aligned}
$$

Results on Factors Contributing to Participation

Table 3.1 presents the ordinary least squares (OLS) regression estimates for the equation predicting participation.[19] All of the hypothesized causal fac-

---

to participate than members of other ethnic groups (though the estimated coefficient on the dummy variable was negative). Given their residence in the north, where there were fewer memoranda submissions, they might have been expected to be less participatory. However, the analysis of the causes of participation captures the relevant aspects of being Nilotic in the other variables included in the model.

19. These results are robust to different specifications of the model. If the variables for secondary school education, own consumer goods, and occupation and measures for the different ethnic and religious groups are included, they are not significant, they add virtually nothing to the predictive power of the

TABLE 3.1. OLS Regression Estimates Predicting Participation

	b	Robust se	Beta
Dependent variable: Participation activities index			
Resources			
Male	.65	(.09)	.22***
Urban residence	.08	(.19)	.02
Age	.01	(.00)	.06*
Primary school education	.48	(.11)	.16***
Access to basic needs	.02	(.01)	.05#
Orientations			
Interest	.21	(.06)	.11***
Mobilization			
Local council position	.22	(.06)	.14***
Close to high official	.29	(.12)	.09*
Community integration	.08	(.03)	.06*
Associational affiliations	.08	(.01)	.17***
Baganda ethnicity	.31	(.11)	.09**
Exposure to news on radio	.06	(.02)	.08*
Exposure to newspapers	.07	(.04)	.08#
Exposure to news in meetings	.17	(.05)	.11***
Road difficulties	−.52	(.26)	−.06*
Distance to headquarters	−.03	(.01)	−.05#
Constant	−1.23	(.34)	

Source: Author's data set.
Note: N = 743; adjusted R^2 = .41.
#p ≤ .10   *p ≤ .05   **p ≤ .01   ***p ≤ .001

tors except urban residence are statistically significant in the expected direction.[20] Resources, civic orientations, and mobilization factors all matter. Together, the three sets of factors explain more than 40 percent of the variance in participation (adjusted R^2 = 0.41). Individuals participated in the Ugandan constitution-making process because they had the resources and the motivation to do so, but also because they were mobilized to become involved.

Substantively, participation is most strongly related to gender, associational affiliations, primary education, and local council position.[21] Furthermore, the joint effect of the mobilization factors appears to be more influential

model, and the effect of the other variables is stable (with the exception of access to basic needs and road conditions). This is also the case if a measure of support for the National Resistance Movement is included. Citizens who did not support the government in power were no less likely to participate than citizens who supported the National Resistance Movement government.

20. The coefficients on the measures of wealth (access to basic needs), exposure to newspapers, and distance to headquarters are significant only at the 90 percent confidence level.

21. The substantive rankings are based on the standarized coefficients.

than the joint effect of the individual-level traits.[22] The analysis suggests that the program organizers, activists, and media were successful in mobilizing disadvantaged citizens who may otherwise have been left out of the process. However, they did not succeed in eliminating gender or educational biases altogether.[23]

In sum, participation is predicted by a number of individual-level demographic, socioeconomic, and attitudinal characteristics and by a set of variables measuring the likelihood that a respondent was mobilized to participate in the constitution-making process. These mobilization factors include the respondent's relationship to the government councils, the local community, and civil society as well as the probability that the respondent received and accepted the messages from the program organizers. These exogenous variables, together with the endogenous democratic attitude variable, form the second equation in each of the simultaneous-equation systems.

3.4. MODEL OF DEMOCRATIC ATTITUDES AND PARTICIPATION

This section presents the first of the three models: the model of democratic attitudes and participation. The aim is to evaluate the hypothesis developed in section 3.1: Does participation in constitution making have a positive estimated effect on democratic attitudes, ceteris paribus?

---

22. The different numbers of variables in each category complicates assessment of the relative magnitude of individual-level characteristics versus mobilization factors. Therefore, I compare the combined effect of the six individual-level variables (the five resource variables and one orientation variable) with the six strongest mobilization variables (local council position, close to high official, associational affiliations, Baganda ethnicity, exposure to news in meetings, and exposure to news on radio). The predictive power of a subset of variables can be measured by the drop in the predictive power from the full model when those variables are excluded. The drop in adjusted R^2 is 0.08 (0.41 − 0.33) when the six individual-level variables are excluded and 0.11 (0.41 − 0.30) when the six mobilization variables are excluded. Together, the variables measuring demographics, SES, and orientations explained less of the variation in participation than the indicators of mobilization. I also compare the Bayesian Information Criterion (BIC) approximations (which can be interpreted as measures of overall model fit) between the two reduced models. The difference of 32 between the BIC values provides "very strong support" for the hypothesis that mobilization offers a better explanation of who participated than individual demographics (Raftery 1995, 140). Finally, the relative precision of the blocks of variables can be assessed with a Wald test on eacdh set of the six variables. The F-statistic is 23.7 for the six mobilization variables, compared to 16.8 for the resource and orientation variables. Thus, the mobilization factors are more statistically precise than the traits of individuals.

23. For a discussion of the obstacles faced by women in particular, see Tamale 1999; Tripp 2002; Tripp and Kwesigna 2002.

Measuring Democratic Attitudes

In a review of research on support for regime principles, Norris (1999, 11) writes that "the basic principles of democratic regimes are commonly understood to include such values as freedom, participation, tolerance and moderation, respect for legal-institutional rights, and the rule of law." My measure of *democratic attitudes* is a multi-item index constructed from five questions designed to measure the respondent's valuation of the attitude dimensions: tolerance, equality, individual rights, public involvement in government, and freedom of speech.[24] The index ranges from 0 to 5, with a high value indicating more democratic. According to the index, 16 percent of the respondents were decidedly democratic, meaning that they had the highest score on four out of five dimensions. Fifteen percent were undemocratic and scored below 2 on the index. The remaining 69 percent can be considered moderate democrats, with scores ranging from 2 to 4.

Influences on Democratic Attitudes

The model predicting democratic attitudes includes the same demographic variables used to predict participation: gender, urban residence, and age.[25] Education is thought to be highly associated with democratic values (Emler and Frazer 1999; Muller, Seligson, and Turan 1987). Thus, the equation predicting democratic attitudes includes the variables *primary school education* and *secondary school education*.[26] The model also employs the measure of interest in politics to control for the respondent's prior political engagement.[27]

---

24. The reliability measure is low (Cronbach's alpha = 0.33), but this is not surprising because I am measuring adherence to different dimensions of democracy and have no reason to assume that the different dimensions will cohere. A democratic person would be high on all dimensions, but being high on one does not necessarily cause one to be high on the others. The reliability analysis shows that the factors are weighed equally.

25. Age is likely to be negatively related to democratic attitudes because older Ugandans experienced a longer period of socialization under nondemocratic regimes and are less likely to change their political attitudes than are younger Ugandans. Urban residence exposes citizens to democratic influences from a variety of sources, while citizens in rural areas tend to be more traditional in their outlook. I was uncertain a priori about the influence of gender on democratic attitudes.

26. Although I expect postsecondary school education to also be related to democratic attitudes, only eight respondents in the sample had some college or university education; thirty-one had some training other than university or college.

27. There is a possible disadvantage to including interest as a control variable in the equations predicting democratic values. If participation causes an increase in political interest, which leads to a change in democratic attitudes, then this indirect effect of participation on democratic values will be excluded from the estimated coefficient on participation. Rather than capturing the total effect, I will find only the direct effect of participation on attachment to democracy. The estimated effect of participation is

Political interest might lead an individual to believe more strongly in equality and the notion that citizens should be involved in government.

Also incorporated in the model are dummy variables for two ethnic identities—*Baganda ethnicity* and *Basoga ethnicity*—which are likely to be negatively associated with democratic attitudes. One question in the democratic attitude index asks about the inclination toward a return to traditional forms of government. The Baganda and the Basoga both had historically strong kingdoms, and allegiances to the monarchy remain high within both groups.[28] Finally, mobile individuals were more likely to be exposed to Ugandan citizens from different ethnic, religious, and political backgrounds. *Mobility* should be positively associated with tolerance, a component of democratic attitudes.

Therefore the two equations to be estimated are as follows.[29]

1. The First Equation:

$$
\begin{aligned}
\text{democratic attitudes} = {} & \beta_{1,0} + \beta_{1,1} \text{ participation} + \gamma_{1,1} \text{ male} \\
& + \gamma_{1,2} \text{ urban residence} + \gamma_{1,3} \text{ age} \\
& + \gamma_{1,4} \text{ primary school education} \\
& + \gamma_{1,17} \text{ secondary school education} \\
& + \gamma_{1,6} \text{ interest} + \gamma_{1,11} \text{ Baganda ethnicity} \\
& + \gamma_{1,19} \text{ Basoga ethnicity} + \gamma_{1,18} \text{ mobility} \\
& + \mu_{1,i}
\end{aligned}
$$

---

statistically and substantively stronger when the measure of political interest is omitted from both equations in the system. The coefficient on the participation activities index is 0.16 (robust se = 0.05, p-value = 0.00), and the coefficient on the alternative measure, respondent-identified participation, is 0.50 (robust se = 0.18, p-value = 0.01).

28. The Baganda and Basoga preference for traditional hierarchies is evidenced by their quick moves to restore their kingdoms when allowed to do so, the level of support given to the royal establishments, and the memoranda from these areas sent to the UCC. Memoranda to the UCC from members of ethnic groups that were not formally kingdoms and those that did not move quickly and effectively to restore their kings (such as the Ankole Kingdom) showed less preference for a political role for their traditional leaders. Members of other ethnic groups with restored kingdoms (such as the Toro Kingdom) are not sufficiently represented in my sample.

29. The model is identified according to the "block-recursive" method (Young, Rao, and Chatufale 1995). The first equation is identified as a result of exclusion from the second equation of the instrumental variables: secondary school education, Basoga ethnicity, and mobility. The second equation is identified because of the measures of access to basic needs; local council position; close to high official; community integration; associational affiliations; exposure to news via radio, newspapers, and meetings; road difficulties; and distance to headquarters.

2. The Second Equation:

$$
\begin{aligned}
\text{participation} = {} & \beta_{2,0} + \beta_{2,2} \text{ democratic attitudes} + \gamma_{2,1} \text{ male} \\
& + \gamma_{2,2} \text{ urban residence} + \gamma_{2,3} \text{ age} \\
& + \gamma_{2,4} \text{ primary school education} \\
& + \gamma_{2,5} \text{ access to basic needs} + \gamma_{2,6} \text{ interest} \\
& + \gamma_{2,7} \text{ local council position} \\
& + \gamma_{2,8} \text{ close to high official} \\
& + \gamma_{2,9} \text{ community integration} \\
& + \gamma_{2,10} \text{ associational affiliations} \\
& + \gamma_{2,11} \text{ Baganda ethnicity} \\
& + \gamma_{2,12} \text{ exposure to news on radio} \\
& + \gamma_{2,13} \text{ exposure to newspapers} \\
& + \gamma_{2,14} \text{ exposure to news in meetings} \\
& + \gamma_{2,15} \text{ road difficulties} \\
& + \gamma_{2,16} \text{ distance to headquarters} + \mu_{1,i}
\end{aligned}
$$

Before turning to the model results, one last note is in order with regard to measures that were not included in predicting democratic attitudes. First, I do not expect that local council officials would necessarily be more democratic than average citizens after controlling for education, mobility, and interest. Membership on a local council is usually a position of respect, but voters typically do not award it based on the candidate's democratic credentials but rather choose leaders who are believed to be capable and to have access to resources. Such individuals are often members of the National Resistance Movement (NRM), have contacts with officials at higher levels of authority, occupy important positions in traditional hierarchies, and are relatively wealthy. None of these factors makes the individual more likely to be democratic. Second, the equation predicting democratic values does not include the index measure of associational affiliations. There are mixtures of associations included in the index: some of them might make an individual more democratic (such as a women's political organization), most are unlikely to have an effect (such as a sports and drinking clubs), and some might dampen attachments to democratic values (such as some ethnic or traditional associations). Third, the equation excludes measures of exposure to news. While I initially thought that news exposure would have a positive influence on democratic attitudes, there is clearly no significant relationship in either the 2SLS or the simple OLS estimates, probably as a consequence of the mixed messages on issues of democracy in the Ugandan media. None of the measures discussed in this paragraph have a significant effect in either the 2SLS or OLS analyses. Furthermore, their inclusion or exclusion does not significantly alter the findings presented here.

Results on Democratic Attitudes and Participation

Table 3.2 presents the 2SLS estimates for the second-stage equation predicting democratic attitudes on the top and the second-stage equation predicting participation on the bottom.[30] Appendix C shows the first-stage equation estimates. The top row of table 3.2 contains the main result of interest for this model—the influence of participation on democratic attitudes. The estimate for participation is statistically significant (coefficient = 0.14, robust se = 0.05, p-value = 0.01), suggesting that participation in constitution making did help build democratic attitudes.[31]

Participation has a modest estimated substantive effect on democratic attitudes. Going from no participation to full participation increases an individual's democratic score by 17 percent across the various dimensions. For example, an individual who participates in all six possible activities would experience a 17 percent increase in his or her support for tolerance, equality, individual autonomy, public participation, and freedom of speech. While not large, these levels of change are sizable when it comes to political attitudes, which are thought to be relatively rigid. Participation has the largest influence on democratic attitudes of any of the variables in the model, as indicated by the standardized beta coefficients.[32] For example, this 17 percent increase in participation is 3.7 times larger than the effect of obtaining a primary school education and 3.8 times larger than the effect of completing secondary school. If these levels of change can be achieved from one participatory program, then enacting repeated long-term partic-

---

30. Given the nature of the hypotheses that I am evaluating, it might be appropriate to use one-tailed tests of significance. However, I decided to present only the more conservative two-tailed test statistics.
31. The coefficients on the exogenous variables in both specifications of the model (with the participation activities index and respondent-identified participation) are in the expected direction, and the coefficients are within conventional levels of statistical significance, except for urban residence. It seems that the key elements that distinguish an urban from a rural citizen in Uganda are already captured in the other control variables. The results for the other variables do not change if the urban residence variable is dropped. I leave it in here because it is theoretically appropriate and may be empirically significant in another setting.
32. The estimated influence of participation is also largest when considering the effect of changing from the minimum value to the maximum value. Substantively, the findings are even more dramatic when the alternative measure of participation, respondent-identified participation, is used (coefficient = 0.43, robust se = 0.19, p-value = 0.02). Moving from no participation to full participation is estimated to change the participant's attitude on 1.3 questions.

ipation in several issue areas has the potential dramatically to change the participant population's attitudes.

The bottom portion of table 3.2 shows that the influence of democratic attitudes on participation is not statistically significant (*p*-value of 0.27); it seems that being a democrat did not make an individual more likely to

TABLE 3.2. 2SLS Estimates Predicting Democratic Attitudes and Participation

	b	Robust se	Beta
Dependent variable: Democratic attitudes			
Participation activities index	.14**	(.05)	.23**
Demographics			
Male	.15#	(.08)	.08#
Urban residence	.10	(.11)	.03
Age	−.01***	(.00)	−.12***
Education			
Primary school education	.23*	(.09)	.12*
Secondary school education	.22#	(.13)	.06#
Initial orientation to democracy			
Interest	.12*	(.05)	.10*
Baganda ethnicity	−.19**	(.08)	−.09**
Basoga ethnicity	−.24*	(.10)	−.08*
Mobility	.06*	(.03)	.10*
Constant	2.43***	(.20)	
Dependent variable: Participation activities index			
Democratic attitudes	.46	(.42)	.29
Male	.54***	(.14)	.18***
Urban residence	.03	(.21)	.01
Age	.01*	(.00)	.09*
Primary school education	.34*	(.17)	.11*
Access to basic needs	.02	(.01)	.04
Interest	.13	(.09)	.07
Local council position	.21***	(.05)	.13***
Close to high official	.22#	(.13)	.07#
Community integration	.07*	(.04)	.06*
Associational affiliations	.07***	(.02)	.17***
Baganda ethnicity	.35**	(.11)	.10**
Exposure to news on radio	.06*	(.03)	.07*
Exposure to newspapers	.05	(.05)	.05
Exposure to news in meetings	.16***	(.05)	.10***
Road difficulties	−.46#	(.27)	−.06#
Distance to headquarters	−.02#	(.01)	−.05#
Constant	−2.23*	(.94)	

Source: Author's data set.
Note: N = 740.
#*p* ≤ .10   **p ≤ .05   ***p* ≤ .01   ****p* ≤ .001

participate in the constitution-making process. Nonetheless, the coefficient on democratic attitudes (0.46) is in the expected positive direction and is substantively large, indicating that democratic individuals are more participatory. It is possible that the standard errors are inflated in the 2SLS procedure as a result of the extra estimation burden, though they are well beyond conventional limits.[33] We nonetheless cannot reject the null hypothesis that democratic attitudes had no effect on participation.

To further investigate whether democratic attitudes promote participation, I performed a Durbin-Wu-Hausman test (augmented regression test) for endogeneity.[34] Based on the 2SLS estimates and the Durbin-Wu-Hausman test, I conclude that the relationship is not endogenous. Participation in constitution making seems to have contributed to higher democratic attitudes, but democratic attitudes did not seem to affect participation.[35]

In sum, the evidence is consistent with initial hypothesis: as the level of participation increases, citizens are likely to be more democratic in their attitudes when controlling for confounding variables and reciprocal effects. The results are robust to different measures of participation, different specifications of simultaneous-equation 2SLS estimations, and the single-equation OLS estimation. Furthermore, the open-ended interviews I conducted support the thesis that participation fostered democratic attitudes. For ex-

---

33. One cautionary note is that R^2 in the first-stage equation predicting democratic attitudes is only 0.19, compared with an R^2 of 0.42 in the equation predicting participation. While the lower figure is within acceptable bounds for individual-level survey data, the discrepancy gives reason for caution about the results. The insignificance of the coefficient on democratic attitudes in the second stage may result from the fact that democratic attitudes are more poorly predicted in the first stage than is participation. However, I can feel more confident about the finding because when I use the alternative measure of participation, the respondent-identified participation, the coefficient on democratic attitudes is negligible and insignificant (coefficient = −0.03, robust se = 0.18, p-value = 0.85). Furthermore, the predictive powers in the first-stage equations, although still low, are more balanced for this specification of the model. The R^2 in the first-stage equation predicting democratic attitudes is 0.19, and the R^2 in the first-stage equation predicting participation is 0.25.

34. To perform the test, I regressed participation on all the exogenous variables in the system and saved the residuals. I then regressed democratic attitudes on participation and the exogenous variables in the equation and included the residuals. The residuals are not related to the outcome variable, democratic attitudes. In the model specification using the participation activities index, the F-test of the residuals has a p-value of 0.34. In the model specification using the alternative variable, respondent-identified participation, the F-test of the residuals has a p-value of 0.27. This indicates no endogeneity.

35. I also reestimated the equation predicting democratic attitudes using a simple OLS procedure. Once again, participation was significantly related to democratic attitudes, and the control variables were statistically significant and in the predicted direction, except for urban residence. Although the coefficient on participation is statistically significant with a higher degree of certainty in the OLS (p-value = 0.00) than in the 2SLS (p-value = 0.01), the coefficient dropped from 0.14 in the 2SLS estimation to 0.11 in the OLS estimation.

ample, a guard in Mbarara District described his experience attending a CA candidates' meeting:

> It was the first time in our lives that we were told to come and be part of making laws to govern us. I had never seen this. . . . At the rally, people were told, "[The draft constitution] is the basis of the future. This is a treasure brought back for the first time." The people were concerned. We were told, "It is time to depend on the law, not on the power of a person or army power." In the campaigns, people were allowed to do their own selection based on ability. So progress is coming in bits, and people are now concerned about replacing repressive regimes with rule by law. (interview, Mbarara District, April 2001)

This analysis provides support for classical and contemporary theorists who argue that participation has a positive developmental effect on the individual, including the development of democratic values.

3.5. MODEL OF CAPABILITIES AND PARTICIPATION

We now turn to the second of the three models: the model of subjective political capabilities and participation. Again, the goal is to evaluate the hypothesis developed in section 1: Does participation in constitution making have a positive estimated effect on subjective political capabilities, ceteris paribus?

Measuring Subjective Political Capabilities

The measure *political capabilities* is an index variable constructed from five questions asking respondents to give self-assessments of their ability to perform a range of political activities: public speaking, leading groups, influencing others, understanding government, and serving on a local council.[36] The respondent values are distributed evenly from 0 to 10 with a mean of 4.9 and a standard deviation of 3.1.

Influences on Capabilities

The equation predicting political capabilities includes the standard demographic variables: gender, urban residence, and age. I expected the coefficient estimates to be positive. In addition, socioeconomic status probably

---

36. The reliability of the index is high (Cronbach's alpha = 0.82), indicating that the different questions are measuring the same underlying concept.

helped individuals to feel more capable. I also expected positive coefficients on primary school education[37] and access to basic needs. Similarly, interested citizens were likely to feel more skilled in politics.

Naturally, individuals who already held leadership positions in civic associations and in local councils were likely to feel better qualified to participate in public life. Individuals who had personal relationships with higher government officials may have also felt more efficacious. Exposure to news can also cause people to have greater confidence in their ability to understand politics and convince others and thus score higher on the scale. The equation includes the three measures of news exposure (from radio, newspaper, and meetings) as well as a measure that records how often the respondents *follow public affairs*.

Given the Ugandan political climate, individuals who supported the current regime might have felt more efficacious in political activities. The model contains a measure of *support for the NRM*.[38] Whether or not individuals support the regime, if they belong to a group that is often deemed as opposing the current leadership, they are likely to feel less politically capable. The territories where the majority of Nilotic respondents live experience frequent civil unrest. Nilotic citizens in general had fewer opportunities to develop political skills, generating an expectation of a negative coefficient on *Nilotic ethnicity*.[39]

With the model predicting participation described here and the earlier model predicting participation, the equations are as follows.[40]

1. The First Equation:

$$
\begin{aligned}
\text{political capabilities} = {} & \beta_{1,0} + \beta_{1,1} \text{ participation} + \gamma_{1,1} \text{ male} \\
& + \gamma_{1,2} \text{ urban residence} + \gamma_{1,3} \text{ age} \\
& + \gamma_{1,4} \text{ primary school education} \\
& + \gamma_{1,5} \text{ access to basic needs} + \gamma_{1,6} \text{ interest}
\end{aligned}
$$

37. The dummy variable for secondary school education was not related to political capabilities in the OLS or 2SLS equation. It seems that primary school education is sufficient to promote political skills.

38. This variable functions much like the familiar party identification variable used in survey research. I had to alter the question wording somewhat to make it relevant in the Ugandan context, where parties are not allowed to sponsor candidates in elections.

39. Many Ugandans and observers of Ugandan politics also argue that Nilotic speakers have been systematically excluded from government since Museveni came to power.

40. I use the "block-recursive" method to identify the model (Young, Rao, and Chatufale 1995). The first equation is identified with the exclusion from the second equation of follow public affairs, support NRM, and Nilotic ethnicity. The second is identified with the exclusion from the first equation of community integration, Baganda ethnicity, road difficulties, and distance to headquarters.

$$+ \; \gamma_{1,7} \text{ local council position}$$
$$+ \; \gamma_{1,8} \text{ close to high official}$$
$$+ \; \gamma_{1,10} \text{ associational affiliations}$$
$$+ \; \gamma_{1,12} \text{ exposure to news on radio}$$
$$+ \; \gamma_{1,13} \text{ exposure to newspapers}$$
$$+ \; \gamma_{1,14} \text{ exposure to news in meetings}$$
$$+ \; \gamma_{1,17} \text{ follow public affairs}$$
$$+ \; \gamma_{1,18} \text{ support NRM}$$
$$+ \; \gamma_{1,19} \text{ Nilotic ethnicity} + \mu_{1,i}$$

2. The Second Equation:

$$\text{participation} = \beta_{2,0} + \beta_{2,2} \text{ political capabilities} + \gamma_{2,1} \text{ male}$$
$$+ \; \gamma_{2,2} \text{ urban residence} + \gamma_{2,3} \text{ age}$$
$$+ \; \gamma_{2,4} \text{ primary school education}$$
$$+ \; \gamma_{2,5} \text{ access to basic needs} + \gamma_{2,6} \text{ interest}$$
$$+ \; \gamma_{2,7} \text{ local council position}$$
$$+ \; \gamma_{2,8} \text{ close to high official}$$
$$+ \; \gamma_{2,9} \text{ community integration}$$
$$+ \; \gamma_{2,10} \text{ associational affiliations}$$
$$+ \; \gamma_{2,11} \text{ Baganda ethnicity}$$
$$+ \; \gamma_{2,12} \text{ exposure to news on radio}$$
$$+ \; \gamma_{2,13} \text{ exposure to newspapers}$$
$$+ \; \gamma_{2,14} \text{ exposure to news in meetings}$$
$$+ \; \gamma_{2,15} \text{ road difficulties}$$
$$+ \; \gamma_{2,16} \text{ distance to headquarters} + \mu_{2,i}$$

Results on Capabilities and Participation

Table 3.3 presents the 2SLS estimates for the second-stage equation predicting subjective political capabilities and the second-stage equation predicting participation.[41] The top of table 3.3 displays the findings for the equation predicting subjective political capabilities. The coefficient estimate for participation is not statistically significant (coefficient = 0.60, robust se = 0.45, p-value = 0.19).[42] Therefore, I am unable to reject the null hypothesis that there is no effect of participation on respondents' assessment

41. For the first-stage equation predicting political capabilities, the R^2 is 0.50; for the first-stage equation predicting political participation, the R^2 is 0.42. See appendix C for the first-stage equation estimates.
42. The results are similar when the alternative measure, respondent-identified participation, is substituted for the participation activities index (coefficient = 1.51, robust se = 1.19, p-value = 0.20).

TABLE 3.3. 2SLS Estimates Predicting Political Capabilities and Participation

	b	Robust se	Beta
Dependent variable: Political capabilities			
Participation activities index	.60	(.45)	.29
Demographics and socioeconomic status			
Male	.93**	(.33)	.15**
Urban residence	−.52#	(.32)	−.06#
Age	−.03***	(.01)	−.12***
Primary school education	.20	(.30)	.03
Access to basic needs	.04	(.03)	.04
Political exposure and experience			
Interest	.30*	(.14)	.07*
Local council position	.40**	(.14)	.12**
Close to high official	.54*	(.22)	.08*
Associational affiliations	.08#	(.04)	.09#
Exposure to news on radio	.19**	(.06)	.11**
Exposure to newspapers	.23**	(.07)	.12**
Exposure to news in meetings	.18	(.12)	.06
Follow public affairs	.49***	(.12)	.12***
Support NRM	.48**	(.17)	.08**
Nilotic ethnicity	−.43#	(.25)	−.05#
Constant	.30	(.74)	
Dependent variable: Participation activities index			
Political capabilities	.09	(.08)	.19
Male	.53***	(.14)	.18***
Urban residence	.15	(.20)	.03
Age	.01*	(.00)	.08*
Primary school education	.44***	(.12)	.14***
Access to basic needs	.02	(.02)	.04
Interest	.16*	(.07)	.08*
Local council position	.18*	(.07)	.11*
Close to high official	.22	(.14)	.06
Community integration	.07*	(.03)	.06*
Associational affiliations	.07***	(.02)	.15***
Baganda ethnicity	.31**	(.11)	.09**
Exposure to news on radio	.04	(.03)	.05
Exposure to newspapers	.05	(.04)	.05
Exposure to news in meetings	.14**	(.05)	.09**
Road difficulties	−.44#	(.27)	−.05#
Distance to headquarters	−.02	(.01)	−.05
Constant	−1.28***	(.34)	

Source: Author's data set.

Note: N = 737.

#$p \leq .10$ *$p \leq .05$ **$p \leq .01$ ***$p \leq .001$

of their civic skills. The results do not validate the claim that participatory constitution making made citizens feel more competent in the political realm.[43]

Despite the lack of statistical significance, the estimate for participation is substantively moderate. For example, by participating in two additional acts, an individual is estimated to move from being able to speak in public "none of the time" to "some of the time." A citizen who went from no participation to full participation would experience a change in more than three skills. Therefore, it is plausible that the increase in standard errors resulting from the estimation burden of the 2SLS procedure is responsible for the results' lack of statistical significance, producing findings that are somewhat ambiguous.

My in-depth interviews with local council officials and with randomly selected citizens throughout the country can help elucidate the slightly ambiguous statistical findings. Qualitative analysis of the interviews indicates that, in general, participation did not usually improve subjective civic competence. Some citizens reported that they gained political skills, as in the case of one local council official who served at both the village and parish levels:

> I am proud that the ideas in the constitution came from the people below. Also it allows us to know what kind of governance there is and to see that things move right. It puts in place the structure. It helps people to know how to be involved with government. (interview, Mpigi District, January 2001)

However, such responses came from a minority of interviewees. Far more reported feeling somewhat confused or frustrated by their conversations on the constitution. A thirty-five-year-old woman from a rural area of western Uganda gave a typical response:

> Most don't understand [the constitution]. I understand some, but with difficulty. They didn't take enough time to teach or to translate it. If it was in Runyankole, maybe I could understand, but still it is difficult. I went to the meeting, and they told us to discuss many important things, but still we didn't understand. (interview, Bushenyi District, April 2001)

---

43. With the exception of age and urbanization, the estimates of the exogenous variables are in the predicted direction.

The constitution is, quite simply, a difficult subject to understand, fairly distant from most people's lives. This is especially the case for individuals who lack prior knowledge about constitutions. For most Ugandans, these events constituted their first exposure to the topic, and many walked away from the constitution-making exercises feeling no more capable of understanding and taking part in the new political system than before they arrived.

Furthermore, an individual typically had only one opportunity to take part in a given participatory activity. In most cases, each village had only one meeting on the subject, one campaign rally, and one chance to vote for the CA. There was little follow-up to the exercise. One of the most common statements expressed by respondents in interviews was a variant of the following: "They never came back after they finished the constitution to show us what was there and to explain it to us" (interview, Iganga District, February 2001). It is quite possible that repeated exposure to politics through participation is necessary to build civic skills.[44] Thus, although I did not find a significant outcome in this study, whether a different program of participation in another context can raise subjective capabilities remains an open empirical question.

The bottom half of table 3.3 demonstrates that the effect of subjective political capabilities on participation is statistically insignificant (coefficient = 0.09, robust se = 0.08, p-value = 0.28).[45] Individuals who felt capable apparently were not more likely to participate in the Ugandan constitution-making process.[46]

---

44. In a study of civic education programs in South Africa, the Dominican Republic, and Poland, Finkel (2003) found that frequent exposure to civic education is associated with larger increases in civic participation and democratic attitude than is limited exposure. Especially for democratic attitudes, a threshold effect seemed to exist whereby a few sessions had no effect but three or more sessions had a large effect. Participation may have a similar threshold effect on subjective political capabilities.

45. In the model specification using the alternative measure of participation, respondent-identified participation, the effect of political capabilities on participation is statistically and substantively negligible (coefficient = 0.01, robust se = 0.03, p-value = 0.78). The results are somewhat different when an ordered probit procedure was used to predict participation. The estimated effect is higher but still does not fall within the acceptable bounds for rejecting the null hypothesis (for the participation activities index, coefficient = 0.12, robust se = 0.09, p-value = 0.15; for the respondent-identified participation variable, coefficient = 0.05, robust se = 0.10, p-value = 0.66).

46. This is an unexpected finding and is somewhat fragile. Three possible statistical issues may help explain the lack of significance. First, the standard errors may be inflated in the 2SLS procedure as a consequence of the extra estimation burden. Yet regardless of whether the standard errors are inflated, the estimated effect is substantively low. Even in the simple OLS, the substantive effect is small but statistically significant (coefficient = 0.11, robust se = 0.02, p-value = 0.00). An individual who felt highly skilled in all five areas would participate in only one more activity than someone who felt totally incapable. A second possible explanation is that civic competence is highly correlated with the exogenous variables in the equation. For example, the variable political capabilities is correlated with being a man (0.38), primary school education (0.37), exposure to news on the radio (0.45), associational affiliations

The result that respondents' subjective political capability did not alter their participation may seem surprising in general but makes sense in the Ugandan case. As I argued earlier, citizens were mobilized into the constitution-making process. Elite decisions and structural factors were paramount for producing participation. Individual attitudes played less of a role. The findings support these claims. In short, feeling capable, in and of itself, was not enough to make an individual participate in the constitution-making process. People who might not normally feel efficacious can be induced to get involved, just as people who are predisposed to participate can also be influenced to stay home by unfavorable political circumstances.

Overall, the findings on political capabilities are troubling for democracy activists who want to jump-start a self-sustaining trend of deepening democratic citizenship. A similar mobilization campaign seems unlikely to have long-term behavioral consequences, no matter how many people it reaches. If those mobilized to participate in the initial campaign feel no more capable of participating in politics after the fact, then the effects of participation may stall at the attitudinal level without generating greater civic behavior down the road.

3.6. MODEL OF INSTITUTIONAL TRUST AND PARTICIPATION

This section covers the last simultaneous equation model. The model of institutional trust and participation is designed to evaluate the hypothesis developed earlier: Does participation in constitution making have a positive estimated effect on trust in government institutions, ceteris paribus?

Measure of Institutional Trust

The endogenous variable, *institutional trust,* is a measure of citizen faith in four government institutions. Citizens were asked how much they trusted

---

(0.40), and local council position (0.36). The problem of multicollinearity might bias the coefficient and standard errors. Another problem might be that the effect of political capabilities on participation is indirect. Several of the exogenous variables might be mediating variables. Feeling capable might make an individual more interested in politics, and being interested might lead someone to participate more. Or most individuals who feel capable might already have been driven by interest to become leaders of the local council or civic associations. In such a case, the increase in participation as a result of capabilities is captured in the coefficient of the mediating variables. The model of capabilities is more fragile than other models presented in this chapter, indicating that specification error may be responsible for the lack of effect. For example, the effect of political capabilities on the participation activities index is significant when the measure of interest is removed from both equations (coefficient = 0.13, robust se = 0.07, p-value = 0.07).

(1) the police, (2) the courts of law, (3) the local council (at the village or neighborhood level), and (4) the Electoral Commission. In my survey, 55 percent of respondents reported trust in the police, 72 percent reported trust in the courts, 86 percent reported trust in the local council, and 78 percent reported trust in the electoral commission. These results resemble those from the Afrobarometer survey conducted less than a year earlier.[47] The responses were summed to create an index variable ranging from 0 to 4.[48] I chose these four institutions because they represent a mix of local and national bodies that are not typically associated in Ugandans' minds with any single individual. The aim is to capture trust in the institutions, not support for the current officeholders.[49] Institutional trust in Uganda is high, with a mean value of 3.1 and a 0.98 standard deviation. In my survey, 36 percent of the respondents reported trusting all four institutions.[50]

Influences on Institutional Trust

The equation predicting trust controls for demographic characteristics (gender, urban residence, and age); socioeconomic status (primary school education and access to basic needs); political interest; relationship to government (local council position and close to high official); exposure to news (from radio, newspapers, and meetings); and respondent mobility. In addition, many scholars argue that institutional trust is positively related to social trust (Brehm and Rahn 1997; Finkel, Sabatini, and Bevis 2000). The equation includes a common measure, *social trust,* which I expected to have a

---

47. In the 2000 Afrobarometer survey, 53 percent or respondents reported trust in the police, 63 percent reported trust in the courts, 76 percent reported trust in the district council, and 74 percent reported trust in the electoral commission (Bratton, Lambright, and Sentamu 2000, 13). Survey evidence from 2002 indicates that trust in the village councils is higher than trust in district councils (Logan et al. 2003, 42).

48. Cronbach's alpha = 0.73, and the loadings on a single factor are police = 0.59; courts = 0.63; local council = 0.44; electoral commission = 0.46.

49. In other surveys, measures of institutional trust often include trust in the presidency, Parliament, parties, the army, the supreme court, and other institutions. In Uganda, for the most part, only one individual led these institutions since the transition in 1986. Thus, it would be impossible to distinguish whether respondents were expressing trust in the institution itself or in the person associated with the institution.

50. In my Ugandan survey, 55 percent reported trust in the police and 72 percent reported trust in the courts. In the 2000 Uganda Afrobarometer survey, 53 percent reported trust in the police and 63 percent reported trust in the courts. From other Barometer surveys, the mean percentage reporting trust in the police was 46 percent in Africa, 53 percent in East Asia, 36 percent in Latin America, and 27 percent in New Europe. The mean percentage reporting trust in the courts was 49 percent in Africa, 56 percent in East Asia, 36 percent in Latin America, and 25 percent in New Europe.

positive coefficient. The model also includes a measure of what I call *exuberant trusting,* or the tendency to report trusting all institutions. This dummy variable identifies all individuals who said that they trusted both the NRM and political parties. Since these two institutions are typically viewed as being at odds with each other in Uganda, individuals who reported trust in both either are particularly trusting or disguised their true feelings.[51]

The equation also has a measure of support for the NRM because movement supporters were more likely to report trust in government institutions (Brehm and Rahn 1997, 1011).[52] The model contains two additional measures related to wealth because individuals whose needs and wants were met may have been more favorably disposed toward their government. Because of the difficulty of obtaining accurate income figures in a country where most citizens work in the informal economy, I use a combination of measures to capture the full range of material well-being. The measure used in previous equations, access to basic needs, records wealth at the lower range of the scale. A second variable, *own consumer goods,* measures wealth at the higher range by summing the value of durable goods owned by household members. Finally, the model includes a measure of subjective economic welfare. I asked respondents to compare their current satisfaction with living conditions with their satisfaction five years ago. Several scholars argue that the perceived economic performance of governments has a consistent and large influence on citizen trust in institutions (Brehm and Rahn 1997, 1011), so I expected a positive coefficient for *improved living conditions.*

The resulting two equations to be estimated are as follows.[53]

---

51. The findings are similar when exuberant trusting is included and excluded.

52. It is possible that support for the NRM is a mediating variable between participation and institutional trust. Participation may cause individuals to support the government that sponsored the participatory process, and support for the government leaders would generate trust in the institutions. If this were the case, then the coefficient estimate for participation would be too low, because it measures only the direct effect and not the indirect effect through the measure of support for the NRM. However, the relationship between participation and support for the NRM is weak, so I do not anticipate that the indirect effect is large, if indeed it exists at all.

53. The model is identified according to "block-recursive" models (Young, Rao, and Chatufale 1995). The first equation is identified because of the exclusion from the second equation of the measures of mobility, social trust, exuberant trusting, support NRM, Ankole ethnicity, own consumer goods, and improved living conditions. The second equation is identified due to the exclusion from the first equation of the instrumental variables: community integration, associational affiliations, Baganda ethnicity, road difficulties, and distance to headquarters.

1. The First Equation:

$$\text{institutional trust} = \beta_{1,0} + \beta_{1,1} \text{ participation} + \gamma_{1,1} \text{ male}$$
$$+ \gamma_{1,2} \text{ urban residence} + \gamma_{1,3} \text{ age}$$
$$+ \gamma_{1,4} \text{ primary school education}$$
$$+ \gamma_{1,5} \text{ access to basic needs} + \gamma_{1,6} \text{ interest}$$
$$+ \gamma_{1,7} \text{ local council position}$$
$$+ \gamma_{1,8} \text{ close to high official}$$
$$+ \gamma_{1,12} \text{ exposure to news on radio}$$
$$+ \gamma_{1,13} \text{ exposure to newspapers}$$
$$+ \gamma_{1,14} \text{ exposure to news in meetings}$$
$$+ \gamma_{1,17} \text{ mobility} + \gamma_{1,18} \text{ social trust}$$
$$+ \gamma_{1,19} \text{ exuberant trusting} + \gamma_{1,20} \text{ support NRM}$$
$$+ \gamma_{1,21} \text{ own consumer goods}$$
$$+ \gamma_{1,22} \text{ improved living conditions} + \mu_{1,i}$$

2. The Second Equation:

$$\text{participation} = \beta_{2,0} + \beta_{2,2} \text{ institutional trust} + \gamma_{2,1} \text{ male}$$
$$+ \gamma_{2,2} \text{ urban residence} + \gamma_{2,3} \text{ age}$$
$$+ \gamma_{2,4} \text{ primary school education}$$
$$+ \gamma_{2,5} \text{ access to basic needs} + \gamma_{2,6} \text{ interest}$$
$$+ \gamma_{2,7} \text{ local council position}$$
$$+ \gamma_{2,8} \text{ close to high official}$$
$$+ \gamma_{2,9} \text{ community integration}$$
$$+ \gamma_{2,10} \text{ associational affiliations}$$
$$+ \gamma_{2,11} \text{ Baganda ethnicity}$$
$$+ \gamma_{2,12} \text{ exposure to news on radio}$$
$$+ \gamma_{2,13} \text{ exposure to newspapers}$$
$$+ \gamma_{2,14} \text{ exposure to news in meetings}$$
$$+ \gamma_{2,15} \text{ road difficulties}$$
$$+ \gamma_{2,16} \text{ distance to headquarters} + \mu_{2,i}$$

Results on Institutional Trust and Participation

Table 3.4 reports the 2SLS estimates for second-stage equations in the model predicting institutional trust and participation.[54] The top line of the table displays the most notable finding of this chapter: the estimated effect of

---

54. Appendix C displays the first-stage equation estimates.

TABLE 3.4. 2SLS Estimates Predicting Institutional Trust and Participation

	b	Robust se	Beta
Dependent variable: Institutional trust			
Participation activities index	−.22#	(.12)	−.34#
Demographics and socioeconomic status			
Male	−.01	(.10)	−.01
Urban residence	.10	(.13)	.04
Age	.00	(.00)	.04
Primary school education	.12	(.10)	.06
Access to basic needs	.04**	(.01)	.12**
Influences on opinion of government			
Interest	.09#	(.05)	.07#
Local council position	.05	(.05)	.05
Close to high official	.06	(.09)	.03
Exposure to news on radio	−.00	(.02)	−.01
Exposure to newspapers	−.06**	(.03)	−.10**
Exposure to news in meetings	.03	(.04)	.03
Mobility	−.04	(.03)	−.06
Generalized trust			
Social trust	.30***	(.09)	.12***
Exuberant trusting	.59***	(.07)	.25***
Support for current leadership			
Support NRM	.24***	(.07)	.12***
Own consumer goods	−.04#	(.02)	−.08#
Improved living conditions	.10***	(.03)	.14***
Constant	2.30***	(.28)	
Dependent variable: Participation activities index			
Institutional trust	−.14	(.10)	−.09
Male	.63***	(.10)	.21***
Urban residence	.08	(.20)	.02
Age	.01#	(.00)	.06#
Primary school education	.50***	(.11)	.16***
Access to basic needs	.03#	(.01)	.06#
Interest	.22***	(.06)	.11***
Local council position	.23***	(.06)	.14***
Close to high official	.27*	(.12)	.08*
Community integration	.07*	(.04)	.06*
Associational affiliations	.08***	(.02)	.17***
Baganda ethnicity	.29**	(.11)	.09**
Exposure to news on radio	.06*	(.03)	.07*
Exposure to newspapers	.05	(.04)	.05
Exposure to news in meetings	.17***	(.05)	.11***
Road difficulties	−.47#	(.26)	−.06#
Distance to headquarters	−.03#	(.01)	−.05#
Constant	−.82#	(.45)	

Source: Author's data set.

Note: N = 730.

#$p \leq .10$ *$p \leq .05$ **$p \leq .01$ ***$p \leq .001$

participation on institutional trust is negative. The estimate for participation is substantial and is just slightly beyond the 95 percent level of confidence (coefficient $= -0.22$, robust se $= 0.12$, p-value $= 0.05$).[55] Participation in constitution making predicts lower trust in government institutions. The finding contradicts the main hypothesis derived from the optimistic participatory perspective. Furthermore, it challenges one of the central goals outlined by the designers, implementers, and funders of the Ugandan constitution-making process.

While the negative relationship between participation and institutional trust is opposite what was initially hypothesized, there are statistical and empirical reasons to believe the results are accurate. First, the statistical results are robust to several specifications of the model. When the ordered probit estimates are used in the simultaneous-equation model, the findings are even more substantial (coefficient $= -0.29$, robust se $= 0.14$, p-value $= 0.04$). When the alternative measure, respondent-identified participation, is used, the coefficient remains negative. Finally, when possible mediating variables are removed (such as interest and social trust), the results hold.

The estimated substantive impact is also large. A citizen who participates fully is estimated to have 1.4 units less trust than an individual who does not participate at all.[56] This difference is equal to more than one-third of the trust scale. The standardized beta coefficients show that the estimated effect of a one-standard-deviation change in participation is greater than the effect of a similar change in all the other variables included in the model.[57] The estimated influence of participation on institutional trust is far from trivial.

Second, the open-ended interviews I conducted provide empirical support for the statistical findings. In Mpigi District alone, eight of eleven citizens who said they participated also expressed dissatisfaction with the ultimate results. Many told me that when they were creating the constitution, they had high hopes for its ability to transform Uganda. They blamed the government for failing to deliver the goods that had been promised during the constitution-making process, including economic and developmental goods (such as money, roads, and jobs) as well as political goods (such as security from arbitrary arrest, freedom to select the leaders of their choice, influence over

55. The two endogenous variables, institutional trust and participation, are acceptably predicted in the first-stage equations with an R^2 of 0.24 and 0.43, respectively.

56. The substantive effects for the alternative measure, respondent-identified participation, are even greater, though not when the ordered probit estimates are used.

57. Exuberant trusting has the next largest substantive effect. Some respondents expressed consistently high trust, even in the seemingly opposing institutions of the NRM and political parties. Such individuals also reported high trust in government institutions.

those leaders elected, and not being forced to pay bribes to corrupt officials). Some interviewees reported dissatisfaction with the process and the constitution itself, but more reported dissatisfaction with its implementation and the government. As one particularly eloquent farmer put it,

> Obote changed the 1962 constitution. I was young, but I heard Obote made the changes by himself, just one person. This one is almost the same. Before it was a plain dictatorship. This one is a dictatorship of language. It is conniving. He comes and sweet-talks you. It's like you go to buy a blouse, and they talk about how nice the silk blouse is, and instead they give you a cotton one. By the time you realize the shirt is cotton, it's too late. He doesn't use force, but language. (interview, Mpigi District, January 2001)

Third, empirical studies by other scholars show results similar to the ones found in Uganda, although the type of participation differed substantially. As mentioned in section 3.1, several scholars found that participation in civic education contributed to decreased trust, while these studies also found that participation contributed to increased democratic attitudes. Bratton and Alderfer (1999) found that Zambian participants in civic education were more likely to distrust government institutions, support the rule of law, and value freedom of expression than were nonparticipants. Finkel, Sabatini, and Bevis (2000) demonstrate that civic education in the Dominican Republic had a negative influence on participant trust in institutions and a positive impact on political tolerance. In sum, the finding that participation lowered trust seems valid, although it was unexpected.

The second equation in the system is displayed in the bottom half of table 3.4. The effect of institutional trust on participation is substantively very small (-0.14) and statistically insignificant (robust se $= 0.10$, p-value $= 0.18$). Trust in government institutions did not predict participation in constitution making. This null finding is robust across various specifications.[58]

---

58. The null finding is robust for the following specifications: (1) the 2SLS procedure that uses ordered probit to predict participation; (2) the simple one-equation OLS estimate; and (3) the standard 2SLS procedure using both measures of participation (the participation activities index and respondent-identified participation). The results differ somewhat when the alternative measure of participation, respondent-identified participation, is substituted for the initial measure, the participation activities index. Trust has a marginally significant and negative effect on participation in the standard 2SLS procedure (coefficient $= -0.09$, robust se $= 0.05$, p-value $= 0.07$). Although the substantive effect is quite small, the negative sign is unexpected. When an ordered probit procedure is used to predict the variable respondent-identified participation in a 2SLS procedure, the coefficient is not significant (coefficient $= -0.18$, robust se $= 0.12$, p-value $= 0.15$).

In sum, I feel confident in the finding that participation in Ugandan constitution making predicts an increase in democratic attitudes as well as a decrease in trust in political institutions, though I am less confident in the null finding with regard to subjective political capabilities. The finding that participants both valued democracy and were more skeptical of government institutions is notable. It provides the motivation for the empirical and theoretical investigations in the next chapter.

3.7. CONCLUSION: THE PUZZLE OF DISTRUSTING DEMOCRATS

This chapter presented empirical evidence regarding the estimated effects at the individual level of participation on democratic attitudes, subjective civic capabilities, and institutional trust. I argue that individuals who participated in the Ugandan constitution-making process were more likely to be distrusting democrats—that is, citizens who possess democratic attitudes but distrust government institutions. The results have several important theoretical implications.

First, the statistical models in this chapter show a positive estimated effect of participation on democratic attitudes and negative estimated effect of participation on institutional trust. The findings indicate that individual attitudes are subject to influence through participation, providing strong incentives to conduct additional empirical studies on attitude formation in transitioning polities and in new democracies.

Second, this study and others like it have notable implications for empirical research on the causes of political participation.[59] Many studies use cross-sectional data to establish the individual-level characteristics that lead to participation. From single-equation estimates, scholars conclude that certain individual characteristics are more likely to cause participation. Even scholars who acknowledge the reciprocal nature of participation and attitudes often fail to correct for this bias in their statistical analysis (see, for example, Verba, Nie, and Kim 1978). The results presented here indicate that single-equation cross-sectional studies may seriously overestimate the influence of these personal attributes on participation. When the equations predicting participation are estimated using a single-equation OLS procedure, the effects of democratic attitudes and political capabilities on participation are positive and statistically significant. However, in the two-equation sys-

---

59. Finkel (1987) makes a similar argument.

tems, they are not statistically significant. When the theorized reciprocal relationship is explicitly modeled, the influence of democratic values and civic competence disappear, suggesting that the OLS results may be spurious. Scholars should not generalize from this case to say that attitudes usually have no impact on participation. (I chose this case in part because attitudes' influences on participation were expected to be lower than those in most cases of participation.) Nonetheless, cross-sectional studies of participation and attitudes that do not test for reciprocal effects are inconclusive.

Third, the empirical results on the consequences of participation are especially crucial given that the untested participatory theories are being used as the basis for numerous policy programs. My study offers a cautionary note to activists and policymakers who want to use participation to legitimize new governments or increase political stability in new democracies. The research indicates that participation is an unreliable means of bolstering support for an existing regime. However, participation is highly effective at building attachment to an idealized model of democracy—a valuable asset for a transitioning country.

Fourth, the finding of distrusting democrats creates a theoretical puzzle for scholars of participation. The optimistic classical democracy scholars and the more recent participatory theorists predict a uniform effect of participation on attitudes: participation is thought to build democratic attitudes, increase civic competence, and heighten institutional trust. The pessimistic scholars assert the opposite: excessive citizen involvement—especially outside of consolidated democracies—leads to intolerance and extremism, fuels frustration and self-doubt, and heightens distrust of the state. In my study of participatory constitution making, I found a combination of influences: participation has a positive estimated effect on democratic attitudes, an insignificant estimated effect on subjective capabilities, and a negatively estimated effect on institutional trust.

The striking contradiction between theoretical expectations of the currently dominant optimistic perspective (that participation increases trust in government), and the empirical evidence (that participation lowered trust) cannot be overstated. The conclusion to a book-length study of constitution making in Uganda, South Africa, Eritrea, and Ethiopia (four participatory constitution-making programs) (Hyden and Venter 2001, 218) proclaims,

> Constitution-making has been a convincing way of earning legitimacy for both regime and government. It has given citizens in these countries hope that their leaders are there for a purpose other than feathering their nests.

My empirical research signals that at least in the case of Uganda, this conclusion is incorrect.[60] Participation in Ugandan constitution making is associated with lower rather than higher government legitimacy. The puzzle is to figure out why participation had this unexpected effect. Chapter 4 delves deeper into the case of participation in the Ugandan constitution making as a way of shedding light on the theoretical puzzle introduced in this chapter.

---

60. Earlier, the editors acknowledge that "this study lacks the systematic data to point out how successful the process was in transforming political attitudes" and note that they are basing their observations on "anecdotal evidence provided, especially from South Africa" (Hyden and Venter 2001, 214).

CHAPTER 4

Creating Informed Distrusting Democrats

The most intriguing finding of chapter 3 is that participants in the Ugandan constitution-making process were more likely to emerge as distrusting democrats—that is, citizens who are democratic in their attitudes but suspicious of their government institutions. This finding runs contrary to the predictions of most current-day theorists and policymakers, who assert that participation generates legitimacy and support for government institutions, not distrust.

Why were participants more democratic yet more distrusting than nonparticipants? This chapter provides an answer. It first discusses the existing literature regarding institutional trust and introduces my generalized theory linking participation, institutional performance, and attitude formation. Next, it reviews the poor democratic performance of the Ugandan government. The bulk of the chapter is devoted to empirical evaluation of the causal links implied by the theory: (1) participation increased democratic attitudes; (2) participation raised civic knowledge; and (3) the joint effect of higher democratic attitudes and knowledge contributes to a decline in trust. The two-stage least squares (2SLS) analysis in chapter 3 provides some support for the first hypothesized mechanism. This chapter presents statistical models to evaluate the latter two hypothesized mechanisms. In addition, the statistical analysis is supplemented and illuminated by qualitative evidence from in-depth interviews.

4.1. SOLVING THE PUZZLE OF DISTRUSTING DEMOCRATS

The optimistic participatory theory—today's dominant view—predicts that participation enhances institutional trust (Almond and Verba 1963; Bowler and Donovan 2002; Clarke and Acock 1989; Pateman 1970; Salisbury 1975; Tyler 1998). A number of scholars and policymakers specifically argue that participatory constitution making builds trust in government (Commonwealth Human Rights Initiative 1999; Deegan 2000; Hyden and Venter 2001; Van Cott 2000). Yet the empirical evidence to date (including my own) does not support the existing theoretical consensus. A few scholars have found that participation enhances trust, but others have found that participation had no effect or had a statistically significant negative influence (Bratton and Alderfer 1999; Brehm and Rahn 1997; Finkel 1987, 2000). We need to revise participatory theory to account for growing (though still limited) evidence that context mediates between participation and institutional trust.

A Theory Linking Participation and Trust

As noted in chapter 1, recent work on the origins of trust from the new institutionalist perspective can shed some light on this issue. Putnam, Pharr, and Dalton (2000) argue that trust depends on three factors: (1) the trustworthiness of the agent; (2) the information that the principal receives about agent trustworthiness; and (3) the principal's evaluation of the available information. A number of scholars argue that institutions affect the first factor, but little attention has been paid to how context affects information access and interpretation.

Participation is likely to affect exactly the two factors that are least studied: the information that the principal receives and the principal's evaluation of available information. First, citizen involvement increases knowledge about government performance. It brings citizens into contact with government agents, enabling people to learn if those agents are competent, democratic, and law-abiding. Participation also teaches citizens about governmental structures and functions, the political issues being debated, and the government's actual performance on those issues. Thus, participants develop a repertoire that includes a broad set of experiences with, examples of, and information about government performance.

Second, participation can change citizens' selection and evaluation of elements in their repertoires by altering the salient standard against which performance is assessed. Participants learn about the benefits of democratic government and become more attached to democratic principles. Engaged citizens also develop clearer ideas about their preferences. Participants are likely to judge the political performance of their government institutions against more highly developed democratic standards than are nonparticipants.

Participation is expected to affect trust by broadening citizen knowledge about government performance and by raising democratic attitudes, thus changing the criteria against which citizens evaluate government. However, the direction of the effect of participation on trust depends on the actual democratic performance of government institutions. In polities where democratic performance is higher than expected, participation brings "good news" about government and heightens trust in institutions. In polities where institutional performance is lower than expected and government agents are behaving undemocratically, participation delivers "bad news" about how government is matching up to the participants' newly developed democratic standards. Thus, the level of democratic institutionalization conditions participation's effect on institutional trust.[1]

In addition to getting bad news about government performance, participants in fledgling democracies are more likely to develop higher expectations about democracy than are participants in established democracies. Through initial participation, citizens are likely to learn about and come to believe in an idealized version of democracy. They lack prior experiences that might temper their expectations. In contrast, citizens socialized under democratic systems probably experience less of a change in democratic attitudes as a result of participation. They already hold many democratic attitudes, and their expectations of democracy will be less grandiose and more jaded by past participatory experiences in an imperfect world. Therefore, the gap between principles and practice appears especially stark for participants in transitioning states, and the resulting decline in trust as a consequence of participation is more dramatic than in comparably functioning but established democratic systems.

In sum, my theory states that participation affects citizens in two ways: (1) it increases citizen exposure to information on actual institutional performance, and (2) it builds attachment to democratic attitudes, thus altering the standards against which citizens judge their government institutions. Individuals evaluate the trustworthiness of institutions based on the perceived disparity between actual and ideal government performance. If actual democratic performance is higher than expected, then participation raises citizens' evaluations and increases institutional trust. If actual performance is lower than expected, then participation widens the gap between desired

---

1. Finkel, Sabatini, and Bevis (2000) make a similar argument about the effects of civic education in the Dominican Republic on institutional trust. My theoretical explanation has benefited greatly from their work. However, their account is somewhat ambiguous about the causal mechanisms; it is unclear from their analysis whether civic education itself or the greater participation that results from civic education is responsible for the increase in democratic attitudes and the decrease in trust.

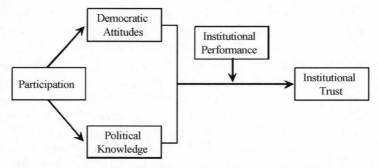

Fig. 4.1. Theoretical argument linking participation and institutional trust

and perceived performance, thus lowering trust. I do not contend that trust in government changes instantaneously as a result of participation. Rather, participation initiates a change in how citizens perceive their government, which over time may shift assessments of institutional trustworthiness. The theoretical argument is represented in figure 4.1.

Government Performance in Uganda

Ugandan participants lost trust in government institutions over time as government performance declined. In this analysis, the relevant type of government performance is democratic political performance (as opposed to economic performance). Participation affects perceptions of political performance first and foremost, and since the constitution-making process, the Ugandan government has behaved increasingly undemocratically.

In general, when asked why they do or do not trust government institutions, respondents mentioned both political and economic concerns. However, evidence indicates that those who participated in constitution making were more concerned with democratic political performance than those who did not participate. First, participants were more likely to mention political concerns to explain their dissatisfaction with the government.[2] Second, the quantitative evidence presented in this chapter indicates that only knowledgeable and democratic citizens are distrustful; knowledge alone does not predict distrust. Only citizens who prioritized democratic behavior distrust their government.

Third, in the quantitative analysis predicting institutional trust (in both chapter 3 and in this chapter), I included a variable to control for percep-

2. See, for example, the quotations from open-ended interviews presented later in this chapter.

tions of economic performance: *improved living conditions.*[3] Evaluations of living conditions are positively and significantly related to institutional trust in all the equations predicting trust. More importantly for this analysis, participation predicts trust even when perceptions of economic performance are held constant. Perceptions of economic performance do not account for the difference in trust between participants and nonparticipants. Fourth, the bivariate relationship between participation and perception of economic improvement is not significant, nor is the relationship between knowledge and perception of economic improvement. Active and knowledgeable citizens are no more likely to say that their living conditions have improved than the inactive and ignorant.

In sum, economic performance is an important factor influencing trust in government, but participation alters evaluations of government through noneconomic channels—that is, through evaluations of democratic political performance.[4] Participants in the Ugandan constitution-making process seem to have become distrustful because of their government's political rather than economic performance.

If democratic political performance is what matters to participants, then it is important to establish the behavior of the Ugandan government along those lines. Political analysts argue that although some definite improvements over past Ugandan regimes have occurred, the current government has not abided by basic democratic, constitutional, and human rights principles. Freedom House rated Uganda "not free" until 1980, when Obote was ousted from power. Since then, it has been rated "partly free," except from 1991 to 1994, when it was again rated "not free." This later episode of "not free" occurred during the major period of activity of the Uganda Constitutional Commission (UCC), the elections of the Constituent Assembly (CA), and the beginning of the CA debates. In 1999–2000, just before I conducted my survey and interviews, Uganda received ratings of five on seven-point scales for both political rights and civil liberties, with seven being the worst (Freedom House 2002).[5] These ratings indicate important deviations from liberal democratic norms.

---

3. Citizens were asked to compare their current living conditions with those of five years earlier.

4. My analysis is consistent with research showing that "committed democrats" in Africa are more concerned about political matters than economic matters (Bratton, Mattes, and Gyimah-Boadi 2005, 276, 307).

5. In comparison, the political and civil liberties ratings respectively in the same year were: 3 and 2 for Botswana; 6 and 5 for Kenya; 4 and 4 for Lesotho; 3 and 3 for Malawi; 2 and 3 for Namibia; 1 and 2 for South Africa; 4 and 4 for Tanzania; 5 and 4 for Zambia; and 5 and 6 for Zimbabwe. With the exception of Zimbabwe and Kenya, all the African countries presented here had "freer" ratings than Uganda (Freedom House 2002).

According to Onyango (1995, 162), the Ugandan government's commitment to constitutionalism has been more rhetorical than real. Several analysts also point out that the government's commitment to staying in power and to economic development have always been greater than its commitment to strengthening democracy and the rule of law (Furley and Katalikawe 1997, 247; Kasfir 2000, 61–62). Furthermore, many careful observers assert that the government's democratic behavior has deteriorated over time (Oloka-Onyango 2000, 44; Tripp 2005). Since 1995, the government is accused of failing to implement important constitutional provisions and of violating both the letter and the spirit of the new law (Human Rights Watch 1999).[6] (See chapter 2 for a discussion of the most egregious and well-known violations of democratic governance.)

In open-ended interviews, respondents noted a number of violations of democratic constitutional principles, including the continuing denial of freedom of political organization under the movement system; the arrest and harassment of journalists, nongovernmental organization activists, and opposition members of Parliament; human rights violations committed by the army in the north and the Democratic Republic of Congo; police abuse, torture, and extortion of bribes; Parliament passing controversial bills without quorum; the narrowing of political space and freedoms available to those who criticize leaders; government-inspired violence, intimidation, and rigging in the 2001 elections; and unwarranted and self-serving constitutional amendments. My respondents revealed that these undemocratic actions on the part of the government were not merely a topic of discussion for analysts and politicians but also influenced the attitudes of a section of Ugandan public—the active public. By the time I interviewed them in 2000 and 2001, participants in the constitution-making process seem to have learned that a large gap existed between their democratic standards and the performance of the Ugandan government. I do not think that participation instantaneously generated distrust. Rather, participation predisposed citizens to be more sensitive to and disturbed by the government's autocratic behavior. Over time, those individuals who had participated in the constitution-making process became more disenchanted with government than those who had remained on the sidelines.

---

6. Odida (2001) told me that the Law Reform Commission identified more than two hundred laws that needed to be repealed or amended to accord with the 1995 constitution. She claimed that almost none had been touched at the time of our interview.

Three Causal Mechanisms

This theoretical argument includes three hypothesized causal mechanisms: (1) participation increases democratic attitudes; (2) participation raises civic knowledge; and (3) in poor-performing states, a combination of higher democratic attitudes and higher knowledge lowers trust in government institutions. Testing the argument requires separately analyzing each of the three links. Chapter 3 evaluates the first hypothesized link—at higher levels of participation in the constitution-making process, Ugandan citizens were likely to be more democratic in their attitudes when controlling for confounding variables and reciprocal effects. The results are robust to different measures of participation, different specifications of simultaneous-equation 2SLS estimations, and the single-equation ordinary least squares (OLS) estimation. I now examine the empirical validity of the remaining two causal links in the theory.

4.2. MODEL OF KNOWLEDGE AND PARTICIPATION

This section evaluates the hypothesis that participation in constitution making had a positive estimated effect on political knowledge, ceteris paribus. The statistical model to evaluate this hypothesis resembles the one used in chapter 3 to evaluate the effect of participation on democratic attitudes. The hypothesized relationship between participation and civic knowledge is also reciprocal. Participation is thought to produce more knowledgeable citizens, but knowledgeable citizens are also thought to be more likely to participate. Consequently, I again estimate a simultaneous equation model using the 2SLS procedure.

Measuring Political Knowledge and Participation

I use two different measures of knowledge to verify that the findings are robust to question bias. The primary measure is an index variable that measures general *political knowledge.* Respondents were asked to identify (1) the elections that had taken place in Uganda since 1986, (2) the name of their member of Parliament, and (3) the names and positions of members of the central government (up to five). The variable ranges from 0 to 7 with a mean of 2.5.

The alternative measure of knowledge is targeted at the information that was mostly likely to be conveyed during the constitution-making process—knowledge of constitutional content. The index variable, *constitutional knowledge,* comprises eight questions where respondents were first asked, in open-ended form, to report some things they knew to be in the constitution and then asked, in closed-ended questions, about specific items in the constitution. In this chapter I report the results using the primary measure of general knowledge. Nonetheless, the results using the measure of constitutional knowledge are generally similar.[7]

Influences on Political Knowledge and Participation

The first equation in the system predicts civic knowledge. It includes the endogenous participation index and the exogenous demographic variables (gender, urban residence, and age), measures of socioeconomic status (primary school education, secondary school education, and access to basic needs), and the indicator of political interest. The equation includes a series of variables that affect whether an individual was likely to be exposed to information about government from sources other than the constitution-making process itself. These include respondents' positions on local councils, their closeness to higher government officials, their associational affiliations, their exposure to news in different contexts, the road conditions leading to their residences, and their frequency of travel.

The second equation predicts participation. It is the same one developed in chapter 3. Therefore, the two equations to be estimated are as follows.[8]

1. The First Equation:

$$
\begin{aligned}
\text{political knowledge} = {} & \beta_{1,0} + \beta_{1,1} \text{ participation} + \gamma_{1,1} \text{ male} \\
& + \gamma_{1,2} \text{ urban residence} + \gamma_{1,3} \text{ age} \\
& + \gamma_{1,4} \text{ primary school education} \\
& + \gamma_{1,17} \text{ secondary school education} \\
& + \gamma_{1,5} \text{ access to basic needs} + \gamma_{1,6} \text{ interest} \\
& + \gamma_{1,7} \text{ local council position} \\
& + \gamma_{1,8} \text{ close to high official}
\end{aligned}
$$

---

7. The analysis in this chapter uses the same two measures of participation used in chapter 3. I will continue to present the results using the primary measure of participation, the participation activities index, which is an index variable created from the sum of six separate survey questions each asking whether the respondent participated in a specific constitution-making activity. I will report the results using the alternative measure, the respondent-identified participation variable, when they differ significantly. The alternative measure captures those activities that the respondent found most memorable and relevant.

8. The model is identified according to the "block-recursive" method (Young, Rao, and Chatufale 1995). The first equation is identified as a result of the instrumental variables: secondary school education and mobility. The second equation is identified because of the measures of community integration, Baganda ethnicity, and distance to headquarters.

$$+ \; \gamma_{1,10} \; \text{associational affiliations}$$
$$+ \; \gamma_{1,12} \; \text{exposure to news on radio}$$
$$+ \; \gamma_{1,13} \; \text{exposure to newspapers}$$
$$+ \; \gamma_{1,14} \; \text{exposure to news in meetings}$$
$$+ \; \gamma_{1,15} \; \text{road difficulties} + \gamma_{1,18} \; \text{mobility} + \mu_{1,i}$$

2. The Second Equation:

$$\text{participation} = \beta_{2,0} + \beta_{2,2} \; \text{political knowledge} + \gamma_{2,1} \; \text{male}$$
$$+ \; \gamma_{2,2} \; \text{urban residence} + \gamma_{2,3} \; \text{age}$$
$$+ \; \gamma_{2,4} \; \text{primary school education}$$
$$+ \; \gamma_{2,5} \; \text{access to basic needs} + \gamma_{2,6} \; \text{interest}$$
$$+ \; \gamma_{2,7} \; \text{local council position} + \gamma_{2,8} \; \text{close to high official}$$
$$+ \; \gamma_{2,9} \; \text{community integration}$$
$$+ \; \gamma_{2,10} \; \text{associational affiliations}$$
$$+ \; \gamma_{2,11} \; \text{Baganda ethnicity}$$
$$+ \; \gamma_{2,12} \; \text{exposure to news on radio}$$
$$+ \; \gamma_{2,13} \; \text{exposure to newspapers}$$
$$+ \; \gamma_{2,14} \; \text{exposure to news in meetings}$$
$$+ \; \gamma_{2,15} \; \text{road difficulties} + \gamma_{2,16} \; \text{distance to headquarters}$$
$$+ \; \mu_{1,i}$$

Results on Political Knowledge and Participation

Table 4.1 presents the 2SLS estimates for the second-stage equation predicting political knowledge on the top and the second-stage equation predicting participation on the bottom. The first-stage equation estimates are shown in appendix C. The top row of table 4.1 shows that participation has a substantively large positive estimated effect on political knowledge that is statistically significant with more than 90 percent confidence (coefficient = 0.48, robust se = 0.28, p-value = 0.08).[9] This result lends additional empirical support for my theoretical argument. Citizens who participated were more likely to know about their government. Based on the size of the coefficient estimate, it appears that participants were likely to know a great deal more about government than were inactive citizens. Going from no participation to full participation increases an individual's knowledge by nearly three units, more than a third of the total knowledge scale. The standardized beta

9. The weak statistical significance may be the result of the extra estimation burden of the 2SLS. In a simple OLS regression predicting political knowledge, the coefficient on participation is extremely significant (coefficient = 0.30, robust se = 0.04, p-value = 0.00). Of course, if there is a positive reciprocal effect of knowledge on participation, then the OLS coefficient is biased upward.

TABLE 4.1. 2SLS Estimates Predicting Political Knowledge and Participation

	b	Robust se	Beta
Dependent variable: Political knowledge			
Participation activities index	.48#	(.28)	.42#
Demographics			
Male	.27	(.20)	.08
Urban residence	−.02	(.20)	−.00
Age	−.01**	(.00)	−.10**
Socioeconomic status			
Primary school education	.38*	(.18)	.11*
Secondary school education	.58*	(.23)	.09*
Access to basic needs	.07***	(.02)	.13***
Exposure to information			
Interest	.13#	(.08)	.06#
Local council position	.12	(.09)	.07
Close to high official	.26#	(.13)	.07#
Associational affiliations	.01	(.03)	.02
Exposure to news on radio	.03	(.03)	.03
Exposure to newspapers	.05	(.04)	.04
Exposure to news in meetings	−.04	(.07)	−.02
Road difficulties	−.68*	(.30)	−.07*
Mobility	.12**	(.04)	.10**
Constant	1.03**	(.38)	
Dependent variable: Participation activities index			
Political knowledge	.19	(.20)	.22
Male	.52***	(.16)	.18***
Urban residence	.06	(.19)	.01
Age	.01*	(.00)	.08*
Primary school education	.37*	(.18)	.12*
Access to basic needs	.01	(.02)	.02
Interest	.16*	(.07)	.08*
Local council position	.20**	(.07)	.12**
Close to high official	.20	(.14)	.06
Community integration	.07*	(.03)	.06*
Associational affiliations	.07***	(.02)	.15***
Baganda ethnicity	.27*	(.11)	.08*
Exposure to news on radio	.05#	(.03)	.06#
Exposure to newspapers	.04	(.04)	.05
Exposure to news in meetings	.16***	(.05)	.10***
Road difficulties	−.30	(.32)	−.04
Distance to headquarters	−.02	(.01)	−.04
Constant	−1.34***	(.33)	

Source: Author's data set.
Note: N = 731.
#$p \leq .10$ *$p \leq .05$ **$p \leq .01$ ***$p \leq .001$

coefficients show that participation had the single-largest effect on knowledge of any measure in the equation, including education, holding a local government position, radio listening, and road conditions. The findings hint that participation is a powerful tool for educating citizens, although we cannot be certain, given the level of statistical significance.

The bottom half of table 4.1 shows the equation predicting participation. Civic knowledge is not a statistically significant predictor of participation, although the effect is in the expected direction (coefficient = 0.19, robust se = 0.20, *p*-value = 0.34). Again, this finding suggests that elite mobilization pulled people who otherwise might not have gotten involved into participating in the constitution-making process. Based on the evidence, I conclude that both knowledgeable citizens and those without knowledge were mobilized to participate in constitution making; once involved in the process, citizens learned about their government and the constitution. Participation appears to have had an educative effect on participants.

4.3. MODEL OF INSTITUTIONAL TRUST

So far, the analysis suggests that participants are more likely to be democratic and knowledgeable than are inactive citizens. But are these two attitudes responsible for the lower level of trust among participants that was revealed in chapter 3? I previously theorized that if citizens in a transitioning polity possess both high democratic standards and knowledge about actual government performance, they will be more skeptical of government than those who lack one or both of these characteristics. Thus, I hypothesize that the joint effect of high democratic attitudes and more political knowledge is associated with lower trust in government, ceteris paribus. To evaluate this hypothesis, I create an interaction term between democratic attitudes and political knowledge and include it in a single equation predicting institutional trust.

The dependent variable, institutional trust, is the same index measure used in the analysis of trust in chapter 3. Citizens were asked how much they trusted (1) the police, (2) the courts of law, (3) the local council (at the village or neighborhood level), and (4) the electoral commission. The responses were summed to create an index variable ranging from 0 to 4. The equation predicting trust includes the interaction term between democratic attitudes and political knowledge as well as each variable individually. The model includes the control factors that were used in the equation predicting trust in chapter 3—demographic characteristics (gender, urban residence, and age), socioeconomic status (primary school education, access to basic needs, and own consumer goods), political interest, relationship to government (local council position and close to high official), exposure to news (from radio, newspapers, and meetings), and respondent mobility. In addition, the model controls for social trust and exuberant trusting, as well as a measure of support for the National Resistance Movement (NRM) because supporters of the current leadership are more likely to report trust in government institutions. Finally, the model includes a measure of subjective economic welfare to control for the perceived economic performance of governments.

The resulting equation to be estimated by OLS is as follows.

$$
\begin{aligned}
\text{institutional trust} = {} & \beta_0 + \beta_1 \text{ democratic attitudes} \\
& \times \text{ political knowledge} + \beta_2 \text{ democratic attitudes} \\
& + \beta_3 \text{ political knowledge } + \beta_4 \text{ male} \\
& + \beta_5 \text{ urban residence} + \beta_6 \text{ age} \\
& + \beta_7 \text{ primary school education} \\
& + \beta_8 \text{ access to basic needs} + \beta_9 \text{ interest} \\
& + \beta_{10} \text{ local council position} \\
& + \beta_{11} \text{ close to high official} \\
& + \beta_{12} \text{ exposure to news on radio} \\
& + \beta_{13} \text{ exposure to newspapers} \\
& + \beta_{14} \text{ exposure to news in meetings} \\
& + \beta_{15} \text{ mobility} + \beta_{16} \text{ social trust} \\
& + \beta_{17} \text{ exuberant trusting} + \beta_{18} \text{ support NRM} \\
& + \beta_{19} \text{ own consumer goods} \\
& + \beta_{20} \text{ improved living conditions} + \mu_i
\end{aligned}
$$

Results on Institutional Trust

Table 4.2 shows the estimated results of the equation predicting institutional trust. As hypothesized, the interaction term has a negative predicted effect on institutional trust. The substantive effect is very large, but it is only significant at the 90 percent level of confidence as a consequence of multicollinearity between the interaction term and the parent variables (coefficient = −0.04, robust se = 0.02, p-value = 0.10). If the parent variables are dropped from the equation, the coefficient is statistically significant with 99 percent confidence (coefficient = −0.02, robust se = 0.01, p-value = 0.01). Ugandan citizens who were both democratic and knowledgeable tended to be less trusting of government than citizens who lacked one or both of these traits.

The parent variables are not individually significant. Individuals who are democratic but who know absolutely nothing about how their government is performing have no reason to be distrustful. Likewise, citizens who know a lot about government but do not care at all if it performs democratically also have no reason to distrust their institutions. It is the combination of the two factors that matters.

The substantive magnitude of the interaction term (which is scaled 0 to 35) is moderate. Going from one extreme to the other on both dimensions (from being totally undemocratic and uninformed to being fully democratic and informed) produces a 14 percent decrease in the total trust scale. Although modest, the effect of the interaction term is the most substantial in the model, as indicated by the standardized beta coefficients. For example, the effect of a one-standard-deviation change in the interaction term

TABLE 4.2. OLS Regression Estimates Predicting Institutional Trust

	b	Robust se	Beta
Dependent variable: Institutional trust			
Democratic attitudes × Political knowledge	−.04#	(.02)	−.25#
Democratic attitudes	.03	(.07)	.03
Political knowledge	.08	(.07)	.13
Demographics and socioeconomic status			
Male	−.10	(.07)	−.05
Urban residence	.11	(.12)	.04
Age	.00	(.00)	.00
Primary school education	.03	(.08)	.02
Access to basic needs	.03**	(.01)	.12**
Influences on opinion of government			
Interest	.06	(.05)	.05
Local council position	.01	(.05)	.01
Close to high official	.03	(.08)	.01
Exposure to news on radio	−.03	(.02)	−.05
Exposure to newspapers	−.07*	(.03)	−.11*
Exposure to news in meetings	−.03	(.04)	−.03
Mobility	−.05#	(.03)	−.07#
Generalized trust			
Social trust	.30***	(.09)	.12***
Exuberant trusting	.60***	(.06)	.25***
Support for current leadership			
Support NRM	.21**	(.07)	.11**
Own consumer goods	−.04*	(.02)	−.09*
Improved living conditions	.11***	(.02)	.16***
Constant	2.44***	(.30)	

Source: Author's data set.
Note: N = 736; R^2 = 0.24.
#$p \leq .10$ *$p \leq .05$ **$p \leq .01$ ***$p \leq .001$

TABLE 4.3. Predicted Values of Institutional Trust

		Democratic Attitudes					
		0	1	2	3	4	5
	0	.00	.03	.06	.09	.12	.15
	1	.08	.07	.06	.05	.04	.03
	2	.16	.11	.06	.01	−.04	−.09
Political	3	.24	.15	.06	−.03	−.12	−.21
Knowledge	4	.32	.19	.06	−.07	−.20	−.33
	5	.40	.23	.06	−.11	−.28	−.45
	6	.48	.27	.06	−.15	−.36	−.57
	7	.56	.31	.06	−.19	−.44	−.69

Source: Author's data set.

is 1.5 times as large as the effect of a similar change in the indicator of economic satisfaction.[10]

Table 4.3 shows the predicted effect of democratic attitudes and knowledge on institutional trust across the full range of values (with all other variables set at 0). As hypothesized, trust is lowered only when the measures of both democratic attitudes and knowledge are high; the negative predicted values on trust (presented in bold and underlined) occur only in the lower right quadrant. When only democratic attitudes are high and knowledge is low, the predicted effect is positive. Also, when knowledge is high and democratic attitudes are low, the predicted values are positive.

Another way to view the joint effects is with the graphs in figure 4.2, which show the predicted values of institutional trust at different levels of political knowledge when democratic attitudes are low, medium, and high. When democratic attitudes are low (in this case zero), increased knowledge about government is associated with higher trust, and there is a positive slope. However, at medium levels of democratic attitudes, a change in knowledge has no estimated effect on trust. At high values on the democratic attitude index, rising knowledge lowers trust, as indicated by the negative sloping line. At these high levels of democratic attitudes, trust dips below zero as knowledge rises.

In sum, the statistical analysis provides some support for the third hypothesized causal mechanism: the combination of higher democratic atti-

---

10. Exuberant trusting is the only other factor that has an estimated substantive effect of similar magnitude. Some individuals are likely to express consistently high trust in all factors, including seemingly opposing institutions such as the NRM and political parties. Such individuals are also very likely to report trust in government institutions.

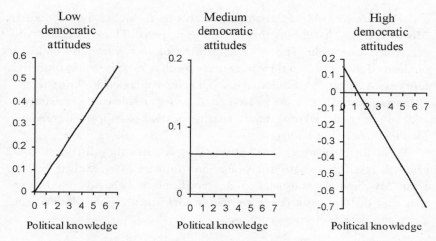

Fig. 4.2. Predicted values of institutional trust. (Data from author.)

tudes and higher political knowledge is associated with lower trust of government institutions in Uganda.

4.4. EXPRESSIONS OF DISSATISFACTION WITH GOVERNMENT

This causal relationship between participation and distrust is corroborated and elucidated by analysis of in-depth interview transcripts. Consistent with the high levels of trust found in the survey results, most interviewees told me that they trusted the police, the courts, their local council, and the Electoral Commission. On average, they also reported trusting "the government," the president, Parliament, and the army.[11] When asked why they trusted the government and its institutions, most explained their attitudes in reference to an improvement from the past.[12] For example, when I asked

---

11. My observations here generally hold true for when respondents were discussing government personnel as well as institutions. In the case of the presidency, Parliament, the army, and the government, it is often difficult to determine whether the person is referencing personnel or institutions. Since the transition began in 1986, there has been only one president, commander in chief, and typically only one member of Parliament; these institutions are thus more likely to be associated with a specific person. For the survey, I chose institutions that were less likely to be associated with a single individual (the police, the courts, the Electoral Commission, and the local councils).

12. The one exception occurred when people were asked to explain their trust for the local council. In this case, they usually talked about their closeness to the individuals on the council, who are village residents, relatives, and friends.

a seventy-six-year-old herdsman why he trusted the police, he responded, "Today is better. In Obote's time there was no peace. Thieves would come and attack us at night. The police and army took money from the children on the road to school, and there were many roadblocks" (interview, Bushenyi District, April 2001). Similarly, a shopkeeper explained his trust in the electoral commission: "Now we have elections for president and Parliament, and we can choose who we want. That never used to happen" (interview, Mbale District, April 2001).

What about the minority of citizens who said that they distrusted government institutions? What explanations did they give for their lack of trust? My respondents usually cited a specific event, behavior, or outcome that they disliked, as a young woman in Lira Town explained about the 2001 presidential elections:

> There was a lot of killing and forcing people to vote. Soldiers came and took the box away. Kids voted. I saw it in Kotido. . . . It has made me lose trust in the government. (interview, Lira District, March 2001)

What is most relevant for this study is that participants were far more likely than nonparticipants to report skepticism about government institutions. Furthermore, when explaining why they distrusted government, participants explicitly mentioned concerns that the government was violating the law, their democratic principles, the constitution, and the rights of the Ugandan people. Several illustrations of how active participants talked about government behavior help to demonstrate this point. A local council official who was very active during the CA elections said of the police,

> I want to trust them, but when I go with a problem, then I have to bribe them. That's not fair. That's not the law. (interview, Lira District, March 2001)

When I asked another active person why he did not trust the courts, he made a similar remark:

> They don't act like they should—like the law says they should. If you have no money, you won't succeed in court. (interview, Sironko District, April 2001)

One elderly man whose signature appeared on his village's memorandum to the UCC complained that the president was behaving undemocratically:

This isn't a democracy. I can't do anything because I don't have an army. [Museveni] has ruled for fifteen years but he is still going. (interview, Mpigi District, January 2001)

An elderly woman who was active in a women's association during the process also complained that the government was undemocratic:

We are not equal. This one-sided government is not helping us equally with the people from the other side because of other things. But we were told we would be equal once we had democracy. (interview, Lira District, March 2001)

A man who served as chair of his village government council (RC-1) from 1986 to 1990 and whose name was on the village (RC-1) and parish (RC-2) memoranda to the UCC said that Parliament and the Electoral Commission violated the constitution he had helped to make:

Like sometimes in Parliament they don't have a quorum, and they pass important laws [anyway]. I heard on the radio. Also in these recent elections— in our area it was done according to the constitution, but I heard in other areas the constitution was not followed. The updating officials—some of them didn't follow rules and regulations, and they did what favored their candidates. I heard from the radio. (interview, Bushenyi District, April 2001)

Similarly, a man who had participated in many activities complained about how the government was undermining the new constitution:

After a constitution is made, it should take a long time to change it. But I recently heard that they broke [the 1995 constitution]. They made a sort of amendment, but they used a wrong process to do it. . . . I heard from radio and newspapers. (interview, Mpigi District, January 2001)

Not all of my participant respondents were distrustful.[13] But on average, highly involved participants were more likely than inactive citizens to

---

13. In both the qualitative interviews and the survey, a small group of highly involved participants also exhibit high trust. For example, a teacher in Mukono Town praised the government: "If you look at what is happening in Uganda now, we are within the constitution. Presidential elections are going according to the constitution. The old constitution was not followed before. I can't imagine. I don't know what the old constitution was saying about changing leaders. Amin still did not follow the constitution. Past constitutions were not being followed, so there was a definite need for a new constitution. And now this one is really helping us, and this government is really following it" (interview, Iganga District, February 2001).

say that they distrusted government because an institution or leader had engaged in actions that undermined democracy, the rule of law, or constitutionalism. Whereas most citizens compared the current government's performance to that of past regimes, those who participated in the constitution-making activities compared the government's performance to their newly developed democratic principles and the newly established constitutional and legal system.

4.5. RETHINKING DEMOCRATIZATION, PARTICIPATION, AND TRUST

In chapter 3 as well as here, I have presented evidence that participation in Ugandan constitution making predicts higher democratic attitudes and increased civic knowledge, and the combination of these two outcomes of participation are associated with lower trust. These empirical findings and my theoretical explanation contribute to the scholarly debates on democratization, participation, and institutional trust in important ways.

First, the research has important insights for scholars and policymakers involved with democratization. Those who seek to understand or to strengthen civic culture must pay more attention to the realities of institutional performance in fledgling democracies. Democracy promoters endeavor to simultaneously raise democratic norms and institutional trust, making new democracies both more democratic and more stable. Similarly, democratic theory teaches that advances in one attitude spill over into the other, so that higher institutional trust builds support for system norms, and greater attachment to democratic attitudes fosters trust in democratic institutions. My research highlights the tensions that exist between the goals of achieving stability by building mass faith in government and furthering democracy by increasing citizen preferences for democratic performance, especially during political transitions. Institutional performance is likely to be low during and just after transition, and the gap between actual performance and democratic ideals can be too great for both democratic attitudes and institutional trust to coexist at the individual level. Only when democratic performance improves will increases in knowledge and democratic attitudes be accompanied by an increase in trust.

My research also illuminates a common finding from new democracies: a gap often exists between preferences for democracy and satisfaction with democratic performance, and the gap grows over time (Bratton, Mattes, and Gyimah-Boadi 2005; Inglehart and Catterberg 2002). Citizens are reacting to the deficiencies in government performance—deficiencies that are likely to become more apparent over time. Many scholars interpret the gap between system and government support as a problem, but my research suggests that it is a realistic position for citizens to hold and that it holds more potential for democratic development than when citizens are satisfied with middling democratic performance. Informed distrusting democrats are more likely than complacent loyalists to demand democratic performance from their institutions and leaders.[14] Thus, they offer protection against reversion to authoritarian rule and are more effective against the common problem whereby political systems stagnate in a semidemocratic condition (Bratton, Mattes, and Gyimah-Boadi 2005; Bratton and van de Walle 1997; Diamond 2002; Levitsky and Way 2002). A pliant and faithful citizenry may seem more stable in the short run but will hinder democratic development in the long run.

Second, this chapter provides an important revision to our theories on political participation. I add the important variable of institutional performance to the equation of how participation affects the individual. The revised theory explains the result of lower trust that emerged in Uganda. Previous scholars of participation overlooked the institutional context because institutional performance did not vary within or between their studies; most normative and empirical studies were based (consciously or unconsciously) on the United States and other developed democracies. By implicitly comparing the consequences of participation in Uganda with previous studies done by scholars based in developed democracies, I highlight the importance of institutional performance for understanding the effects of participation on the individual. Analyzing individual-level evidence on the consequences of participation allows me to unpack the causal mechanisms and understand how context matters.

Third, this work adds to the growing literature on trust in two ways. Most of the new institutionalist literature about trust focuses on what makes institutions trustworthy. In explaining the effect of participation, I look to the two understudied components in the new institutionalist perspective: the principals' knowledge of agent performance and the criteria principals

---

14. After reviewing the relationship between attitudes about regime and attitudes about government in twelve African countries, Bratton, Mattes, and Gyimah-Boadi (2005, 240) conclude, "One can feel reassured, therefore, that committed democrats are unlikely to throw out the baby (the democratic regime) with the bathwater (an underperforming government). More likely, committed democrats will used newfound electoral rights to change governments while retaining, and reinforcing, the procedures of democracy."

use to evaluate agent trustworthiness. I provide empirical evidence that participation is related to citizens' access to information about government and their evaluations of that information and that both of these components influence institutional trust. This chapter offers valuable empirical evidence on the links among individuals, institutions, and trust.

While there are many new institutionalist studies on the causes of political trust, the role of participation is both undertheorized and inadequately tested. I find that participation in Uganda is negatively related to institutional trust, and I provide a theoretical explanation that is relevant beyond the specific case. The addition of a comprehensive theory linking participation, institutional performance, and trust is the most notable theoretical contribution of this work.

4.6. CONCLUSION

This chapter began by arguing that participation affects institutional trust in two ways: (1) changing the standards against which citizens judge their government institutions and (2) increasing citizen exposure to information on actual institutional performance. Rather than inducing people to trust their institutions, participation gives citizens a different benchmark and new tools for evaluating the trustworthiness of their current system. According to my thesis, the level of disjuncture between democratic norms and actual government performance conditions the effect of participation on institutional trust.

This chapter then provided empirical evidence from a political system undergoing transition where institutional performance is low. The evidence suggests that participants in Ugandan constitution-making activities had higher democratic attitudes and knowledge of government. Furthermore, the combination of more democratic attitudes and more information about government was associated with lower institutional trust. Participation in the Ugandan constitution-making process seems to have created informed distrusting democrats.

Chapter 5 investigates further the factors that contribute to institutional distrust, exploring whether the participants who became dissatisfied with institutional performance also became disenchanted with the fundamental rules that emerged from the process. The chapter asks how citizen participation in the Ugandan constitution-making process influenced public support for the constitution. Did participation make citizens distrustful of the rules as well as the rulers?

CHAPTER 5

Constructing Constitutional Support

> The constitution is based on most of the views we gave. It was the first time for our people to make a constitution for ourselves. We sent our Constituent Assembly delegates to work on it—not by their own views but by the views of the people. Everyone had a chance to give ideas. (interview, Bushenyi District, April 2001)

> The Constitutional Commission didn't tell how they got the draft. I don't think they took into account our opinions. The commission didn't go with the views of the people. There was some pressure from behind [from government officials]. The Constituent Assembly people battled it, but the pressure was still there behind. (interview, Lira District, March 2001)

These two statements show very different attitudes about the constitution-making process and the constitution itself. The first came from a school headmaster in Bushenyi District. He placed great value on the people's involvement in the making of the constitution, believed that everyone had an equal chance to contribute, and concluded that the constitution was legitimate. The second was from a local council member in Lira District who had been a campaign agent during the Constituent Assembly (CA) elections. His statement notes the high level of contention between the government and opposition during the process. He complained that the process was unfair, resulting in a bias in favor of the current government. Both the satisfied headmaster and the dissatisfied councillor gave these responses when asked about their support for the constitution. In the face of these very different views of both the process and the constitution, an important question emerges: How did the Ugandan constitution-making process affect constitutional legitimacy? More specifically, did participation increase citizen support for the constitution, and if it did, through what mechanisms?

The question of how participation influences constitutional support is important for two reasons. First, developing widespread public support for the new constitution was the primary goal of those who designed the Ugandan program and is a central objective of those advocating the participatory model in other contexts. One of the main challenges facing transitioning states is to create sizable constituencies of citizens to support and defend the new systems being adopted. Participation is an often-prescribed remedy. How successful was the Ugandan participatory constitution-making process in achieving its central policy goal, constitutional legitimacy?

Second, examining how participation affected citizens' views of the constitution can help us better understand the relationship between participation and institutional distrust that has been established in the preceding chapters. Participants might be dissatisfied with the participatory experience itself and therefore oppose the social contract that emerges from that participation; conversely, they may be satisfied with the fundamental rules of the democratic game they helped create but unhappy with how their government is performing in light of those rules. Do participants in the Ugandan process distrust the fundamental rules of the new system, or are they skeptical of government institutions because they do not like how the rules are being implemented?

Like the preceding chapter, this one posits that participation (1) furnished Ugandan citizens with additional information about their institutions and (2) altered the criteria by which citizens evaluate information. The data indicate that participants are more likely to know about their constitution than are nonparticipants. Participants are also more likely to evaluate their constitution based on procedural rather than distributive criteria. While participation may have helped citizens form opinions about the constitution and made those opinions more durable, I argue that the leaders in the area, rather than participation, primarily influenced whether citizens came to view the constitution as legitimate or illegitimate. Once again, we see that the content of the messages to which participants were exposed determined the direction of attitude change.

This chapter begins by describing the actions and expectations of those who designed the Ugandan constitution-making process. The second section shows that on average, constitutional support is much higher in Uganda than in seven other African countries. However, statistical analysis of survey data in the third section indicates that an individual's level of participation does not significantly predict support for the constitution. The question arises as to why aggregate support is so high in Uganda when participation is not associated with constitutional support at the individual level. Sections 5.4 and 5.5 respond to this question by analyzing the influences on constitutional support with quantitative and qualitative data, respectively. Section 5.6 examines those individuals who were left out of the previous analysis because they were ill informed about the constitution and thus were unable to offer opinions about it. Section 5.7 discusses how participation altered citizens' criteria for judging the constitution, thus making attitudes more durable. The final section reviews the ways in which participation did and did not influence support for the constitution.

5.1. LEGITIMACY THEORY AND PARTICIPATION

Lack of mass attachment to and support for constitutions presents a major obstacle to democratization in Africa (Barya 1993; Ghai 1996; Hyden and Venter 2001; Klug 1996; Okoth-Ogendo 1991; Oloka-Onyango and Ihonvbere 1999; Shivji 1991). Without constituencies willing to support and defend their constitutions, leaders can tamper with or ignore with impunity constitutional limits on their power (Weingast 1997). Also, constitutions cannot play the crucial role of mediating between different interests in society if they are not viewed as mutually acceptable and binding social contracts (Calvert 1995). In long-standing democracies, childhood socialization helps ensure that populations view their constitutions as legitimate and worthy of adherence and protection. New democracies rarely have such reservoirs of constitutional support. The recent academic and policy attention to constitutional development has focused largely on how to build constitutional support among adults in democratizing countries.

Ensuring constitutional legitimacy was a central aim of the Ugandan constitution-making process (Nsibambi 2001; Odoki 2001; Ssempebwa 2001; Waliggo 1999). The preamble to the Uganda Commission Statute of 1988, which established the Uganda Constitutional Commission (UCC) and launched the constitution-making process, states participation's importance for the legitimacy and protection of the constitution:

> WHEREAS the history of Uganda is characterized by political and constitutional instability: AND WHEREAS since independence, Uganda has had a series of constitutional instruments, many of which have failed to take account of or satisfy the national aspirations of the time: AND WHEREAS in the past the people of Uganda have been afforded very little or no opportunity to freely participate in the promulgation of their national constitution: *AND WHEREAS National Resistance Government recognizes the need to involve the people of Uganda in the determination and promulgation of a national constitution that will be respected and upheld by the people of Uganda* . . . (National Resistance Council 1988; emphasis added)

A decade later, Benjamin Odoki (1999, 16), the UCC chair and one of the key architects of the program, echoed these ideas:

> The manner in which a constitution is finally adopted by the people is very important in demonstrating the legitimacy, popularity and accept-ability of the constitution. A constitution which is imposed on the people by force cannot form the basis of a stable, peaceful and democratic gover-nance of the people. To command loyalty, obedience, respect and confi-dence, the people must identify themselves with it through involvement and a sense of attachment. A good and viable constitution should be gen-erally understood and accepted by the people. . . . The involvement of the people in constitution-making is therefore important in conferring legit-imacy and acceptability to the constitution.

Odoki stresses participation's transformative effect on participant attitudes and knowledge rather than its effect on constitutional content. His statement echoes the optimistic participatory theorists, who argue that engaging in po-litical activity raises an individual's interest in and knowledge of the system, produces a psychological attachment to the community and its institutions, inculcates a sense of duty to abide by the rules, and fosters dedication to the well-being of the organism (Barber 1984; Mansbridge 1995; Pateman 1970; Radcliff and Wingenbach 2000; Thompson 1970). The developmental theory of participation holds that engaging in political activity directly affects the attitudes of the participants, irrespective of any effect on policy outcomes.

The architects of the Ugandan process clearly had the developmental the-ory of participation in mind when designing their program. The UCC re-jected a proposal to collect public views through a survey based on scientific sampling and instead chose a more difficult and intensive process of holding seminars and collecting memoranda. Odoki acknowledged that the chosen method produced a less representative description of what all Ugandans wanted, since only the ideas of those who chose to participate were collected. He argued that the need for people to engage in collective and public debate on constitutional issues and to submit their views in their own words was more important than obtaining a scientific sample of interests (Odoki 2001; see also UCC 1992b, 345). The primary goal was to encourage active in-volvement to develop citizens who would support the constitution. Produc-ing a representative constitutional document seems to have been secondary.

In sum, the developmental theory of participation—and the architects of the Ugandan program—assert that participation develops support for the constitution by changing the attitudes of active citizens. This chapter seeks to evaluate this claim by assessing whether participants in the Ugandan constitution-making process have a deeper commitment to the constitution than do nonparticipants.

5.2. COMPARING CONSTITUTIONAL SUPPORT

How do Ugandans feel about their 1995 constitution? This section describes my measures of constitutional support and then examines attitudes toward the constitution in Uganda in relation to seven countries for which we have comparable data.

Measuring Support for the Constitution

Support for the constitution is multidimensional, so the survey instrument includes four different questions measuring whether respondents feel that the constitution (1) includes their views; (2) represents the national political community as a whole; (3) is worthy of compliance; and (4) should be preserved. The four questions address different aspects of support, but I initially expected them to be correlated and to be similarly affected by participation. Figure 5.1 shows the distribution of responses by category for each of the four measures.[1]

The first measure, *individual inclusion,* represents a respondent's perception of whether his/her views were incorporated. The question asked, "Are your views included in the current constitution of Uganda? Would you say: 'all of your views,' 'most of your views,' 'some of your views,' or 'none at all'?" The variable ranges from 0 (none) to 1 (all), and the mean value is 0.42, which indicates that the average person believed at least some of his/her ideas were included.[2]

The second measure of support is *national aspiration.* The interviewer asked respondents to agree or disagree with the following statement: "Our constitution expresses the values and aspirations of the Ugandan people." After respondents answered, they were asked if they agreed (or disagreed) "strongly" or "just somewhat."[3] This variable also ranges from 0 (strongly

---

1. See section 6 for a discussion of what led individuals to answer the questions.
2. The mean value is calculated from answers coded as follows: strongly agree = 1, agree = 0.75, neither agree nor disagree = 0.5, disagree = 0.25, strongly disagree = 0.
3. During the testing of the questionnaire, we found that respondents (particularly those with lower education) were better able to answer questions presented in two parts than when four options were presented at once. The first question determines direction of sentiment, and the second question probes for intensity. The option "it depends" was not given verbally but was coded as such with a written explanation that was later checked. Thus, the variable has five possible values.

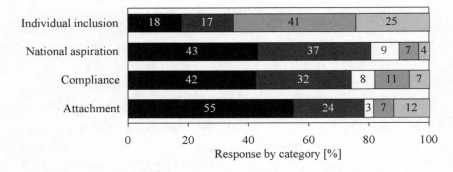

Fig. 5.1. Four measures of support for the constitution in Uganda. (Data from author. *Note:* Represents only individuals who were willing and able to answer the questions about the constitution.)

disagree) to 1 (strongly agree). The mean for national aspiration is 0.77, indicating that the average respondent felt that the constitution represents the Ugandan people. This question is identical to one asked on some Afrobarometer surveys, thus enabling valuable cross-national comparison.[4]

Compliance is the third measure of constitutional support. It was designed to measure whether citizens view the constitution as legitimate and worthy of their observance. Again, the interviewer asked respondents to agree or disagree with a statement: "People should abide by what was written in the constitution whether they agree with what was written or not." A question about intensity of views followed. The variable ranges from 0 to 1 and the mean is 0.73: the average Ugandan believes that people should comply with the constitution.

The last measure, *attachment,* measures the respondent's connection to the current constitution. Respondents were asked whether they agreed most with statement A or statement B. The interviewer then read statement A ("Our present constitution should be able to deal with problems inherited from the past") followed by statement B ("Our constitution hinders development so we should abandon it completely and design another"). After expressing a preference for A or B, respondents replied whether they agreed "strongly" or "just somewhat" with their chosen statement. Attachment

---

4. The Round 1 Afrobarometer survey was conducted in twelve African countries. The project is coordinated by the Institute for Democracy in South Africa, the Centre for Democratic Development, and Michigan State University. See http://www.afrobarometer.org/countries.html for more details.

ranges from 0 (strongly agree with statement B) to 1 (strongly agree with statement A). The variable has five possible values, with a mean of 0.74 indicating general attachment to the current constitution.

Finally, I add up these four measures of support for the constitution to create an index variable, the *constitutional support index*,[5] that captures all the different aspects of constitutional support or legitimacy. The variable ranges from 0 to 4, with higher values indicating more support for the constitution. The mean is 2.73.

Comparative Assessment of Constitutional Support

In general, Ugandans expressed strong support for their constitution. Eighty percent agreed with the statement about national aspirations, 74 percent agreed with the statement signifying compliance, and 78 percent agreed with the statement indicating attachment.[6] These aggregate levels of support for the constitution seem quite high, but how do they compare to other countries? The question used to measure national aspiration is identical to a question asked on some of the Afrobarometer surveys. Thus, I can compare my 2001 findings with those of the Ugandan Afrobarometer survey in 2000[7] as well as with Afrobarometer survey results from Botswana in 1999, Lesotho in 2000, Malawi in 1999, Namibia in 1999, South Africa in 2000, Zambia in 1999, and Zimbabwe in 1999.

Figure 5.2 compares the aggregate results from my Ugandan survey with

---

5. Cronbach's alpha = 0.55.

6. The level of support measured by the individual inclusion variable is much lower than for the other three measures. Only 35 percent reported that "all" or "most" of their views were included in the current constitution of Uganda, while 65 percent reported that only "some" or "none" of their views were included. Perhaps this question sets the bar too high for expressing support for the constitution. Individuals who said that "some" of their views were included may also have been expressing support for the constitution. If this is the case, then 75 percent expressed support or strong support for the constitution (by saying that at least some of their views were included), while only 25 percent said that none of their views were included.

7. A high degree of similarity exists between the Afrobarometer Uganda 2000 survey results and mine. In my survey, 43 percent agreed strongly, 37 percent agreed somewhat, 9 percent were neutral, 7 percent disagreed somewhat, and 4 percent disagreed strongly. In the Afrobarometer survey, 37 percent agreed strongly, 54 percent agreed somewhat, 7 percent disagreed somewhat, and 2 percent disagreed strongly. Unfortunately, the Afrobarometer survey for Uganda alone did not record the neutral category, which somewhat complicates the comparison. It is difficult to know what percentage of the neutral category in my survey would have been coded as "agree" and which as "disagree" if "it depends" was not permitted. If we take one extreme—all neutral answers were coded as "agree"—then the percentage that "agree" or "strongly agree" in my survey (89 percent) is close to that of the Afrobarometer survey (91 percent). However, if we take the other extreme—all neutral answers coded as "disagree"—then the support in my survey (80 percent) is lower than that of the Afrobarometer survey. The actual distribution is probably somewhere in between.

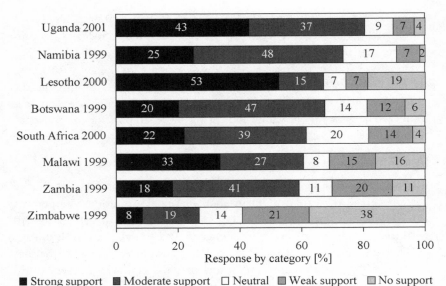

| | Strong support | Moderate support | Neutral | Weak support | No support |

Fig. 5.2. Comparing support for constitutions across Africa. (Data from author and from Afrobarometer survey.)

the aggregate results from those Afrobarometer surveys.[8] The countries are displayed in order of support for the constitution. This figure shows that support for the constitution in Uganda is higher than in all seven other countries. As mentioned earlier, 80 percent support the constitution (agree or strongly agree with the statement "Our constitution expresses the values and aspirations of the Ugandan people"), while 11 percent are hostile. The mean value on a scale of 0 to 1 is 0.77.[9] The next-highest support for the constitution is in Namibia (mean = 0.72). Following close behind are Lesotho (mean = 0.69), Botswana (mean = 0.66), and South Africa (mean = 0.65). At the bottom of the range are Malawi (mean = 0.62), Zambia (mean = 0.59), and Zimbabwe (mean = 0.35).[10]

---

8. For ease of comparison, figure 5.2 replicates the column for national aspiration in Uganda from figure 5.1. I use my survey results rather than the Afrobarometer Uganda survey as the base of comparison because the inclusion of a neutral category in my survey facilitates comparison to the other surveys that also include the neutral category. Support for the constitution is higher in the Ugandan Afrobarometer survey than in mine, so the figure displays the more conservative comparison.

9. In the Uganda Afrobarometer data, 91 percent support the constitution and 9 percent are hostile. The comparable mean is 0.79.

10. Finding comparable data outside of Africa is difficult. However a 2001 survey in Russia conducted by the Public Opinion Foundation found that 28 percent of respondents liked the Russian constitution

The level of support for the constitution in Uganda exceeds the levels found in Botswana and Namibia, two countries with higher per capita economic wealth and much longer experiences with democratic rule. It is also higher than in South Africa, Zimbabwe, and Lesotho, all of which have higher per capita wealth, economic growth, literacy, and civil and political rights.[11] The levels of support for the constitution in South Africa are also relatively high for a new democracy. South Africa also employed an extensive participatory constitution-making process (though it did not last as long or involve as large a percentage of the population as was the case in Uganda). This finding suggests that participatory constitution making may increase constitutional support.[12]

In sum, Uganda's average level of constitutional support is higher than the level in other African countries despite its relatively recent transition to democracy and its low levels of rights, wealth, and education. This cross-national evidence suggests that the extensive public participation in the Ugandan constitution-making process may be responsible for building support for the constitution. The next section examines this claim more closely by evaluating the effect of participation on support for the constitution at the individual level of analysis.

5.3. TEST OF INDIVIDUAL-LEVEL EFFECTS

As discussed earlier, participatory theory predicts that by participating, individuals become more supportive of policy outputs and more attached to the fundamental principles of the political system. Thus, we should expect

---

and 38 percent disliked it. The remainder did not offer opinions about the constitution. The survey found that 8 percent thought the constitution should be left alone, but 67 percent advocated revisions. A total of 47 percent of respondents reported that the constitution is a formal document that has no bearing on the actual life of the country (Yablokova 2001).

11. The civil and political ratings for Zimbabwe and Uganda were the same in 2000–2001, when I conducted the survey; all other countries had better ratings (Freedom House 2002). The economic rankings are based on the World Bank Development indicators' measure of gross domestic product per capita in purchasing power parity current international dollars (World Bank 2002). The figures for 2000 are as follows: South Africa (9,401), Botswana (7,184), Namibia (6,431), Zimbabwe (2,636), Lesotho (2,031), Uganda (1,208), Zambia (780), and Malawi (615). Gross domestic product per capita growth and literacy rates were also measured in the year of the survey (World Bank 2002). Uganda's level of support for the constitution is thus even higher than the numbers indicate, ceteris paribus.

12. It is understandable that levels of constitutional support in Botswana and Namibia would exceed those in South Africa, given their comparatively stable and democratic political histories. However, it remains a mystery why the level of support for the constitution is so high in Lesotho, a country with a tumultuous constitutional history. Lesotho also had the highest percentage of individuals who could not answer the questions about the constitution (28 percent), and the connection may be meaningful.

individuals involved in Uganda's constitution-making process to be more supportive of the constitution than those who were not involved. In this section, I evaluate the hypothesis that the higher an individual's level of participation, the more supportive s/he is of the constitution, ceteris paribus.

To evaluate this individual-level hypothesis, I employ the survey data from Uganda used in previous chapters. Because I was unable to measure the attitudes of individuals before and after they participated in the constitution-making process, I gauge the impact of participation by comparing individuals with different levels of involvement while controlling for possible confounding factors. The hypothesized relationship between participation in constitution making and support for the current constitution is not reciprocal and is therefore not like the relationships between participation and democratic attitudes, efficacy, social trust, institutional trust, and political knowledge examined in previous chapters. The participation in question happened prior to the existence of the 1995 constitution, so individuals could not have already held attitudes about the constitution when they decided to participate. Therefore, I estimate the statistical models using a single-equation ordered probit or ordinary least squares (OLS) procedure where appropriate.[13]

Influences on Support for the Constitution

The key independent variable of interest is the respondents' reported participation in the constitution-making process. As in the analysis from previous chapters, I use two different measures of participation: the participation activities index and respondent-identified participation. Following the convention of earlier chapters, I present the results using the participation activities index and report the results from analysis with the respondent-identified participation variable only when they differ significantly.[14]

The model controls for factors that might be related to both support for the constitution and participation. Three demographic variables are commonly associated with political attitudes: gender, urban residence, and age. I expected that women would be more supportive of the constitution because there are a number of provisions that are favorable to women, especially when compared with previous constitutions. In addition, the main women's organizations in Uganda support the constitution

---

13. I use ordered probit for the four individual measures: individual inclusion, national aspiration, compliance, and attachment. These dependent variables have four or five values each. I use OLS for the combined index variable, constitutional support index, which has forty-three values.

14. See chapter 3 for a more detailed description of the two measures of participation.

and have been actively informing citizens about its impact on women's rights. I had no clear prior ideas about the net influence of urban residence and age.

The model also includes two measures of socioeconomic status. I initially expected that those citizens with higher socioeconomic status would be more supportive of the constitution, since they are comparatively better off under the current rules than are those with lower socioeconomic status. Socioeconomic status is measured with a dummy variable for primary school education[15] and a continuous variable of wealth based on a weighted scale of the number of durable consumer goods owned by the respondent's household. The education variable measures not only socioeconomic status but also political sophistication. It was unclear a priori whether education strengthened attachment to the constitution (as with attachment to democratic attitudes) or led to a more critical evaluation of the constitution (as it made citizens more distrusting of government institutions).

The model includes a series of variables to control for political exposure. More politically exposed individuals might have picked up cues about the legitimacy of the constitution from sources other than the constitution-making process. Included in this category are variables measuring the degree to which they follow public affairs and their exposure to news on the radio, in newspapers, and in meetings. There is also a measure of mobility, since mobile individuals were likely to encounter a wider variety of opinions. I also expected that individuals would be exposed to talk about the constitution in associations, during local council meetings, and with government officials, so the model controls for associational affiliations, local council position, and close to high official.

Next are variables that measure support for the current government and satisfaction with government performance.[16] I surmised that supporters of

---

15. I also ran the model with a dummy variable for secondary school education. The effect of secondary school was significant only in the models predicting the measures individual inclusion and constitutional support index. The inclusion of the secondary school measure did not influence the results regarding the effect of participation on constitutional support in any of the models, but it is correlated with other control measures in the model.

16. Support for the National Resistance Movement and assessments of current conditions might be mediating variables between participation and constitutional support. Participation may cause individuals to support the government that sponsored the participatory process and to feel that their living conditions are improving. Support for the government might then generate support for the constitution. If so, then the coefficient estimate for participation does not capture the total effect of participation on constitutional support. The indirect effect is captured in the coefficients on support for government. However, without empirical validation that participation led to support for the current regime in government, I prefer to err on the side of caution and include these variables as controls.

the current leadership were more likely to feel positively about the constitution that was created and adopted during the regime's tenure. Thus, the model includes support for the National Resistance Movement (NRM). I also predicted that individuals who are satisfied with current conditions might attribute their improved fortunes to the constitution.[17]

Finally, the equation contains dummy variables for four of the thirteen districts where the survey was conducted. The inclusion of these district variables was motivated by systematic qualitative analysis of the in-depth interviews. In reading through the responses to questions about the constitution, I noticed that negative attitudes about the constitution were highly concentrated in certain locations. Whereas the overwhelming majority of respondents in most locations gave positive assessments of the constitution, the overwhelming majority of respondents in these four districts were decidedly negative. As I explain later, these areas include the constituencies of some of the government's fiercest political opponents both historically and at the time of the constitution-making process. I include the four dummy variables (*Mpigi District, Luwero District, Nakasongola District,* and *Lira District*) to test the hypothesis that context had a large influence on support for the constitution as well as to control for the possible confounding effect of district on the relationship between participation and constitutional support.[18]

The resulting equation to be estimated is as follows.

$$
\begin{aligned}
\text{constitutional support} = \beta_0 &+ \beta_1 \text{ participation} + \beta_2 \text{ male} \\
&+ \beta_3 \text{ urban residence} + \beta_4 \text{ age} \\
&+ \beta_5 \text{ primary school education} \\
&+ \beta_6 \text{ own consumer goods} \\
&+ \beta_7 \text{ follow public affairs} \\
&+ \beta_8 \text{ exposure to news on radio} \\
&+ \beta_9 \text{ exposure to newspapers}
\end{aligned}
$$

17. The improved living conditions measure asked respondents to express their level of satisfaction with their current living conditions as compared with their living conditions five years earlier (prior to the implementation of the new constitution).

18. These four districts were identified to be associated with lower attitudes about the constitution prior to analyzing the survey data. The survey data show that one additional district, Apac, has a consistently negative effect on the constitutional support measures, though it is only statistically significant in the equation predicting compliance. If the Apac District variable is included, the effects of participation on attachment and the constitutional support index are only very slightly lower. Because the model is designed to test a theoretical hypothesis held prior to examining the quantitative data, I prefer to include only the four districts that were identified from the qualitative analysis.

$+\ \beta_{10}$ exposure to news in meetings
$+\ \beta_{11}$ mobility
$+\ \beta_{12}$ associational affiliations
$+\ \beta_{13}$ local council position
$+\ \beta_{14}$ close to high official
$+\ \beta_{15}$ support NRM
$+\ \beta_{16}$ improved living conditions
$+\ \beta_{17}$ Mpigi district $+\ \beta_{18}$ Luwero district
$+\ \beta_{19}$ Nakasongola district
$+\ \beta_{20}$ Lira district $+\ \mu_i,$

where constitutional support is measured by the variables individual inclusion, national aspiration, compliance, attachment, and the constitutional support index, in turn.

Results on Constitutional Support and Participation

Table 5.1 presents the ordered probit estimates[19] for the equations predicting individual inclusion, national aspiration, compliance, and attachment and the OLS estimates for the equation predicting the constitutional support index.[20] The top row of results shows the estimated effect of participation on constitutional support. Overall, there is only weak and uneven support for the initial hypothesis correlating an individual's high level of participation with elevated support for the constitution. The ordered probit estimates for participation are positive and statistically significant in the equations predicting only two of the four measures. The analysis indicates that citizens who participated were more likely to agree (1) that their views had been included and (2) that people should abide by the constitution. However, in the equation predicting national aspiration, the estimate for participation is negative, though indistinguishable from zero. Also, in the equation predicting attachment, the coefficient is positive but statistically insignificant. Citizens who participated were not more likely to agree that

19. The results are nearly identical if ordered logistical regression is used instead of ordered probit.
20. The analysis includes only those individuals who answered the questions. Those who responded "don't know" were dropped. In addition, three observations were dropped from the analysis because they were outliers that exerted undue influence on the results. The analysis is meant to capture general trends, not the relationships of only a few individuals. All three had very high participation, and they were the only three who scored 0 on the constitutional support index. When these observations are included, the effect of participation on compliance drops below significance (coefficient = 0.06, robust se = 0.04, p-value = 0.14), as does the effect on the constitutional support index (coefficient = 0.03, robust se = 0.03, p-value = 0.39).

TABLE 5.1. Ordered Probit and OLS Estimates Predicting Support for the Constitution

	Individual Inclusion	National Aspiration	Compliance	Attachment	Constitutional Support Index
	Ordered Probit	Ordered Probit	Ordered Probit	Ordered Probit	OLS Regression
Participation activities index	.13***	−.03	.08*	.02	.05#
	(.04)	(.04)	(.04)	(.04)	(.03)
Demographics and socioeconomic status					
Male	−.04	.00	.04	−.02	−.07
	(.11)	(.11)	(.10)	(.10)	(.08)
Urban residence	.01	.21	.21	.27	.18
	(.17)	(.18)	(.17)	(.17)	(.13)
Age	.00	−.00	.00	.00	.00
	(.00)	(.00)	(.00)	(.00)	(.00)
Primary school education	.05	.01	.17	−.17	.01
	(.12)	(.12)	(.12)	(.12)	(.09)
Own consumer goods	−.06*	.03	.04	.04	.02
	(.02)	(.03)	(.03)	(.03)	(.02)
Political exposure					
Follow public affairs	.18*	.39***	.17**	.25***	.25***
	(.08)	(.07)	(.06)	(.06)	(.05)
Exposure to news on radio	.03	−.01	−.04	−.00	−.01
	(.04)	(.03)	(.03)	(.03)	(.02)
Exposure to newspapers	.01	−.12**	−.06	−.07*	−.06#
	(.04)	(.04)	(.04)	(.04)	(.03)
Exposure to news meetings	.02	.06	−.03	.05	.04
	(.06)	(.06)	(.05)	(.05)	(.04)
Mobility	−.04	−.05	−.00	−.11*	−.06*
	(.04)	(.04)	(.04)	(.04)	(.03)
Associational affiliations	.04**	−.01	−.04*	.03	.01
	(.02)	(.02)	(.02)	(.02)	(.01)
Local council position	−.13**	.06	.05	.07	−.02
	(.05)	(.06)	(.05)	(.06)	(.04)
Close to high official	.07	.28*	.41***	.08	.20**
	(.11)	(.12)	(.11)	(.12)	(.08)
Support for current leadership					
Support NRM	.36***	.20*	.07	.43***	.29***
	(.10)	(.10)	(.09)	(.10)	(.07)
Improved living conditions	.02	.08*	.07*	.10**	.07**
	(.04)	(.04)	(.03)	(.04)	(.02)
District of residence					
Mpigi	−.68***	−.55***	−.18	−.33*	−.38***
	(.15)	(.13)	(.13)	(.13)	(.10)
Luwero	−.70***	−.45**	−.38*	−.34*	−.39**
	(.20)	(.16)	(.15)	(.17)	(.13)
Nakasongola	−.61*	−.42*	−.12	−.57***	−.31*
	(.29)	(.18)	(.14)	(.18)	(.14)
Lira	−.34*	−.18	−.92***	−.30#	−.47***
	(.14)	(.17)	(.14)	(.17)	(.13)
Intercepts (robust se)	.13 (.33)	−.91 (.29)	−.85 (.27)	−.19 (.27)	1.62 (.23)
	1.37 (.34)	−.31 (.28)	−.22 (.26)	.13 (.27)	
	1.98 (.33)	.15 (.28)	.05 (.27)	.25 (.27)	
		1.30 (.28)	1.00 (.27)	.97 (.28)	
N	526	607	669	667	458
Pseudo R^2 or R^2	.08	.07	.06	.06	.25

Source: Author's data set.

Note: Entries are ordered probit and unstandardized OLS coefficients with robust standard errors in parentheses.

#$p \leq .10$ *$p \leq .05$ **$p \leq .01$ ***$p \leq .001$

(1) the constitution represents the Ugandan people or (2) the current constitution is acceptable or should be replaced.

In the equation predicting the constitutional support index, the OLS estimate for participation is positive but is statistically significant only at the 90 percent level of confidence (coefficient = 0.05, robust se = 0.03, p-value = 0.08). The substantive influence of participation on constitutional support is low. Going from no participation to full participation increases an individual's constitutional support index score by 0.30 units, or 7 percent of the total index. In sum, there is only weak and uneven evidence from this statistical analysis that participation is related to constitutional support at the individual level of analysis.[21]

There are reasons to think that the two measures not related to participation (national aspiration and attachment) are better measures of constitutional legitimacy than those that are significantly related to participation (individual inclusion and compliance). Individuals may think that their views are included but still fail to view the institution as legitimate, and vice versa. Citizens may also be motivated to comply with an institution that they do not deem legitimate. In a study of citizen attitudes about the South African Constitutional Court, Gibson and Caldeira (2003, 23) found that "acquiescence does not necessarily mean legitimacy. . . . Many are willing to accept a Court decision irrespective of how much legitimacy they ascribe to the institution." The authors theorize that compliance can be motivated by habit, coercion, and cost-benefit calculations in addition to or instead of legitimacy. The framing of the question in terms of what people "should do" rather than what the respondent "would do" suggests an answer based on legitimacy, but we cannot be certain.

In conclusion, the relationship between participation and support for the constitution is weak, inconsistent, fragile, and often indistinguishable

---

21. I examined whether these findings were robust to the different measures of participation and different specifications of the models. In the model specification using the alternative measure, respondent-identified participation, the only significant effect of participation is in the model predicting individual inclusion (coefficient = 0.18, robust se = 0.07, p-value = 0.01). The effects on the other dependent variables were not significant (national aspiration: coefficient = −0.02, robust se = 0.08, p-value = 0.82; compliance: coefficient = 0.13, robust se = 0.09, p-value = 0.16; attachment: coefficient = 0.04, robust se = 0.10, p-value = 0.71; constitutional support index: coefficient = 0.06, robust se = 0.06, p-value = 0.32). I also ran the model including individually variables that had been significantly related to participation in analysis from previous chapters but for which I had no strong expectation that they would affect support for the constitution. These variables include interest in politics, access to basic needs, and ethnicity. In addition, I included measures for constitutional knowledge, institutional trust, and democratic attitudes. Including these variables did not significantly affect the relationship between participation and constitutional support.

from zero. Therefore, I take the more conservative interpretation of this statistical analysis: As the level of participation increases, Ugandans are not significantly more supportive of their constitution. The analysis in this section does not bolster the original hypothesis, which was based on the optimistic claims of those from Uganda and elsewhere that participation fosters support. While this analysis is not conclusive, it does shift the burden of proof to those who assert that participatory constitution making creates constitutional legitimacy.

5.4. ALTERNATIVE INFLUENCES ON CONSTITUTIONAL SUPPORT

If participation is not a good predictor of constitutional support at the individual level, what is? The statistical results provide some answers to this question. First, the variable measuring the extent to which individuals follow public affairs has a consistent and significant positive effect. Citizens who reported following public affairs were significantly more supportive of the constitution across all the measures of support. It is unclear how to interpret this finding. It is possible that these individuals are more supportive because they are exposed to government pronouncements about the value of the constitution.[22] In addition, the variable might be another indicator of support for the system. Given the NRM's rhetorical emphasis on public involvement in politics, individuals who support the system may feel that it is socially desirable to report following public affairs.

Second, the two measures of support for the government are positive in all the equations and statistically significant in three of the four equations predicting single-question measures. They are also positive and statistically significant in the equation predicting the index variable. Individuals who supported the current leadership (the NRM) and who felt that their living conditions had improved under the current regime were more supportive of the constitution. This important finding means that initial support for the leadership and feelings of well-being translate into support for the constitution. It can also mean that citizens who oppose the leaders in power or who feel that their conditions are deteriorating will reject the constitution regardless of whether they participated in its creation.

---

22. Gibson, Caldeira, and Baird (1998, 345) found that those who are more attentive to the high courts are more supportive of them. They argue that individuals who are attentive are exposed to a "series of legitimizing messages focused on the symbols of justice, judicial objectivity, and impartiality." I expect the same to hold true for the constitution in Uganda.

Third, my conjecture from the qualitative analysis—that the level of support for the constitution is associated with where the respondent resides—also receives strong support in the statistical analysis. Citizens who live in the four districts identified from the qualitative analysis are significantly less supportive of the constitution than are individuals who live in the other nine districts. In short, location of residence is a strong predictor of constitutional support.[23]

What about district of residence influences constitutional support? Do district residents share some individual-level characteristics that are missing from the model? Does something about the geographical context itself change attitudes, above and beyond the influence of individual traits? In the next section, where I discuss the data from in-depth interviews, I present evidence that elite opinions are responsible for the district effect. For the moment I limit myself to talking about what is not responsible for the district effect.

Ethnicity is the most likely individual-level trait to be responsible for the district effect, since ethnicity is regionally concentrated in Uganda. There is some indication that the Baganda are less supportive of the constitution and the Banyankole are more supportive, but this is not uniformly the case.[24] Also, adding dummy variables for the five main ethnic groups to the sample does not systematically alter the results for the district dummy variables.[25] Thus the district effect does not seem to result from the effect of ethnicity.

---

23. The 2002 Afrobarometer survey also reveals deep divisions in attitudes about the constitution based on political affiliation and location of residence. The survey found that 76 percent of citizens affiliated with the NRM agreed that their constitution expresses the values and aspirations of the Ugandan people, while only 48 percent of opposition sympathizers agreed. While 90 percent of Ugandans from the west agreed with the statement, only 57 percent of those in the east, 59 percent of those in the center, and 44 percent of those in the north agreed. In short, partisan and regional differences about the legitimacy of the constitution were not transient and even seem to be increasing over time (Logan et al. 2003, 47).
24. When only the dummy variable for Buganda is included, the variable is negative for all the equations except the one predicting compliance. However, the coefficient on Buganda is not statistically significant in any of the equations. When only the dummy variable for the Banyankole is included, the coefficient is positive and significant for the equations predicting individual inclusion and national aspiration and is positive but not significant in the equations predicting attachment and the constitutional support index. The Buganda leadership favored a political role for traditional leaders and a federal system, both of which were not granted in the constitution. President Museveni and many top government officials are Munyankole.
25. I added the dummy variables separately and altogether (excluding one category). When ethnic variables were added together or separately, the district variables remained negative throughout. When added all together, the statistical significance of only one of the district measures changed and did so only for the equations predicting national aspiration, attachment, and the constitutional support index. (Nakasongola district was no longer statistically significant.) When added separately, the significance of the district variables usually stayed the same but occasionally changed either from insignificant to significant

Religion is another plausible explanation, though it is not as regionally concentrated in Uganda as is ethnicity. Using the same tests with religious dummy variables produced no significant changes. Thus, religion is also not responsible for the district effect. Nor is the distance from regional headquarters or the road conditions leading to the respondent's house. These variables are insignificant when included and do not alter the effect of district variables. Other possible suspects such as wealth, education, and urbanization are already included in the model as controls.

In sum, the statistical results indicate that participation had only a weak and uneven impact on constitutional support. Following public affairs, satisfaction with the current government, improved living conditions, and location of residence had more consistently significant and larger effects on support for the constitution than did participation.

5.5. LOCATION OF RESIDENCE AND ELITE INFLUENCES

The discrepancy between the national-level comparisons (section 5.2) and the individual-level analysis (section 5.3) is puzzling: Why is support for the constitution so high in Uganda if being involved in the process did not make individuals any more supportive of the constitution? To answer this question, I supplement the quantitative analysis of survey data with qualitative analysis of in-depth interviews. Earlier, I noted that location of residence is significantly related to constitutional support. Yet we still lack an adequate explanation of why location is important. This section examines in more detail the effect of context on support for the constitution.

Based on qualitative analysis of in-depth interviews, it appears that the views of leaders active in a given area shaped citizen evaluations of both the constitution-making process and the constitution.[26] Citizens lacked skills and information to evaluate the constitution on their own, so they turned

---

or vice versa. (They changed most often in the equation predicting compliance.) The effect of participation on constitutional support was only slightly lower when the models included the ethnic variables individually and as a group. When the Buganda or Banyankole variables were included individually, the effect of participation on constitutional support was slightly higher. To further investigate the effect of ethnicity, I ran the model using responses from members each ethnic group one at a time and from members of all ethnic groups excluding one at a time. With the exception of where there were too few respondents in a given category, the results did not change significantly between subsamples.

26. A venerable scholarly literature discusses the influence of opinion leaders and elites on public opinion. Some of the most influential works of this tradition include Berelson, Lazarsfeld, and McPhee 1954; Katz and Lazarsfeld 1955; Lupia and McCubbins 1998; Mutz, Sniderman, and Brody 1996; Weimann 1994; Zaller 1992.

to local elites for cues. In addition, elites had an interest in persuading citizens to share their views. Where elites supported the constitution, they imparted positive messages to the citizens about the process and constitution, but where elites were antagonistic, citizens learned that the process was unfair and that the resulting constitution was flawed.[27] The location of residence variable appears to be a proxy for elite spheres of influence.

Limited Sources of Information and Interpretation

Most Ugandans had limited access to information about the constitution-making process and the constitution itself. Few had access to official documents such as the constitution, draft constitution, UCC reports, and educational materials on the constitution. The reach of private media and civic associations was also limited at that time. Furthermore, interpreting the legitimacy of the constitution is difficult for individuals everywhere in the world and is especially difficult for Ugandans, who had littel prior experience with constitutional rule.

The survey data provide many clues about the lack of citizen knowledge about the constitution and citizens' difficulty in evaluating it. Only 19 percent of survey respondents said that they had seen the constitution, and only 11 percent had read some part of it. In a question that asked respondents to agree or disagree with the statement, "The constitution is too complicated for most people to understand," 54 percent agreed and 14 percent did not know, leaving only 32 percent who believed that most people could understand the constitution. Only some survey respondents were willing and able to provide responses to the four questions measuring support for the constitution.[28] At a more basic level, only 67 percent could provide an appropriate response to the question, "In your opinion, what is the purpose of the constitution?"[29]

In the in-depth interviews, citizens frequently talked about how they

---

27. Finkel (2003) makes a similar argument with respect to why civic education led to lower trust in the Dominican Republic but higher trust in South Africa. He argues that participants in civic education programs were highly influenced by the attitudes of those organizing the activities.

28. In the survey, 69 percent answered the question measuring individual inclusion, 80 percent answered about national aspiration, 89 percent answered about compliance, and 89 percent answered about attachment.

29. An appropriate answer was defined fairly broadly and included references to laws, supreme laws, rules guiding citizens or leaders, means of choosing leaders, governance, democracy, rights and duties, nation building, peace and security, conflict resolution, helping citizens, and justice. It did not include responses about the current government, such as "Museveni" or "NRM," if that was the only response given. It also did not include answers such as "to collect taxes" that were far off the topic or admissions of ignorance, such as "We were not taught about that one."

had to rely on "local experts" for information and assessments of the constitution. For example, a local council chair from Iganga expressed strong support but admitted that most people in his village had trouble contributing views and understanding the constitution:

> From the current situation it seems to be the right constitution. According to me, I think that in most places [the government officials conducting the constitution-making activities] tried [to collect views], but you never know about other places. At the constitution-making time, there was not enough information for people to give views. The government tried to teach us, but if there are many people, then only a few can understand. We need representatives to come to each parish and teach us. People want to know what is going on in government. (interview, Iganga District, February 2001)

In the open-ended interviews, many respondents remarked that they lacked the experience and knowledge to know which issues are constitutional issues and which lie outside the constitutional domain.

Most citizens also found it difficult to evaluate the fairness of the constitution-making process. Participants had their own experiences as a reference, but many reported feeling uncomfortable generalizing from their personal experiences to the country as a whole. For example, in response to my question about whether or not the CA elections had been free and fair, most responded affirmatively about their particular voting locations but qualified their answers by saying that they did not know about other places except what they had been told by leaders.

In addition, many respondents said that they could not track the outcome of their efforts. For example, a fifty-year-old man said, "I haven't had enough chance to get information on the constitution, so I don't know if [his views] are [true] there. The [members of Parliament] should come back and tell us" (interview, Iganga District, February 2001). My archival research demonstrated that the UCC did a good job of documenting the submissions it received and how the draft constitution was developed. However, most Ugandans never had access to these materials. Only two of eighty-one in-depth interview respondents said that they had read at least some part of the draft constitution or reports containing statistics and commentary about the memoranda. The respondents often complained that they did not have a chance to read the constitution (either because they could not get a copy or because the copy available was in English), so they could not judge the final outcome for themselves.

Where did Ugandans get information about the process and the constitution, then, if not from these official documents? In the interviews, respondents reported that their CA delegates and members of Parliament (often the same individual) were the preferred sources of information because they had the greatest knowledge. Several of the clusters of negative evaluations of the constitution in my data had CA delegates who strongly opposed the regime. For example, the CA delegate for some of my respondents in Mpigi District was Paul Ssemogerere, former president of the Democratic Party and the main opposition candidate in the 1996 presidential elections. The CA delegate from Lira Town was Celia Ogwal, former assistant secretary-general of the Uganda's Peoples Congress. These two groups were the largest opposition parties and maintained strong support in their areas, often based on political affiliations formed before the current regime came to power. In interviews, both Ssemogerere (2001) and Ogwal (2001) denounced the constitution-making process, expressed dissatisfaction with the constitution, and accused the current government of being undemocratic. Their constituents held some of the most negative views of the constitution found in my survey.

Respondents made specific reference to these and other CA delegates when telling me how they came to their opinions about the constitution. My discussion with a forty-year-old man from Mpigi District is illustrative.[30]

Interviewer: Why did you choose statement B, "Our constitution hinders development so we should abandon it completely and design another"?
Respondent: There is a lot left to be desired for it to be a good constitution. It is a biased constitution. It is not a fair constitution. Although we were told we were going to elect people to make the constitution, there was a game behind it. In the elections, some people were put there by the government to run for the CA. The majority of the people who went through were from the government.
Interviewer: Was your CA delegate put there by the government?
Respondent: It was not here that the government pushed through their candidates, but elsewhere. In this place it was okay for the CA elections. Our CA delegate took our views but he couldn't win because the government side beat him. It wasn't fair. That is what he told us when he came back. (interview, Mpigi District, January 2001)

---

30. This respondent was active in the process. He reported participating in meetings about memoranda, the CA delegates meeting, and the CA elections.

This man's perception of the fairness of the elections was based on what he was told by his CA delegate, not on his personal experience.

The degree to which constituents had contact with their CA delegates and members of Parliament varied tremendously. The respondents' chief complaint about the process was that their CA delegates failed to come back to inform them of what happened. For example, one man in Mpigi said that the delegate "never came back to tell us what he did. If you give someone a hoe to go dig in your garden and you never see them again, you can't know if he did the work or not. Probably he just ran away with the hoe" (interview, Mpigi District, November 2000).

When CA delegates were not available, respondents reported that they learned about the process and the constitution from local council and government officials, active and educated community members, and the leaders of organizations active in their communities. When asked how he heard about the constitution-making activities, a farmer in Luwero said, "The local council was the main way of informing people. The councillors minded about the layman. They did a lot of work and encompassed everyone, even the illiterate" (interview, Luwero District, January 2001). Survey respondents who had heard about the constitution listed their sources as radio (88 percent),[31] government officials (67 percent), friends and family (65 percent), and local council meetings (63 percent). Civic educators, religious leaders, posters, pamphlets, television, and newspapers ranked far lower as sources of information. Interview respondents noted that they looked first to their elected officials for information because they were perceived as having the most knowledge. High-placed officials were preferred because of their presumed expertise, but they were less accessible than were local elected leaders, who typically filled the role of informer and influencer when the CA delegate was absent. Friends, family, and community members were most accessible but often suffered from the same lack of knowledge and interpretive skill. Educated, active, and connected community members provided some assistance.[32]

Another interesting piece of evidence indicates that leaders' opinions

31. Although most respondents said that they had heard about the constitution from the radio, radio listening had no influence on either the level of support for the constitution or the likelihood of offering an opinion about the constitution according to the survey analysis. Furthermore, in the in-depth interviews, respondents rarely cited the radio when asked how they came to know a specific piece of information about the constitution. While most survey respondents heard the constitution mentioned on the radio, it did not seem to be the most influential medium for imparting information and opinions.

32. Local elites sometimes acted as intermediaries between the CA delegate and others, as this woman indicates: "From each district, one [CA delegate] is elected and then that person goes and brings back what is there and then it is passed through from person to person" (interview, Lira District, March 2001).

mattered: within a given location, people typically referred to the same topics, used similar language, and offered equivalent arguments about the constitution-making process or the constitution, but much more variation occurred between different locations. One dramatic example comes from an area in the central region that had a negative view of the constitution. I heard from four different respondents that the majority of Ugandans had wanted *federo* (federalism) and that the UCC ignored the wishes of the majority of the people by recommending a unitary system. In other areas, I heard the opposite portrayal of public sentiment: leaders and citizens stated that most Ugandans opposed *federo*. The statistical summary of views in the UCC report does not clearly indicate what most Ugandans preferred,[33] although strong regional preferences unquestionably existed.[34] In my survey, 51 percent of my respondents in the central area knew that "Buganda did not get a federal system," while only 30 percent of those in other regions had that information. In sum, people in the central region were more likely to know that Uganda was a unitary rather than a federal system, but they also shared the misconception that the majority of Ugandans in all regions unambiguously wanted a federal system.

These different perceptions of public opinion on federalism mirrored the various views I heard expressed by elites in personal interviews, in the media, during the CA debates, and in written sources. For example, Mujaju (1999, 3), former head of the Department of Political Science and Public Administration at Makerere University, wrote, "So as to design a draft constitution, the constitutional commission which was chaired by a High court judge received views, 97 percent of which supported a federal system of government. But the Constituent Assembly rejected this option." The public learned these various "interpretations" of public opinion (whether accurate or not) from political elites.

In sum, most Ugandans who formed opinions about the constitution seem to have relied primarily on local experts (or regional experts who came to their locations) for information about the process and about the outcome. Without alternative sources of information and the skills necessary to evaluate the constitution, they had few resources with which to question what they were told.

---

33. According to the UCC's final report, 65.8 percent of the village councils (RC-1s) that sent in memoranda wanted a federal system, whereas 49 percent of the higher councils (RC-2s to RC-5s) wanted a federal system.

34. In the central portion of the country, 90 percent of the higher councils wanted a federal system. In the east, north, and west, only 16 percent of those councils wanted such a system.

Divided Elites and Their Influence on Public Opinion

So far I have presented a demand-side explanation for why citizens adopted elite views as their own: citizens, eager for information, looked to leaders for cues. There is also an important supply-side explanation: political leaders actively worked to convey their opinions to the public and to prevent the public from hearing alternative views. The public's formal involvement in the making of the new constitution created incentives for leaders to convey their opinions to their constituents, to convince citizens to share their views, and to mobilize the public in support of or in opposition to certain constitutional provisions. After all, public opinion shaped the memoranda submitted to the UCC, the draft constitution, the composition of the CA, and the CA debates. As elite wrangling became more polarized and contentious, so did public opinion. In short, leaders struggling for power found that it was in their interest to convince the public to think as they did about the process and about the constitution.

Ugandan leaders had a keen interest in ensuring that their favored rules were embodied in the constitution, because constitutional rules shape future power balances. During the course of the constitution-making process, leaders' views became more polarized and antagonistic. During the CA elections and the debates, the NRM leaders became more actively involved in the process to ensure that the provisions included in the constitution would help them maintain their hold on power. As opposition groups realized that they were in danger of being shut out of power in the long term, they fought back by actively criticizing the constitution-making process and later (when they failed to secure protections) the constitution itself. They hoped that undermining support for the constitution would provoke an opportunity to enact their desired changes. The opposition accused the government of self-serving, undemocratic, and illegal behavior, complaining that the general environment favored the NRM, that the UCC was biased, that the CA campaigns and elections were unfair, and that the government unduly influenced the constitutional commissioners and CA delegates.[35] Critiques of the process were expressed in the media, at seminars and conferences, during campaigns for office, at local meetings,

---

35. These critiques of the process are based largely on reviews of the process by Furley and Katalikawe (1997); Makara and Tukahebwa (1996); Okeny (1995); Oloka-Onyango (2000); and Tripp (2005) as well as on interviews with Besigye (2001); Njuba (2001); Ogwal (2001); and Ssemogerere (2001). For a more expansive list of the common critiques of the process, see section 2.4.

and in informal discussions with citizens as well as in formal protest actions, petitions, walkouts, and boycotts.[36]

My data show that the majority of citizens did not internalize these complaints and formal protest actions. Citizens in most areas adopted the government rhetoric that the process was free and fair and the constitution represented all people's interests. However, in areas where the opposition was stronger, citizens were deeply influenced by accusations against the government, the process, and the constitution. Thus, citizen attitudes about the constitution-making process and the constitution became polarized, like those of the leaders from whom they obtained their information.

In the areas where opposition elites dominated, their critiques are echoed in both the survey questions about constitutional legitimacy and the open-ended interview transcripts. For example, a local chair in Sironko told me that he was dissatisfied when his CA delegate "came back and said we have made the laws but it is like a body without a head" (interview, Sironko District, April 2001). His CA delegate was one of those who had walked out of the CA in protest over the political system issue. Another constituent of the same CA delegate responded to my questions as follows.

Interviewer: When the CA finished its work, did you hear anything more about the constitution?

Respondent: Our representative came, and we were with him here in the trading center. He came and briefed us on some of the issues, and he read us some of the articles. He talked of one that caused him to move out [walk out of the CA]. He said one article contradicts the other. . . .

Interviewer: Does the constitution represent all the groups in Uganda?

Respondent: The multipartyists don't very well agree with it. . . . They say when we are in power, we will change the constitution because it is a movement constitution and it favors the movement.

Interviewer: Where did you hear that?

Respondent: I heard it from the rally for [members of Parliament]. When they were campaigning, the candidates said, "When we go there, we want to change the constitution because it was made by movement people." (interview, Sironko District, April 2001)

---

36. The UPC and many of its followers boycotted the UCC seminars and did not send memoranda. They also filed a petition against the CA election rules, boycotted the CA, and refused to send their allotted two delegates. Sixty-four delegates walked out of the CA proceedings to protest the political system debate, and a small number of CA delegates boycotted the promulgation of the 1995 constitution.

Citizens seem to have believed what they were told by local or regional leaders because most lacked alternative sources of information about the process and about the constitution. In addition, individuals were probably predisposed to accept the views of officials who had only recently been elected. In areas where people had deep historical ties to political parties—the Democratic Party and Uganda People's Congress—they elected opposition leaders. These partisan attachments were formed in the thirty years prior to the constitution-making period and were reinforced by ethnic, religious, and regional connections. Opposition elites probably had little difficulty reviving these latent affiliations during the constitution-making process to mobilize their constituents against unfavorable provisions in the constitution. Citizens in these areas readily accepted that the NRM used underhanded means to influence the outcome. Citizens in other areas who had elected NRM stalwarts were predisposed to discount any criticisms they heard over the radio and to trust in the positive assessments they heard from their elected officials.

In sum, it makes sense that political leaders were the most influential sources with regard to the constitution. Both government and opposition leaders worked hard to ensure that the public thought as they did about both the constitution-making process and the resulting constitution. Citizens rarely heard opinions contrary to those of the local leaders because few alternative sources of information existed and because people had little inclination to question what they were told by elected leaders. Furthermore, it is understandable that the public was highly polarized in its views of the process and the constitution, considering the polarization of the leaders. In most areas of Uganda, progovernment leaders persuaded citizens that the process had been conducted in a fair manner and that the constitution accurately reflected the public's views. However, in some areas where the opposition was stronger, dissatisfied leaders convinced citizens that government had secured its favored provisions by unfair means, thus making the constitution illegitimate.

Reconciling Aggregate and Individual-Level Results

We now return to the puzzling juxtaposition of the aggregate and individual-level data: Why is aggregate support for the constitution higher in Uganda than in other African countries when individuals who participated are not more supportive of the constitution than those who were not involved?

One possible answer is that it is not the act of participation (as suggested by the developmental theory of participation) but rather the perception of inclusiveness that increases the legitimacy of the constitution. Perhaps it was enough for citizens to believe that they had the opportunity to participate and that others did participate in the constitution-making process. The act of participating itself may be superfluous to an individual's judgment of constitutional legitimacy. Another related answer is that participation does not directly affect the individual participant but rather affects the final document in a way that makes it more suitable to the circumstances in Uganda. In this case, the constitution would be viewed as appropriate in the eyes of all Ugandan citizens, regardless of whether they personally had participated in its creation.

To be fair, these alternative mechanisms by which participation might strengthen constitutional legitimacy would not seem alien to the key architects of the Ugandan process. Their rhetoric on the process is consistent with the developmental theory of participation as well as with these alternative mechanisms of change.[37] In addition, these alternative mechanisms are mentioned in the theoretical literature on the benefits of participation.[38]

Nonetheless, the Ugandan policymakers and theorists of participation missed an important component that this research highlights. If only perception mattered, then citizens in all areas where participation took place would support the constitution. If only content mattered, then all individuals who knew about the content would be equally supportive. My analysis shows that neither holds true. There were pockets of negative attitudes about the constitution even in areas with high rates of participation and with relatively knowledgeable citizens. Simply including participation in the constitution-making process was not sufficient to ensure support.

The answer to the question lies in the strength of the progovernment leadership vis-à-vis the political opposition, not participation per se. Participants did not assume that they were listened to just because they contributed their views in meetings, memoranda, and voting booths. Leaders provided information and opinions that helped citizens interpret the effects of their participation and the suitability of the constitution. The inclusion of participation may have helped progovernment leaders to convince citizens that the process was fair and the constitution legitimate, but it did not prevent

---

37. The methodology chosen by the Ugandan constitution makers clearly indicates that they thought that the act of participating was one of several important possible mechanisms.

38. The developmental theory of participation holds that the act of participation directly affects the individual, and the evidence does not support these contentions. However, these alternative mechanisms are also mentioned in the theoretical literature on the consequences of participation. Unfortunately, theorists are often not clear about the individual-level mechanisms by which participation might influence attitudes.

opposition leaders from convincing their followers otherwise. The high level of popular support for the constitution in Uganda most likely resulted from the high level of support among the Ugandan elites. In a context where the political opposition is stronger, participatory constitution making may lead to far more extensive antagonism to the constitutional order.

5.6. PARTICIPATION AND CONSTITUTIONAL KNOWLEDGE

This analysis shows that local elites, not participation, influenced whether citizens came to support or oppose the constitution. Does this mean that participation in the constitution-making process had no effect on public support for the constitution? In this section and the next, I argue that the previous analysis fails to capture the full effect of participation for two reasons: (1) the sample is truncated, disproportionately excluding those with lower levels of participation; and (2) the quantitative analysis captures changes (or lack thereof) in the magnitude of support but misses changes in the quality of support for the constitution. This section argues that participation was crucial for teaching citizens about the constitution and helping them to form opinions, even if it did not determine whether those opinions would be positive or negative. The next section discusses how participation altered evaluation criteria.

The quantitative analysis presented earlier in this chapter included only those respondents who were able and willing to answer questions about the constitution. Sizable proportions of the respondents failed to answer the questions about the constitution and are coded as "don't know," "refuse to answer" or "skip."[39] Only 69 percent answered the question measuring individual inclusion; 80 percent answered regarding national aspiration;[40] 89 percent answered regarding compliance; and 89 percent answered regarding attachment. Altogether, 60 percent of the respondents provided answers for all four questions and are included in figure and analysis of the constitutional support index.[41]

39. "Refuse" and "skip" do not necessarily mean that the respondents were unable to answer the questions. However, these codings are few. Almost all of those missing were coded as "don't know."

40. Similarly, 82 percent answered the question on national aspiration in the Afrobarometer survey conducted in Uganda a year before my survey. The proportion from other countries who answered the question in the Afrobarometer surveys is also low, ranging from 72 percent in Lesotho to 96 percent in South Africa.

41. Far fewer respondents answered the questions about the constitution than answered questions about other political attitudes. More than 90 percent (and often 98 or 99 percent) answered the questions about democratic attitudes, trust, and political capabilities. Ninety-nine percent answered a question about understanding what is going on in government, whereas only 86 percent answered a nearly identically worded question about understanding the constitution.

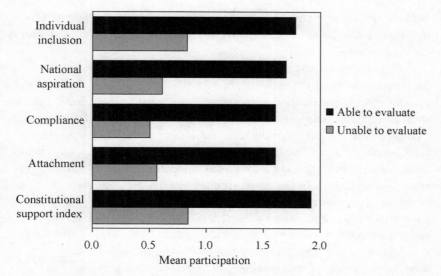

Fig. 5.3. Mean participation and propensity for constitutional opinions. (Data from author.)

Those who answered had considerably higher rates of participation than did those who failed to answer. Figure 5.3 shows the mean value of participation for those who answered and those who did not for each of the four individual questions and the index variable. For example, those who answered the question about national aspiration participated in an average of 1.8 activities, while those who failed to answer participated in 0.61 activities. In short, participation is associated with a greater propensity to offer opinions about the constitution.

The correlation between participation and holding opinions about the constitution exists not only in the bivariate relationship but also in a multivariate analysis that controls for possible confounding factors such as demographics, socioeconomic status, and political exposure.[42] A probit model predicting whether an individual answered all four constitutional questions shows that participation had a large positive significant estimated effect (coefficient = 0.19, robust se = 0.05, p-value = 0.00).[43] In sum, strong

---

42. The control variables include male, urban residence, age, primary school education, own consumer goods, follow public affairs, mobility, associational affiliations, local council position, close to high official, and exposure to news on radio, through newspapers, and in meetings.

43. All of the control variables were in the expected direction except for mobility. Following public affairs, exposure to newspapers, associational affiliations, and close to high official were significant at the 95 percent level.

evidence shows that participation in constitution making predicts an individual's willingness and ability to offer opinions about the constitution,
ceteris paribus.[44]

What are the mechanisms by which participation helped citizens to
form opinions about the constitution? Participation seems to have taught
citizens what a constitution is and what is included in their document, as
indicated by the comments from a twenty-nine-year-old man from Luwero:
"The first time I heard about the constitution was at the CA delegates meeting [campaign rally]. The candidates explained it to us. Then, after, I heard
more about it from the radio and the CA delegate" (interview, Luwero District, January 2001). In the in-depth interviews, a large number of respondents reported that they had first learned about the purpose of the constitution in such participatory forums, and in analysis of the survey data,
participation had a robust and significant estimated effect on whether an individual could give an appropriate answer to the question, "In your opinion,
what is the purpose of the constitution?" Furthermore, the evidence in chapter 4 indicates that participation predicts increased knowledge of the content of the 1995 constitution, controlling for confounding factors and reciprocal effects. When variables for knowledge of constitutional purpose
and knowledge of constitutional content are included in the equation predicting propensity for constitutional opinions, they are significant, and the
effect of participation declines substantively and drops below conventional
levels of statistical significance. This finding seems to result from the mediating effect of knowledge on opinion formation.[45] The evidence supports
the contention that participation in constitution making taught citizens
about the purpose and content of the constitution, knowledge that enabled
them to offer opinions about it.

Teaching citizens what a constitution is, helping them to form opinions
about the current constitution, and thus raising the salience of constitu-

44. A Heckman selection model provides even stronger evidence that when individuals are able to
evaluate the constitution, participation has no additional effect on support for the constitution. The
Heckman model estimates the probit equation predicting propensity for constitutional opinions and includes the predicted values in the equation predicting constitutional support. The results of the Heckman model indicate that participation has a significant positive effect on those who offer opinions about
the constitution but that participation has no effect on the constitutional support index (coefficient $=$
-0.01, robust se $= 0.05$, p-value $= 0.76$). Although this Heckman model is suggestive, the results
should be viewed with caution because it is not well identified. I was unable to find sufficiently independent instruments predicting propensity for constitutional opinions.
45. The full test of mediation specified by Baron and Kenny (1986) indicates that participation affected
constitutional knowledge, knowledge affected who provided answers, and the initial relationship between participation and who answered was reduced by the inclusion of the knowledge variables.

tionalism among the general population is an important contribution of the participatory constitution-making process. In a review of the Ugandan, South African, Ethiopian, and Eritrean constitution-making processes, Hyden and Venter (2001, 212) express this sentiment:

> Making people conscious of the importance of a constitution was in itself a necessary first step, because the political legacy the incoming regimes inherited had paid little or no attention to how civic rights and the use of power could meaningfully be regulated through adherence to a constitution. . . . People had to be persuaded that this was a break with the past; that the arbitrary use of power would no longer be possible without incurring high costs in political terms.

A local council member echoed these sentiments when I asked if it was necessary to make a new constitution:

> Yes, it was very necessary. In the past, we would just hear things and try to follow them, but we wouldn't really know. Now if it is something that is made by us at the grassroots, it is easier to follow. (interview, Bushenyi District, April 2001)

Recent scholarship in the new institutionalist tradition suggests that the main goal during transitions should be to break out of the old undemocratic equilibrium behavior and create a new equilibrium based on democratic principles and rule of law. One way to generate a critical moment of change is to make the new rules highly salient—a new focal point for expectations of political behavior that can act as a coordinating devise (Bardhan 1997; Bates 1990; Bratton and van de Walle 1997; Calvert 1995; Nabli and Nugent 1989; Ordeshook 1992; Putnam 1993; Weingast 1997). Increasing awareness of the constitution is a necessary first step toward making the constitution into a new focal point for the political game.

In sum, participatory constitution making in Uganda provided citizens with basic knowledge of the constitution's purpose and content and thus helped Ugandans to develop attitudes about the constitution. Ugandans who offered opinions on the constitution, on average, expressed support for it. In general, those who participated can and do support the constitution, whereas many of those who did not participate in constitution making do not support the constitution because they do not know what it is.[46] Therefore, evidence

---

46. Of course, they are also unable to oppose the constitution without knowing what it is.

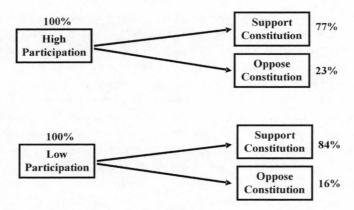

Fig. 5.4. Participation and constitutional support for only those who know the constitution. (Data from author.)

indicates that participatory constitution making did help build support for the constitution in Uganda by creating a new group of individuals who know and care about the constitution (but not by changing previously held opinions).

Figures 5.4 and 5.5 reveal how participation built constitutional support even though the relationship was insignificant in the earlier statistical analysis.[47] Figure 5.4 shows the dichotomous effects of high and low participation on constitutional support when only those who could answer the questions are included. Participation appears to have had a negative (though insignificant) effect on constitutional support: 77 percent of those with high-level participation supported the constitution, whereas 84 percent of those with low-level participation supported it. Figure 5.5 shows the same relationship when the entire sample is included (those who answered the questions and those who did not). Seventy-one percent of those with high-level participation supported the constitution, whereas 59 percent of those with low-level participation supported it. Participation helped citizens form opinions, and most with opinions are supportive. While participation clearly led to greater support in Uganda, participation bolstered constitutional support only because most Ugandan elites were supportive. There is no guarantee that the context will be conducive to supportive attitudes in other cases of participatory constitution making.

47. High participation is above average, and low participation is at or below average. Support for the constitution is based on the measure of national aspirations, where high and low were determined in the same way.

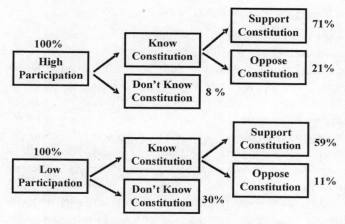

Fig. 5.5. Participation and constitutional support for all respondents. (Data from author.)

5.7. CRITERIA FOR EVALUATING THE CONSTITUTION

There is one final reason to think that the initial statistical analysis did not capture the full effect of participation. Participation seems to have altered the terms by which citizens evaluate the constitution rather than changing the level of their support.[48] The statistical analysis presented earlier can capture only changes in the level of support, but the in-depth qualitative interviews capture changes in the criteria on which these evaluations are based.[49] The interview transcripts show that Ugandans with higher levels of participation tend to discuss the legitimacy of the constitution in procedural terms, whereas those with lower levels of participation typically refer to distributive concerns. Support based on procedural evaluations is more durable than that based on distributive concerns (Lind and Tyler 1988; Tyler, Casper, and Fisher 1989). Therefore, participation seems to have helped produce a more enduring kind of support by altering the criteria by which citizens evaluated the constitution.

---

48. I am again talking here only about the section of the population willing and able to offer opinions about the constitution.

49. Respondents for in-depth interviews included (1) citizens randomly sampled within a given location (but not in proportion to the population in that area); (2) local leaders who were likely to know about constitution-making activities in the area; and (3) individuals sampled off lists of participants. The interview sample is not representative of the general population, as is the survey sample. The interviews loosely followed a list of questions, but follow-up questions were asked and question ordering was altered depending on the responses. The in-depth interviews are more vulnerable to interviewer bias than is the survey. See the introduction for more details on the research methodology.

Patterns in the Qualitative Data

This inquiry relies primarily on data from qualitative interviews. The analysis occurred in three stages. In the first stage, I read each interview in full, assigned a level of participation to each, and coded all passages where the respondent discussed the constitution.[50] In the second stage, I reread a list of only those passages that referred to the constitution and assigned a level of support for the constitution. I also coded each mention of procedural or distributive concerns, paying special attention to which concerns the respondent emphasized.[51] In the third stage, I connected codings about evaluations of the constitution with those about level of participation that I had assigned earlier.

Three patterns emerged from this analysis: (1) active participants tended to evaluate the constitution based on the fairness of the constitution-making process—they based their evaluations on procedural terms; (2) less active or inactive participants tended to evaluate the constitution based on their current circumstances, or distributive concerns; and (3) most of those interviewed supported the constitution, but geographic pockets of negative evaluations included both participants and nonparticipants.[52]

First, individuals who engaged in many constitution-making activities typically talked about the fairness of the process. In the open-ended interviews, I asked the same four questions about the constitution that were asked in the survey and then asked follow-up questions about why they gave the answers they did. Citizens who had participated talked about whether (1) the process was inclusive; (2) different groups were represented equally; (3) the elections for CA were free and fair; (4) their views were considered by appointed and elected officials; (5) the president and his cabinet exerted undue influence on the outcome; and (6) the process was transparent. For example, an old man from Bushenyi who had served as the local council chair and who was actively involved in constitution-making activities agreed with the statement that "Our constitution expresses the values and aspirations of the Ugandan people." When I asked him why he agreed, he responded,

> It was very important for the CA to read through the draft constitution and affirm what was there or even add some. The CA was chosen by people to represent us. It was important to send representatives to confirm that

---

50. I used Nvivo program for the coding and retrieval of sections of the transcripts.
51. In the second stage, my initial codings of levels of participation were not deliberately investigated, though I remembered some of them. In other words, the two stages of coding were not fully independent.
52. This third finding motivated the inclusion of the district variables in the earlier statistical analysis.

the constitution was based on people's ideas and not something else. Now I know that it was based on the ideas of people from the village local councils on up. (interview, Bushenyi District, April 2001)

Second, individuals who engaged in few or no constitution-making activities typically talked about their current circumstances when asked to explain their opinions of the constitution (if they offered opinions). They discussed whether there was peace and security, if their economic conditions had improved since the adoption of the constitution, and the current leadership. In a follow-up to the question about attachment, one thirty-eight-year-old man said, "We should change the constitution because the tax rates make prices high. I don't believe in the constitution myself because of these tax things" (interview, Iganga District, February 2001). To the extent that low-level participants talked about the constitution itself, it was about the resulting document, not the means by which it was created. For example, respondents who had not participated mentioned that the constitution did not create a federal system, that parties are not allowed to campaign, and that women and children have new rights.

The third pattern that emerged was that most of the respondents were positive about the constitution except for geographic pockets of nearly unanimous negative sentiment. These pockets included both participants and nonparticipants. However, their explanations for their dissatisfaction mirrored the distinctions discussed earlier: participants were more likely to say that the constitution-making process was unfair, while nonparticipants usually said that the outcomes went against their interests.

Table 5.2 depicts these patterns, containing quotations representing respondents who expressed support and dissatisfaction with the constitution and who had high and low participation rates. The bottom row illustrates the first pattern, the top row shows the second pattern, and the difference between the columns reveals the third pattern.

Evaluations of Procedure and Outcomes

How can we interpret these findings from the qualitative analysis? The theoretical literature on institutional support indicates that perceptions of procedural fairness can help build and maintain diffuse support in the face of an unfavorable outcome (Tyler 1989). The fact that participants cited procedural fairness as the primary basis for their support suggests that participation produced a more enduring support for the constitution by raising the salience of procedural considerations.

Tyler, Casper, and Fisher (1989) argue that two main sources of institutional legitimacy exist: childhood socialization and adult experiences. Adult experiences include perceptions about the fairness of procedures and the favorability of outcomes. Studies of adult encounters with the police, the courts, workplace management, and political campaigns show that individuals judge these institutions as much by the fairness of the process as by the outcome itself (Lind and Tyler 1988; Tyler, Casper, and Fisher 1989). In these studies, the potentially negative impacts of unfavorable decisions were counteracted by views that the procedures used to make the decisions were fair. Thus, perceptions of procedural fairness help build durable support for institutions even in the face of fluctuations in outcome favorability.

In the case of Uganda, childhood socialization (a crucial source of constitutional legitimacy in long-standing democracies) probably had little impact on how citizens view the constitution—constitutionalism had little influence on politics when today's adult Ugandans were young. Opinions of the constitution in Uganda are based primarily on adult experiences, including perceptions of procedural fairness and outcome favorability. *Procedure* refers to the constitution-making process, and *outcome* refers to current circumstances for the citizen. Outcomes include such issues as whether one's favored candidate is allowed to run for office, whether one's traditional leader can collect taxes, and what rights one has over the land that one farms.

Constitutions may be relatively stable, but constitutional outcomes fluctuate over time—at one point a citizen will find outcomes favorable and at

TABLE 5.2. Evaluations of the Constitution by Constitutional Support and Participation

Level of Participation	Support for the Constitution	
	Low	High
	Distributive opposition	Distributive support
Low	"There should be a new one. We have a lot of problems and there is no peace."	"The other constitution was bad. This one is better. Things are better now. Before you couldn't get necessities such as soap and salt."
	Procedural opposition	Procedural support
High	"We gave our views, but the government didn't listen. When we gave our views to the subcounty, they edited out some. The [national] government edited out others."	"The past constitutions were made by only a few people, but this one gathered the views of all the people."

another point unfavorable. In the case of term limits, for example, at one point a term limit may prevent one's favored candidate from running again, whereas at another time it may prevent one's opponent from running. In contrast, evaluations of the procedures are not likely to change, since constitution making happens infrequently. A view that the constitution-making process was fair can create a buffer between unfavorable outcomes and constitutional legitimacy. However, this buffer exists only to the extent that citizens value procedural integrity over their assessment of current outcomes. Participation appears to have made procedural concerns salient, so we should expect more durable support for the constitution among those who participated.

5.8. CONCLUSION

We can now answer the question that is asked at the beginning of the chapter: How did participation in constitution-making affect attitudes about the constitution? The evidence suggests that participation helped build support for the constitution but did not do so as initially expected. The developmental theory of participation assumes that procedures are fair, that participants can judge them as such, and that perceptions of fairness will increase support for policy outcomes. In Uganda, the constitution-making process was not unambiguously fair, and Ugandans found it difficult to evaluate the process and the resulting constitution. These deviations are important for understanding how participation affected constitutional legitimacy.

Among those individuals who offered opinions about the constitution, participants were no more likely than those who stayed home to say that the constitution is legitimate. Participation was not a magic bullet that automatically produced support for governing institutions. Rather, participation indirectly built support for the constitution by teaching citizens about the constitution and helping them to form opinions about it. The vast majority of those who learned about the constitution have positive opinions. In short, participation built support for the constitution by contributing to the creation of a new class of supporters among citizens who otherwise would not have known about the constitution.

I found that participation not only contributed to the total number of supporters but also made support more durable. Participation seems to have transformed support based on distributive concerns into support based on procedural legitimacy. Nonparticipants were more concerned about their current personal circumstances, whereas participants were more concerned about the legitimacy of the process in which they had taken part. Existing literature suggests that support based on distributive outcomes is fragile, whereas support based on procedural legitimacy is more enduring. Therefore, to the extent that participation led citizens to focus on the legitimacy of the constitution-making process, their opinions about the constitution are thought to be more stable. Since support for the constitution in Uganda is currently quite high, solidifying these positive sentiments probably facilitates the system's future stability.

However, not all participants had positive views of the constitution-making process or the constitution. For some, participation also led to a solidifying of negative sentiments. The participants who view the constitution-making process as unfair presumably will have more enduring negative views than the nonparticipants who are not currently getting what they want but may do so in the future.

This brings us back to the two quotations that opened this chapter. Participation is associated with the attitudes reflected in both these statements; both men offered strong opinions about the constitution, and both were evaluating constitutional legitimacy based on procedural grounds. The school headmaster from Bushenyi viewed the constitution as legitimate because he believed that the process was inclusive and representative. The campaign agent from Lira believed that the process was biased and unfair and consequently concluded that the constitution was illegitimate. Some observers may feel heartened that many more Ugandans reflect the attitude of the headmaster than that of the campaign agent. In this sense, participation contributed to robust support for the constitution. However, they should be cautioned by the finding that even a minority of participants held attitudes like those of the agent from Lira. Participatory constitution making in Uganda helped instill an enduring antagonism to the constitution among a small class of individuals who otherwise might not have known or cared about the constitution.

More generally, this research offers important lessons for scholars and advocates of participatory constitution making. Participation does not happen in a vacuum. Nor do citizens form their views of the constitution in a vacuum. Citizens have difficulty evaluating constitutions and consequently rely on elected leaders for information and opinions. It is important to pay attention to what local elites communicate to citizens about the impact of their participation, the fairness of the process, and the resulting constitutional document as a way of predicting whether participation will strengthen or weaken constitutional legitimacy. Based on the evidence from Uganda, chapter 6 examines in more detail the benefits and drawbacks of the participatory constitution-making model.

CHAPTER 6

Participation, Constitution Making, and Democracy

The previous chapters examine the effect of participation in constitution making on Uganda's political culture. The empirical evidence indicates that participants tended to be informed distrusting democrats, most of whom were supportive of the constitution but some of whom were antagonistic. This chapter asks what these resulting individual traits mean for democratic constitutionalism. In which ways did public involvement in the process help or hinder democratization in Uganda? How and where can policymakers best utilize participatory constitution making to further democratic development in other contexts? What does this research tell us about the consequences of participation more generally?

After briefly reviewing the key findings of the research, this concluding chapter responds to these questions. I argue that a more democratic and informed citizenry is certainly advantageous for democratization. Though my discovery of lower institutional trust was somewhat unexpected, I contend that it too is beneficial for democratic development in Uganda, especially in the long term. By monitoring government performance, skeptical citizens can help protect against backsliding. Conversely, the Ugandan program seems to have fed the polarization of citizen views of the constitution, which may increase instability and hinder constitutionalism. Most participants were deeply attached to the constitution, but a minority of citizens harbored enduring enmity to the new system's fundamental rules.

In addition, I infer that polarization of the mass public's constitutional preferences is more likely when public participation is a major component in the constitution-making process. As such, the biggest drawback to the participatory constitution-making model is the increased risk that a significant number of citizens may come to strongly reject the constitution. The percentage of citizens who develop antagonistic views of the constitution is likely to be higher outside of Uganda, where the organized political opposition was small and weak, a situation that is unlikely to be the case in other places. This chapter suggests a number of policy options for minimizing polarization among the mass public. Ultimately, however, the considerable benefits derived from participatory constitution making (rendering citizens more democratic, knowledgeable, and discerning) must be weighed against the risk that a section of the population may emerge with strong views against the constitution and thus become distrustful of the rules as well as the rulers.

The chapter concludes by reiterating my theory about how participation (in constitution making or otherwise) affects participants' attitudes. Participation has the potential to change the attitudes of the participant population, even in the short term, by increasing the likelihood that citizens are exposed to political information and by changing the criteria citizens use to evaluate that information. The content of the messages to which participants are exposed determines the direction of attitude change. Accordingly, I urge policymakers and theorists to pay more attention to message content as a means of predicting participatory outcomes.

6.1. SUMMARY OF KEY FINDINGS

Advocates of the participatory constitution-making model make bold claims about participation's ability to alter political culture. Public involvement in the process is said to (1) foster democratic attitudes such as tolerance, appreciation of rights, support for public participation, and equality; (2) encourage feelings of efficacy so that citizens will act in support of their beliefs; (3) expand knowledge about the constitution and the public sphere; (4) build support for the constitution and constitutional principles; and (5) enhance trust in institutions and legitimize the new government. The Uganda Constitutional Commission (UCC) (1992a, 13) claimed that the Ugandan constitution-making process accomplished these goals:

> The consultation of Ugandans on the new constitution has been unprecedented. This participation has made people more politically mature and given them a sense of dignity that their views really matter in the democratic organization of society. Once they recognize that their views have formed the basis for the new constitution, they will be in a position to respect and defend it. People now generally know what a constitution is, its usual contents, and its objectives and principles. They have come to understand that democratic constitutions ought to emerge from the people. This

belief is the strongest safeguard of a national constitution, which has evolved from the people themselves.

The UCC report continued (1992a, 36),

The methodology employed has yielded tremendous results. People have become politically aware. They are eager to assert and defend their rights. They are convinced of their right to participate in their own governance. Never again will they allow major decisions which concern them to be decided upon without their being consulted. Participatory democracy and a search for a consensus have gradually become a new culture in Uganda. The ordinary citizens have found the exercise most reassuring. Their views on the new constitution did not appear to be much different from those of the elites. They can now confidently participate in all other national exercises, fully convinced that their views will carry weight. The exercise has taught people tolerance of views that differ from their own.

Was the UCC correct in its optimistic assessment of how participation in constitution making altered the attitudes and knowledge of ordinary citizens?

The analysis presented in this book indicates that the Ugandan constitution makers realized some but not all of their goals. The data in chapter 3 suggest that leaders mobilized citizens to participate in the process beyond what we would expect from individual-level traits. The UCC's assertion that "consultation of Ugandans on the new constitution has been unprecedented" is supported by empirical analysis. Chapters 3 and 4 present evidence that participatory citizens were likely to be more democratic and politically knowledgeable than inactive citizens, even when controlling for reciprocal effects and confounding factors. The evidence is consistent with the commissioners' claims that participation in constitution making raised preferences for participation, tolerance, and individual rights as well as made Ugandans more politically aware.

The data also indicate that participation contributed to a decline in institutional trust. This finding is contrary to my initial expectations derived from the optimistic participatory theories but does not necessarily conflict with the UCC's assessment. The Ugandan government did not behave democratically. In chapter 4, I argue that participation contributed to the erosion of trust precisely by making citizens more democratic and more knowledgeable. Participants learned that a sizable gap exists between their newly developed democratic ideals and their government's actual performance. The gap probably grew when democratic performance declined in the period prior to my survey. Those who participated in the constitution-making process seem to have been more sensitive to this democratic decline than those who did not. In this sense, participation appears to have made citizens "more politically mature" and "eager to assert and defend their rights" against undemocratic government actions.

In contrast to these important effects of participation, chapter 3 reveals that participation did not significantly enhance feelings of political capability, as the UCC alleged. Citizens who were involved in the process apparently felt no more confident in the political realm than those who did not participate. The development of competence was probably hindered by the difficulty of the topic (the constitution), the newness and infrequency of the activities, the lack of feedback following the promulgation of the constitution, and the government's continuing authoritarian tendencies. It seems that ordinary citizens did not necessarily find "the exercise most reassuring" and do not feel able to "confidently participate in all other national exercises." The failure to advance competency represents a serious shortcoming. Supportive attitudes and knowledge will not beget civic behavior if participants feel incapable of acting in the public realm and effecting change. As a result, even democratic citizens may not act in defense of democracy.

Finally, the evidence in chapter 5 supports the contention that participation helped citizens to form opinions about the current constitution by teaching them what it is and what it contains. It may also have made those opinions more durable by increasing the salience of procedural over distributive criteria of evaluation. However, participation did not significantly predict whether citizens came to support or oppose the constitution; rather, leaders in a given area influenced the direction of citizen sentiment. Because of the lack of alternative sources of information, the difficulty of interpreting constitutional legitimacy, and deliberate attempts by polarized elites to alter citizen attitudes, ordinary people relied on local elites for information and opinions. In most areas, citizens came into contact with elites who supported the current government and developed positive assessments of constitutional legitimacy. However, in areas where opposition elites were strong, participants developed an enduring antagonism to the constitution. Participation appears to have helped citizens to learn "what a constitution is, its usual contents, and its objectives and principles" but did not ensure that "a search for a consensus [has] gradually become a new culture in Uganda." The data indicate quite the opposite. Citizens seemed more polarized and steadfast rather than more consensual in their views of the constitution. The Ugandan constitution-making process seems not to have fulfilled a primary objective of its organizers.

6.2. IMPLICATIONS FOR DEMOCRATIC DEVELOPMENT IN UGANDA

This book details a number of ways in which participation in the Ugandan constitution-making process seems to have affected political culture as well as some ways it did not. How do the consequences of participatory constitution making advance or hinder democratization in Uganda?

The Benefits of Informed Distrusting Democrats

Democracy requires a set of normative values and behaviors as well as formal democratic institutions. So far, democracy advocates have had far more success in reforming institutions than in altering ordinary citizens' attitudes and actions. The participatory constitution-making model has garnered extensive interest among policymakers precisely because it promises to build a supportive political culture at the same time as it constructs the new rules and institutions. My research indicates that participants in the Ugandan constitution-making process were more democratic, politically aware, and skeptical of government institutions than their inactive counterparts. I argue that the combination of these three attitude changes helps to facilitate democratization in Uganda.

Increasing democratic attitudes and political awareness among participants was a major achievement for the Ugandan program. By nearly all accounts, more democratic and knowledgeable citizens enhance Uganda's prospects for democratic development. Citizens who value tolerance, equality, individual rights, public involvement in government, and freedom of speech are more likely to behave in ways that are conducive to democracy. This includes participating actively in the polity, respecting the rights of others (including political opponents), condemning infringements on civil liberties, and punishing leaders who govern by undemocratic means (Almond and Verba 1963; Dahl 1971; Dalton 2000; Diamond 1993; Lipset 1994; Tyler 1989). Empirically, these democratic values are strongly related to measures of democracy at the aggregate level of analysis (Inglehart 2003) and to action in defense of democracy at the individual level of analysis (Gibson 1996). In addition, political knowledge facilitates civic engagement. Citizens who know their leaders are better able to contact them and hold them accountable, and citizens who know the rules of governance are better equipped to both use and defend them (Almond and Verba 1963, 1980).[1]

The impact of lowered institutional trust on the democratization process is not as readily apparent. Some are likely to view this outcome of participation as negative: for current leaders interested in ensuring reelection and citizen compliance, the decrease in citizen faith in government certainly is not beneficial. More neutral observers might worry that distrust of government will cause citizens to feel alienated from politics. The fear is that disenchanted citizens will drop out of politics or even act against the system in destabilizing ways and that distrust in institutional performance may spill over into dissatisfaction with democracy. Popular support for fledgling democratic institutions may be important for ensuring stability and fending off authoritarian reversals during bad times (Linz and Stepan 1996; Lipset 1959; Mishler and Rose 2001; Norris 1999).[2]

Nonetheless, I disagree with the conventional view that distrust of government is necessarily damaging to democracy or stability; dissatisfaction with government institutions does not automatically produce apathetic or disruptive citizens. In most parts of Uganda, the risk that citizens will withdraw or rebel seems to be especially low for two reasons.[3] First, citizen trust in government institutions remained extremely high in most areas. Participation seems to have tempered trust, bringing it down slightly from an

---

1. I do not argue that citizens need to be fully informed to participate in politics. Studies of political awareness in the United States show that citizens rely on schema, heuristics, and cues to make decisions where they lack information (Dalton 2000). Rather, I argue that better informed citizens are better able to act, especially in new democracies where schema, heuristics, and cues developed under authoritarian regimes are ill suited to the new system. Survey evidence from twelve African countries indicates that political knowledge is associated with willingness to act in defense of an independent press, legal system, and Parliament: "Defenders of democracy are drawn almost exclusively from Africans who are intellectually engaged in public life and who possess high levels of information" (Bratton, Mattes, and Gyimah-Boadi 2005, 309).

2. There are few empirical investigations of the relationship between institutional trust and democracy. In the concluding chapter of her book, Norris (1999, 257–70) uses cross-national statistical analysis to test the claim that institutional trust is associated with more conventional participation, fewer protest actions, and greater compliance with government. She finds substantively weak but statistically significant results supporting these claims; however, political interest, social trust, ideology, and social background are more influential. She concludes that policies directed at factors other than trust are likely to have a greater impact but that support for institutions is nonetheless important for democratic stability, especially in young systems.

3. A few regions of Uganda have rebel movements fighting against the government. However, these movements predate the constitution-making process. The process may have enhanced disenchantment among the general population in these areas, but there is no evidence that it influenced the rebel leaders.

extremely high level to moderate skepticism, not outright cynicism. Of those who responded, 72.1 percent reported trusting the courts, 55.3 percent the police, 85.7 percent their village councils, and 77.5 percent the Electoral Commission.[4] Second, Ugandans who participated were more critical of government performance but were simultaneously more attached to democratic principles and generally supportive of the constitution. Most of those who participated in constitution making were not disenchanted with the fundamental rules of the game but were merely dissatisfied with the behavior of the current players.

Although an unexpected outcome of participation, distrust can be beneficial for democratization, especially if citizens remain engaged and attached to democratic and constitutional principles while being critical of government leaders and institutions.[5] There is reason to believe that this is the most beneficial combination of attitudes in transitioning or hybrid systems. Critical citizens are more likely than naive or loyal individuals to monitor their leaders and enforce acceptable standards of behavior. Thus, distrust can fuel greater citizen participation rather than alienation and inactivity (Bratton, Mattes, and Gyimah-Boadi 2005; Levi 1998; Pharr and Putnam 2000; Tarrow 2000).[6] Furthermore, citizens who are committed to democracy and the constitution will tend to use democratic means of influencing leaders and thus become active within the system rather than against it. Informed distrusting democrats who support their constitution are well situated to support democratic development by exerting pressure on their leaders to uphold the newly adopted constitutional rules and to continue to create democratic structures. Moderate skepticism—coupled with democratic norms and political awareness—provides better protection against

---

4. From the Barometer surveys, the mean percentage reporting trust in the police was 47 percent in Africa, 53 percent in East Asia, 36 percent in Latin America, and 27 percent in New Europe. The mean percentage reporting trust in the courts was 49 percent in Africa, 56 percent in East Asia, 36 percent in Latin America, and 25 percent in New Europe. Bratton, Mattes, and Gyimah-Boadi (2005, 229, 235) note that overall African levels of trust in government institutions are similar to levels in the member countries of the Organization for Economic Cooperation and Development, and the authors query whether Africans are "too trusting" given their ill-performing institutions. The authors also note that institutional trust is associated with support for the single-party state.

5. For a careful theoretical consideration of the positive and negative effects of trust, see Levi 1998.

6. Recent survey data demonstrate that Ugandans are more participatory than other Africans even years after the constitution-making activities took place. Among the twelve African countries surveyed in the first round of the Afrobarometer, Ugandans had the fourth-highest reported voting, the highest reported election rally attendance, and the highest reported campaigning rates. More Ugandans than Africans from other countries reported that they attended community meetings and contacted government officials (Afrobarometer 2002). Without further research, it is impossible to say with certainty that the constitution-making program contributed to this high level of current activity. Nonetheless, it is a positive sign.

stagnation or backsliding in the democratization process than does blind faith. Critical citizens are especially important during the current period of democratization; countries undergoing transitions in the third wave are more likely to stabilize under hybrid systems that combine authoritarian and democratic elements than to fall victim to complete authoritarian reversals (Bratton, Mattes, and Gyimah-Boadi 2005; Bratton and van de Walle 1997; Diamond 2002; Levitsky and Way 2002). Naive publics that overestimate the quality of democratic governance pose a larger threat to democratic progress than do skeptical citizens.

Many of the informed distrusting democrats in my study seemed inclined to monitor their leaders' democratic and constitutional behavior. For example, a man whose name appeared on a list of UCC subcounty seminar attendees responded to my questions about the fairness of the constitution as follows.

> I'm not seeing any grumbling about the constitution as we go around, only grumbling about the leaders. People are grumbling about the leaders and saying, "This is not in the constitution." The constitution was made to favor all Ugandans, but people are grumbling that the implementation is bad. It is the failure of some individuals. The constitution itself is made to cater for all. (interview, Mbale District, April 2001)

Respondents often mentioned specific violations of the constitution, such as those mentioned by a thirty-two-year-old local council chair:

> The [Ugandan army] was sent to Congo by the president without Parliament, but that is not allowed in the constitution. I blame that on commander in chief, not on [members of Parliament]. Also, there is a ban on political parties and yet the N[ational] R[esistance] M[ovement] is behaving like a party. The [constitution-making] process was good because we were consulted as citizens, but after, the government leaders put in clauses that benefited them—you know, amendments. (interview, Luwero District, January 2001)

Participants also note that the constitution-making process empowered them vis-à-vis their leaders by providing them with knowledge and a feeling of ownership of the constitution. For example, this local council vice chair insisted,

It was very important to have representatives from each region go and make [the constitution]. If they had just made it on their own, people down here would have refused it, saying it didn't include our ideas. The grassroots should also have knowledge about the constitution so as to be aware of what is happening in Uganda. If people don't know, then those clever ones will use it to deceive them by saying, "Oh, that is not in the constitution." (interview, Lira District, March 2001)

While the participants' cognitive traits appear to be conducive to democracy, the question remains as to whether citizens will act on their new knowledge and attitudes. Some respondents indicated that they will. For example, this individual whose name was listed on the memoranda for his parish responded eagerly to my questions.

Interviewer: Do you agree or disagree with the following statement: "People should abide by what was written in the constitution whether they agree with what was written or not."

Respondent: Oh, I definitely agree! After passing the constitution *everyone* has to follow *everything.* If you don't abide by it, you have gone astray. On the radio I listened to the broadcast of the adoption of constitution at Kololo airstrip. They said everyone who goes against the constitution will be jailed, and this includes even the leaders. If the president fails to stand down, then it is an answerable case.

Interviewer: What would you do if he fails to step down?

Respondent: I would participate in a demonstration with others. Those are the people's ideas in the constitution, so we must demonstrate! (interview, Mpigi District, January 2001)

But most others did not feel so empowered, especially given the realities of power in Uganda. A fifty-nine-year-old man who expressed attachment to the constitution believed that he lacked the capacity to protect it:

Interviewer: Do you agree or disagree with the following statement: "Our constitution expresses the values and aspirations of the Ugandan people."

Respondent: Our constitution cares about people's views and what they want. It was made by the people and then given to the president. We elected people, and those are the ones who made the constitution.

Interviewer: Do you think Uganda should keep this constitution or make a new one?

Respondent: It's not up to me. This president came to power by rule of the gun, so it is impossible to do anything. If the president wants to be president, then we can't do anything. We can just beg him to change some things. (interview, Iganga District, February 2001)

Others echoed these sentiments, including a man from Bushenyi who expressed a strong preference for the current constitution and democratic procedures but had little faith in his ability to advance his preferences.

Interviewer: If a future government violated the constitution, what would you do?

Respondent: There is nothing I can do, especially if it is another government. But I feel that if the government doesn't want it or wants to change it, they should come back to the people. This constitution could serve all governments. It is the constitution for Uganda. But if they don't agree and want to change it, they should come back to the people. (interview, Bushenyi District, April 2001)

In response to the same question, another man in Bushenyi stated the dilemma even more forcefully: "Ugandans would oppose the government going against the constitution because it is the constitution of the people— unless they shoot them" (interview, Bushenyi District, April 2001). My queries about what citizens would do to defend their constitution or democracy often evoked expressions of powerlessness and fear.

While respondents who had been active in the constitution-making process frequently complained that the government did not respect their constitution, they often felt incapable of doing anything about it. In this light, the failure of the Ugandan program to increase feelings of political capability is quite important (see chapter 3). Participants are more likely to want their leaders to behave democratically and in line with the constitution, but they are uncertain about their ability to act in the public sphere to influence politicians.[7] In short, participation in Ugandan constitution making seems to have contributed to the development of informed distrusting democrats who are attached to the constitution. These citizens are pre-

---

7. The threat of military interference still looms large for most Ugandans. Based on the 2000 and 2002 Afrobarometer surveys, Logan et al. (2003, 17) argue that the 2001 elections led to a further erosion of subjective political capabilities in the Ugandan public.

disposed to work for democratic government, but because participants do not feel more efficacious, it is uncertain whether these favorable attitudes will translate into action.

Even if knowledgeable distrusting democrats are willing to act in defense of democratic and constitutional principles, we must still query whether there are enough of them to affect the behavior of political leaders. The Ugandan constitution-making process may have engendered a supportive democratic political culture among participants but its reach may have been too limited and shallow to alter Uganda's troubling political trajectory. Participation in the Ugandan process was impressive in comparative terms. However, with the exception of voting for Constituent Assembly (CA) delegates, only a minority of respondents said that they had participated in constitution-making activities. Support for leaders and institutional trust remain very high in Uganda despite the moderating influence of the process on those who were involved. So while participatory constitution making seems to have nudged participants in the right direction, the push may not be broad or large enough to alter Ugandan leaders' strategic calculations.[8]

The Drawbacks of a Polarized Public

The evidence suggests that participatory constitution making benefited democratic development by helping to produce informed distrusting democrats. Unfortunately, participation also seems to have had a detrimental effect, as revealed in chapter 5: citizen views of the constitution-making process and the constitution itself are polarized. Participation seems to have made attitudes more enduring, but elites influenced whether citizens viewed the constitution as legitimate or illegitimate, and elites were themselves polarized. The large majority of the attentive public in Uganda was exposed to positive messages about the constitution, so preserving current sentiment is probably beneficial for stability. However, in the few areas where hostile elites dominated, participants concluded that the process and resulting constitution

---

8. For example, President Museveni and his supporters recommended a change to the constitution to abolish the two-term limit on the presidency. Politicians, both within and outside of Museveni's movement, tried to organize against such an amendment on democratic grounds. They initially suggested a mass public campaign, but my research indicates that they would have had very limited success mobilizing citizens around the issue of term limits. In my survey, only 39.5 percent of the population even knew that there was a two-term limit. This number is far higher among those with above-average participation in the constitution-making process (53.4 percent) than among those with below-average participation (27.2 percent). Participatory constitution making probably helped to create a group of citizens predisposed to action, but it did not help enough to prevent Museveni from abolishing term limits and winning a third term.

were unfair. Individuals who feel close to opposition parties were also likely to reject the constitution. We ought to be concerned about the fact that some of those citizens who were engaged in the process emerged with a negative view of the constitution, even if the number of such individuals is small.

My research indicates that the Ugandan constitution-making process became increasingly politicized and contentious over its eight-year period. The evidence indicates that this excessive politicization of the process affected not only the elites in Uganda but also the attitudes of the Ugandan public. The politicization of the process contradicts the conventional understanding of what promotes a culture of constitutionalism. According to most theorists, leaders and citizens should view the constitution and constitutional issues as something above everyday political struggles. Constitution making should be characterized by a search for consensus with the objective of the common good, not by struggle for personal advantages at the expense of others.[9] The Ugandan process contrasted sharply with this ideal. Competition regarding constitutional issues became intertwined with daily political struggles and partisan divisions. Oloka-Onyango (2000, 49) lamented,

> Over time, the constitutional issues became so wrapped up with the political that it was impossible to distinguish between the two. This explains how the CA eventually became a highly-politicized forum, in which the main issue became how best the various forces involved in the struggle for power could position themselves for the ultimate prize of political power.

Other Ugandans also bemoaned the contentious struggles during the constitution-making process, especially those between movementists and multipartyists during the CA.[10]

The excessive politicization of the constitution-making process has had

---

9. It is possible to question whether such an idealistic process of constitution making ever occurs. Constitution making determines the future power map and is thus always a political activity. However, it is fair to say that different levels of conflict arise in different cases of constitution making. Most critics argue that the Ugandan process became overly politicized and conflictual.

10. Makara (1996, 86) argues that the CA election was the origin of the politicization: "That the CA elections were a real testing ground for N[ational] R[esistance] M[ovement]'s popularity is undoubtable. NRM had before the CA elections, never tested the tempo of the electorate within a framework where other political forces pursued their own interests. The fact that the NRM wanted to show that it was popular is also very crucial. Given this background, the NRM could be said to have its own agenda. The agenda was not only in the zeal to win elections but also to influence the debate in the Constituent Assembly after the elections. This was also crucial given that there were constitutional issues in the draft constitution where NRM as a political organization had a stake."

many negative repercussions for the future of democracy in Uganda. First, it produced intense competition for constitutional provisions along party lines. Thereafter, elites failed to work in the interest of the country as a whole, and developing consensus on constitutional issues became extremely difficult (Makara and Tukahebwa 1996, 15; Tukahebwa 1996, 75). Major General David Tinyefuza, one of the government-appointed army representatives, publicly expressed this sentiment:

> What I fear is this polarization which is not principled. Like when you know that this is wrong; but since it has been advanced by a [fellow] multipartyist you must all support it. Or even when you know something won't take us that far, but because it has been articulated by a [fellow] Movement man, then everybody supports it. The whole thing defeats the purpose of the CA. The Assembly was a learning forum, a reconciling forum and ultimately a saving forum. But if we are going to the CA with fixed positions, we could as well have done this outside the CA, say in the N[ational] R[esistance] C[ouncil].[11]

Second, the politicization of the process tempted leaders to use their influence in ways that undermined the fairness of the process. Both the government and the opposition are accused of self-serving, undemocratic, and illegal behavior, but the government's activities received the most attention and posed the biggest threat to the perceived legitimacy of the process and the constitution. The most egregious violations of fair play involve the severe limitations on party activity throughout the process, UCC reliance on government organs to collect views, the use of bribery and the disregard for electoral regulations during the CA campaigns, and the president's undue influence during the CA debates (Barya 2000; Furley and Katalikawe 1997; Kasfir 2000; Mujaju 1999; Oloka-Onyango 2000). These are valid criticisms of the process. More important, to the extent that the general public came to know about them, these violations undermined the perceived legitimacy of the process and the constitution.

Third, critics argue that the politicization of the process led the majority to overrun the rights of the minority (Barya 2000, 34–36). In particular, critics point to the fact that a fundamental human right, the right of association

---

11. Tinyefuza continued, "Politics is a cold-blooded game" (quoted in Oloka-Onyango 1998, 15). The National Resistance Army High Command subsequently reprimanded Tinyefuza, and he was forced to make a public apology for making statements that went against the directives of the National Resistance Army Council.

and political organization, was put to a vote in the CA and that the majority voted to suspend this right.

Fourth, some observers argue that in addition to the "politicization of constitutional issues," the Ugandan process resulted in the "constitutionalization of political issues." In particular, critics argue that the UCC and CA constitutionalized the continuation of Museveni's movement system and by extension his rule (Besigye 2001; Mugaju and Oloka-Onyango 2000, 1; Ogwal 2001; Olet 2001; Ssemogerere 2001). The perception by a section of the population that what resulted from the process was a partisan constitution can have grave implications for the legitimacy and acceptance of the constitution and the political system as a whole (Mujaju 1999, 1–4; Oloka-Onyango 2000, 54).

Fifth, the politicization of constitution making led to a conflation of constitutional and nonconstitutional domains. Many citizens mistook the constitution makers (CA delegates) for regular lawmakers (members of Parliament), and the same individual often served in both positions. CA candidates used their campaigns and their time in the CA to pave the way for their future election to Parliament. They often discussed and made promises about nonconstitutional issues during their bid for the CA, and constitutional issues were often ignored. Thus, in addition to confusing the CA with Parliament, citizens failed to grasp which issues were being decided in the CA. Many of my respondents confused constitutional issues with political issues and the constitution with bylaws.[12]

---

12. With regard to the difference between the CA and Parliament, nearly all investigators of the campaigns remarked on the misleading statements by CA candidates and the confused citizenry (Byarugaba and Makara 1996, 136; Furley and Katalikawe 1997, 260; Katorobo 1996, 115; Makara 1996, 87; Makara and Tukahebwa 1996, 13; Mujaju 1996, 53; Mukwaya 1996, 129; Nsibambi 2001; Tukahebwa 1996, 74–75). For example, Oloka-Onyango (1995, 171) writes, "Given the nature of the stakes involved, the run-up to the election became much more than a struggle over the issues in the draft Constitution alone and became instead the battle ground for the first bids for the capture of state power. This explains the nature of the issues that were the predominant focus of the campaigns: promises of grand hospitals, refurbished roads and new schools. In sum, nobody really cared about the contents of the draft Constitution—it was a straight battle between the idea of "no-partyism" represented by Museveni and his adherents and "multi-partyism" as transmitted by the various political parties. Unfortunately, this scenario prevented the emergence of any alternative force to either the NRM or the traditional parties. It also blocked serious consideration and discussion of the critical and far-reaching constitutional issues that were supposed to be at the foundation of the election."

I also found that many of the respondents to my survey and interviews confused the CA with Parliament. However, evidence from the open-ended interviews indicates that Oloka-Onyango overstates the extent to which constitutional issues were ignored. Many citizens reported learning about the constitution and constitutional issues during the campaign. Also, the political system was a constitutional issue, so debates over "no-partyism" versus "multi-partyism" were entirely appropriate.

Finally, the politicization of the process prompted political and associational leaders to organize citizens along political lines to support or oppose certain constitutional principles. The adoption of the 1995 constitution (to the extent that it was unable to accommodate all views) produced a feeling that there were winners and losers. After eight years of advocating a given constitutional provision, it was very difficult for the losers to accept the outcome and move on. Following the promulgation in 1995, many continued to push for major constitutional revisions (Uganda Constitutional Review Commission 2001). For example, the Buganda kingdom continues to advocate a federal system and a political role for traditional leaders (Englebert 2002; Kingdom of Buganda 2001). The constitution cannot serve as a solid foundation for democratic governance when the fundamental rules continue to be subject to debate, advocacy, and everyday partisan politics. Schmitter and Karl (1996) identify "bounded uncertainty" as a central principle that makes democracy feasible. In Uganda, citizens and leaders are still fighting to move the constitutional boundaries in fundamental ways.

It is difficult to say with certainty what role public participation played in the politicization of the constitution-making process because we cannot observe the counterfactual case of contemporary constitution making in Uganda without participation. There are many plausible reasons for the politicized and contentious nature of the Ugandan process, and the main divisions that were revealed during the course of the process have deep historical roots. Nonetheless, the inclusion of the general public throughout the process may have made the resolution of contentious issues more difficult for elites. First, early on, politicians were forced to publicly declare their preferences on constitutional issues, and it became politically costly for them to revise their positions. Second, the mobilization and participation of ordinary people took time. Over the course of the eight years, the ostensibly parallel spheres of constitution making and everyday politics became increasingly intertwined. Whatever public-spirited orientations existed at the beginning of the process were squandered by the end. Third, majority leaders felt emboldened by evidence of public support—in the memoranda or at the ballot box—to ignore the views of the minority rather than to seek a compromise. Even more importantly, participation seems to have served as a conduit by which divisions at the elite level penetrated down to the popular level. Elites mobilized citizens in support of constitutional provisions, such as federalism and a multiparty system, thus arousing latent animosities, clearly defining divergent preferences among different populations, and hardening opinions on constitutional issues.

The stability of the new system is endangered when some citizens perceive the constitution-making process as unfair and the results as partisan, even if these disgruntled citizens are a small percentage of the total population. The geographic concentration of constitutional antipathy is also troubling: individuals in close proximity are better situated to organize against the new system than if they were dispersed. Intense and concentrated dissatisfaction with the constitution (not distrust of government leaders) is the real threat to political stability in Uganda.

While acknowledging that popular rejection of the constitution potentially threatens political stability, we should also question whether the type of constitutional support found in Uganda is beneficial for long-term democratic constitutionalism. In many ways, the 1995 constitution represented an improvement over Uganda's previous constitutions. However, the 1995 constitution also contained significant limitations on political freedoms. Perhaps we should be concerned that in most areas, at the suggestion of their leaders, Ugandans seemed to wholeheartedly embrace a constitution that did not fully protect basic civil rights. Furthermore, it may be that leader-mediated support is less effective at providing protection for democratic constitutional provisions than is support derived from firsthand knowledge of constitutional arrangements. When many of the leaders who told citizens to support the constitution in 1995 asserted ten years later that the constitution could be improved by fundamental changes, many (though not all) citizens appear to have easily acquiesced.[13] It remains an empirical question whether those citizens who were involved in the initial constitution-making process were more likely to oppose fundamental constitutional changes in 2005 as a result of their greater knowledge of the constitution and greater reliance on procedural legitimacy.

6.3. BEST PRACTICES IN CONSTITUTION MAKING

What lessons does this analysis of participation in the Ugandan process hold for practitioners involved in constitution making elsewhere? What are the likely benefits and drawbacks of implementing a participatory program in other contexts? Are there ways to heighten the benefits and minimize the risks? What factors must be considered when evaluating the usefulness of public involvement in constitution making for a given polity? This section

---

13. Logan et al. (2003, 47) report that the percentage of Ugandans who agree that the constitution reflects the values and aspirations of the Ugandan people dropped form 74 percent in 2000 to 64 percent in 2003.

responds to these questions of concern to policymakers, activists, and donors.

Participation and a More Engaged Citizenry

Participatory constitution making has the potential to foster a more engaged citizenry by increasing political knowledge, raising democratic values, and inculcating a critical perspective among participants. However, these beneficial outcomes are by no means guaranteed. Several factors contributed to the success of the Ugandan process, and policymakers need to be attentive to the conditions and activities that are most conducive to beneficial change when designing other constitution-making programs.

First, much of the participation in the process was organized by appointed officials and civic groups rather than by politicians seeking votes. This was especially the case during the UCC stage of the process. These officials had an interest in mobilizing a broad section of the population to become involved, whereas politicians aim to mobilize only those supporters who are already likely to vote. The UCC and partner nongovernmental organizations specifically targeted women, rural residents, and the uneducated, and the extensive use of small, local meetings facilitated the involvement of those who had difficulty traveling to towns, responding in written form, or speaking up before large audiences. Extensive mobilization of public participation in any process will require major efforts, resources, and forethought but will also depend on who organizes citizen actions. Attention should be paid to ensuring that leaders have an interest in mobilizing politically disadvantaged populations so that the program counteracts rather than reinforces existing political inequalities.

Second, the architects of the constitution-making process designed their participatory activities with the goals of educating the public and building democratic attitudes. The many materials designed by the UCC and the CA commission attest to this focus (Uganda Constitutional Commission 1989, 1991a, 1991b; United Nations Development Programme 1994). It makes sense that programs are more likely to alter political culture when those goals are explicit and programs are designed accordingly.

Third, as a consequence of decades of dictatorial government, levels of political awareness and democratic values were probably low when the constitution-making process began. Furthermore, trust in the current government was likely to be high just after the transition. If the population's initial attitudes tended toward the ends of the spectrum, it would have been easier for participation to push these attitudes toward the middle and thus raise knowledge and democratic attitudes and lower trust. In polities that already have a sizable percentage of engaged citizens, we would expect the effects of participation to be less dramatic.

Finally, the Ugandan process failed to achieve all the attitudinal benefits that it might have because of one important failure: lack of sufficient follow-up.[14] It is crucial to continue constitutional education and dissemination of constitutional materials following the promulgation of the constitution. Several program organizers and civic leaders expressed regret that extensive attention to fostering constitutional debate and education prior to the adoption dwindled when the constitution was adopted (Akabway 2001; Maitum 1999; M. Mugisha 1999; Odoki 2001). Many Ugandans told me in interviews that they were eager to have copies of the constitution, civic education on constitutional issues, and contact with CA delegates so that they could learn what had been included. An active participant in the constitution-making process articulated this view: "During those discussions, we were just starting to make a constitution. If you have a garden, you need to keep weeding it. They should go back to tell the people what [the constitution] is. It needs to be reaffirmed" (interview, Bushenyi District, April 2001). Unfortunately, most citizens heard little about the constitution after it was enacted. The constitution is a difficult concept, and ongoing education is necessary so that citizens can learn about and feel confident with the topic. Citizens who hear about the results of their participation in the constitution-making process are likely to feel more capable of participating in the future. The benefits of the Ugandan program, as impressive as they are, could have been even greater if constitutional or civic education (as opposed to just voter education) had been extended beyond the constitution-making process.

Participation and Citizen Rejection of the Constitution

Participatory constitution making has risks as well as potential benefits. The polarization of citizen attitudes about the constitution that we witnessed in Uganda was probably exacerbated by the inclusion of public participation in the process and was not specific to the Ugandan context. Variants of the criticisms and problems that emerged in Uganda will probably also occur when participatory programs are implemented elsewhere. Polit-

14. Voter education programs were implemented following the adoption of the constitution, but most of these programs focused narrowly on voting procedures and rules rather than broadly on the new political framework and the constitution (Akabway 2001; M. Mugisha 1999; Nekyon 2001; Odoki 2001; Onegi-Obel 2001; Oneka 1999).

ical wrangles can pervade all kinds of constitution-making processes, but I argue that the risks of a polarized citizenry are higher with participatory programs. As such, policymakers must take into account the likely outcome that some citizens will develop an enduring dislike of the constitution. Policymakers should consider the likely magnitude of the negative attitudes for the polity under consideration as well as methods to mitigate the effects.

Constitutions set the rules of the political game and inevitably influence who will be its future winners and losers. Thus, constitution making is an intensely political act, and leaders should be expected to act strategically to ensure that their preferred institutions are included. It would be a mistake to assume that any constitution-making process (participatory or otherwise) would be free from the influences of societal cleavages and political differences (Elster 1993). However, when the outcome of the process depends on political participation, leaders have a greater interest in mobilizing the public to share their views on the constitution and to support certain provisions. Political wrangles and accusations that might otherwise remain at the elite level are more likely to be passed on to the general public. Furthermore, leaders will find it more difficult to make concessions and build a consensus when negotiations occur under the watch of a mobilized and passionate public. As a result, public participation in constitution making has the potential to make the resolution of societal and political conflicts more difficult by expanding the number of interests that must be considered and by intensifying citizens' preferences.[15] Any program that involves significant public participation runs the risk that the public will become polarized in how it views the constitution.[16]

The magnitude of the risk depends in part on the size, strength, and perspective of the political opposition. Ugandan opposition leaders felt deeply alienated by the process and the outcome, which they felt excluded them

---

15. The mobilization of citizens by elites is not limited to constitution-making processes that include formal participation. Even if public participation is not officially part of the process, leaders may find that it is in their interest to mobilize their supporters. However, when participation is a formal component of the process, public opinion is more likely to affect the outcome, and thus leaders have more of an incentive to mobilize citizens. This is especially likely if the constitution-making process involves an election.

16. Survey evidence from South Africa is suggestive (though not conclusive) regarding this phenomenon. South Africa also had a participatory constitution-making program, and public sentiments about the constitution also reflect elite influences. For example, in South Africa, support for the constitution is highly correlated with party identification. Significant differences exist in constitutional support between those who said they would vote for the African National Congress, Inkatha Freedom Party, and the Democratic Party. Race is also associated with constitutional support, with Africans expressing the highest support, followed by colored, Indians, and whites, respectively. Constitutional support is also related (to a lesser degree) to province of residence, language, and economic satisfaction (Afrobarometer 2002).

from political power. In my survey, a small percentage of citizens expressed intensely negative sentiments about the constitution-making process and the constitution. Their numbers and locations reflect the opposition's limited strength at the time of the constitution-making process. The opposition was weak for several reasons: the popularity of the National Resistance Movement's reforms after it came to power, the limitations on party activities, and the weakness of Ugandan civil society at the time. In other polities, the opposition is likely to be stronger, so the percentage of citizens who come to oppose the constitution will be larger. Thus, participatory constitution making is likely to pose an even greater threat in other contexts.

My research in Uganda suggests a number of steps that can be taken to minimize the politicization of the process and the corresponding polarization of public views of the constitution. First, leaders should strive to reach some degree of consensus on the constitution-making process and on the final constitutional arrangement before involving the public. Such preparation will prevent a group of elites from rejecting outright the process and the constitution and from convincing the public to do likewise. Reaching a consensus also allows leaders to make necessary concessions before going public with their platforms. Furthermore, a fundamental consensus and commitment to the process must be maintained throughout the time needed to create the constitution.

For example, in South Africa's constitution-making process, an initial consensus was reached and maintained with moderate success. The formal multiparty negotiations of the Convention for a Democratic South Africa established the formula for the constitution-making process and for the basic constitutional principles that had to be respected.[17] The Constitutional Court received jurisdiction to determine whether the final draft complied with the basic principles, so the majority was required to respect previous agreements and minority rights. Experience suggests that the party in power is likely to work to maintain the support of the opposition only when it needs to do so. In Uganda, where the NRM had a supermajority following the CA elections, it felt less inclined to pay attention to minority views. However, Uganda's experience suggests that establishing elite agreement is important not only for obtaining necessary votes but also for securing public support and constitutional legitimacy.

Second, attempts should be made to insulate the constitution-making process and the constitution makers from the ongoing political process and

---

17. The process was much more successful in securing the support of the leaders of the National Party than it was with the leaders of Inkatha Freedom Party (Klug 1996; Reynolds 1994).

political leaders. Several factors in the design and implementation of the process in Uganda are said to have exacerbated the politicization of the constitutional debate: (1) the president appointed the UCC without consulting with the opposition; (2) local government structures were used to solicit views for the UCC; (3) members of the sitting Parliament (the National Resistance Council) were allowed to become CA delegates;[18] (4) CA delegates were not prevented from running for Parliament in the period just after the CA; (5) the CA electoral constituencies were the same as those for Parliament; and (6) the caucuses that formed in the CA pressured members to vote with their groups rather than according to their consciences (Oloka-Onyango 1998, 15; Oloka-Onyango 2000, 51; Wapakhabulo 2001, 4). The government in power should appoint constitution makers (such as the UCC) and monitors (such as the Electoral Commission) only after consulting with the opposition. In addition, constitution makers should be prevented from holding political positions at the same time or in the immediate aftermath of the constitution-making process. Finally, government leaders should face sanctions for interfering in the process.

Third, the time allowed for public input should be well defined and limited. In Uganda, the period allotted for the UCC and the CA was extended several times. After nearly a decade of organizing to secure constitutional issues, organizations found it very difficult to reorient their programs to deal with nonconstitutional issues after promulgation. Furthermore, leaders who began with magnanimous goals became more concerned with maintaining power as time wore on. Finally, citizens found it hard to distinguish the constitutional issues about which they had for so long been hearing from broader political issues. Participation takes time to organize, but a year or two of formal public input should be sufficient.

Finally, constitutional education and dissemination of constitutional materials after the promulgation will dampen elites' influence on citizen attitudes. My research shows that having been denied access to neutral information on the constitution, citizens depended on elites' political agendas for information. Continuing civic education will not only raise knowledge and efficacy (as suggested previously) but also counteract the polarization of citizen opinions of the constitution.

In sum, my research suggests that including public participation in the constitution-making process increases the likelihood that citizens will

---

18. Wapakhabulo (2001, 8), the chair of the CA, notes that 101 of the 284 CA delegates were also members of the sitting National Resistance Council; some were ministers, including the vice president and prime minister.

develop polarized views of the resulting constitution. The risk of generating strong antipathy to the constitution within the general public is greater where a section of the leadership feels alienated from the process and where the opposition is stronger and better organized. These risks can be reduced if (1) leaders can obtain minimum consensus on the process and outcome before involving the public; (2) constitution makers are insulated from everyday politics; (3) public input is solicited during a specific and limited time frame; and (4) constitutional education continues long after the constitution is adopted. While the risk of intensifying negative attitudes about the constitution among the general population can be reduced, it will be difficult to eliminate altogether.

Weighing the Benefits and Drawbacks of the Model

Even supporters of the participatory constitution-making model acknowledge some drawbacks. Programs that provide for the extensive involvement of the public take longer to complete. Organizing participatory programs takes time, delays the establishment of the new rules, and prolongs the transition phase. Participatory processes are also costly in terms of material resources and human expertise. These resources must be diverted from other important programs or solicited from outside sources.[19] Finally, to the extent that the constitution includes public input, the resulting documents are likely to be longer, more cumbersome, and more inconsistent than those developed without mass input.[20] The supporters of the partic-

---

19. The UCC received most of its funds from the Ministry of Constitutional Affairs, but it also obtained funds from the governments of Australia, Canada, Denmark, Germany, India, Norway, Sweden, the United Kingdom, the United States, and the Commonwealth Secretariat (Odoki 2005, 43–44; UCC 1992a, 21). The total cost for the CA elections was estimated to be US$15–20 million, with the government contributing approximately US$8.4 million and donors contributing US$11.6 million (Mukholi 1995, 42, 99; United Nations Development Programme 1994, 12–13). Foreign funds were also essential for covering the cost of the CA deliberations (Wapakhabulo 2001, 11). Some Ugandans complained that the dependence on donor funds gave foreign powers undue influence in the process (Furley and Katalikawe 1997, 259; Oloka-Onyango 1995, 162–63; Wapakhabulo 2001, 11).

20. Odoki (1999, 12) lamented the fact that the exercise led to an extremely detailed draft constitution: "The UCC was disposed to write a short, precise constitution in simple language, but due to the vast constitutional issues raised by the people who waited, and the need to address them fundamentally in the constitution, it ended by preparing a fairly long draft constitution with a hope that the CA would weed out any unnecessary provisions which could be dealt with by ordinary legislation. The CA did not successfully achieve this."

Instead, the CA delegates included additional provisions to demonstrate to constituents that they were working in their interest (Odoki 2001). The 1995 constitution has 287 articles and seven schedules. It is ten times longer than the U.S. Constitution and more than double the length of most Western European constitutions (Furley and Katalikawe 1997, 257).

ipatory constitution-making model argue that these results are acceptable because the benefits of participation outweigh the costs. These supposed benefits include, first and foremost, change in the attitudes of the participant population.[21]

Participatory constitution making is likely to be consequential for political culture but the effect is not inevitably positive. My research indicates that involving the public in the making of a new constitution can have important benefits: it may make citizens more democratic, knowledgeable, discerning, engaged, and attached to the constitution. However, participation has the potential to increase public acceptance of the new constitutional rules only when opposition elites feel included and supportive (or are too weak to influence citizens). Where the process and outcome leave elites feeling polarized and antagonistic, participatory constitution making can exacerbate rather than heal mass divisions and reduce rather than enhance constitutional support.

Instead of recommending extensive participation in every constitution-making exercise, reformers need to be more discerning about the existing context in which participation will take place. In addition, programs need to be carefully designed to ensure positive changes in attitudes and diminish the polarization of public attitudes toward the constitution. This research warns academics and policymakers against completely abandoning the traditional approach to constitution making, with its emphasis on elite

---

21. The other benefit attributed to the participatory model is its effect on the content of the constitutional document and suitability to the country in question. The designers of participatory processes have gone to great lengths to demonstrate that the public's views were incorporated into the constitutions. Analysts of these programs have disputed these claims, arguing that public input had only marginal or cosmetic impact on the final products, which are determined primarily by international norms and elite bargains. I am unable to adequately evaluate the impact of public participation on the soundness of the Ugandan constitutional arrangements themselves. While evidence shows that public input shaped some provisions, it is extremely difficult to determine if these changes resulted in a more viable constitutional arrangement for Uganda (independent of any effects on constitutional legitimacy). However, the program's designers have an interest in arguing that public input was consequential as a means of achieving the desired change in attitudes. If citizens believe that leaders were sincere in seeking citizens' views and that leaders considered citizen input when writing the constitution, participation is more likely to have a positive influence on citizen attitudes about democracy and efficacy and support for government and the constitution. If, conversely, citizens believe that they were tricked into engaging in activities that had no effect on the final constitution, the consequences of participation would be expected to differ. Most of those who argue that participation is beneficial because of its effect on the content of the constitution also rely on attitude change as contributing to the supposed benefits: public input makes the constitution more appropriate to the context, which makes it more legitimate in the eyes of the public. By evaluating the effect of participation on constitutional legitimacy, I also tested some (though not all) of the supposed positive effects of participation on document content. For fuller discussions, see Gloppen 1997, 255–67; Klug 1996, 53–58.

negotiations and inclusive institutions.[22] Mass citizen participation during the constitution-writing process cannot substitute for agreement among leaders about the institutional outcomes. It is not possible to bypass opposing elites and build constitutional support from the ground up, as some might hope.

6.4. PARTICIPATION AND DEMOCRATIC CULTURE

Constitution making is only one of many spheres where participatory programs are prescribed in the hopes of building democratic culture. Policymakers, activists, and donor agencies direct efforts and resources at programs to increase political participation—especially in transitioning countries, where changes in mass attitudes, behavior, and knowledge are thought to be essential for democratic development. Does participation offer a cure for the attitudinal ills of unconsolidated democracies?

My research suggests that participation can alter participants' attitudes, even in the short run. However, it demonstrates that the changes were not always those predicted by the optimists; attitude changes are difficult to craft. Participation raised democratic attitudes but had no effect on subjective political capabilities. It also did not determine an individual's support for the constitution, although it helped citizens to form attitudes and made existing attitudes more durable. Finally and most unexpectedly, participation lowered rather than increased trust in government institutions. While I assert that a more skeptical citizenry is favorable for long-term democratization in Uganda, this finding contradicts standard predictions derived from participatory theory.

This book offers a theoretical explanation for these expected and unexpected findings. Participation (1) increases citizen interest in and exposure to information messages and (2) changes the criteria citizens use to evaluate those messages. Participation can provoke attitude change through these two mechanisms, but the content of the messages influences the direction of those changes. Thus, attitudinal outcomes depend on the participatory environment.

In Uganda, participants in the constitution-making process were ex-

---

22. This interpretation receives additional support from Widner (2005b), who investigates the effect of the constitution-drafting process on postratification levels of violence at the national level. She finds that the scope of consultation has little or no effect on reducing violence. The representativeness of the reform model has more of an influence on violence than does participatoriness in Africa, the Americas, and the Pacific Islands.

posed to overwhelmingly positive messages about democracy and democratic attitudes. In contrast, the messages about government institutions were negative. Participants learned that the government was behaving undemocratically and was less trustworthy than desired. The messages to which participants were exposed with regard to the constitution-making process and the constitution depended on where they were living and their party affiliations. Most elites who conveyed the messages supported the constitution and transferred this positive outlook to citizens. However, some elites viewed the process as unfair and the constitution as illegitimate. Citizens exposed to negative messages expressed negative attitudes about the constitution.

This research shows that participation can be a powerful tool for changing political culture. Nonetheless, controlling the outcomes of participation is not easy. Reformers who want to use participation to change attitudes must pay careful attention to the messages that participation will convey to the participants. These messages are a function of both the general context in which participation takes place (such as institutional performance) and the sources of the messages (such as media and local elites). To predict the outcomes of participatory programs, we must anticipate where participants will acquire information and how they will interpret that information. In short, participation can be a powerful drug, but it is not an automatic panacea for attitudinal ills.

APPENDIX A
Sampling Methodology and Survey Design

The survey, which I designed and managed, is based on a national probability sample to represent a cross-section of adult Ugandans. The objective is to give each adult Ugandan an equal chance of being included in the sample by using random selection procedures at each stage of the process. All interviews were conducted between January 13 and May 13, 2001. The resulting sample comprises 820 adult Ugandans aged twenty-six and older. The minimum age limit was designed to include only those individuals of voting age during the constitution-making period. The sampling universe did not include noncitizens, individuals under twenty-six years old on the date of the interview, and people who lived in institutions such as hospitals and prisons. In addition, nine districts in the north and west (Gulu, Kitgum, Kotido, Moroto, Bundibugyo, Hoima, Kabalore, Kasese, and Kibaale) were excluded from the sampling frame because of instability and rebel attacks at the time when I conducted the sampling. Therefore, the resulting data is not representative of these troubled areas.[1]

To ensure that every adult Ugandan had an equal chance of selection, I employed a clustered, stratified, multistage, area probability sampling design. After stratifying by urban/rural localities and region (north, east, center, and west), a probability proportionate to population size method was used to randomly select districts, subcounties, and parishes in successive stages. Population size was based on the most recent census data. This method ensures that units with larger populations have a greater probability of being chosen. A single primary sampling unit (PSU) was randomly selected from each parish (population data did not exist at the PSU level). PSU boundaries were those of the lowest level of the local council system and were typically a single village in rural areas and a neighborhood in urban areas. In the end, the randomly selected PSUs included six urban and sixty-two

---

1. Other areas in the sample provide a vague idea of how conflict and violence might have affected the constitution-making process: districts such as Lira were safe enough at the time of my research to include in the sampling frame but had experienced low-level insurgency at the time of the constitution-making process and at various times thereafter.

rural sites within thirteen districts: Kampala, Jinja, Mpigi, Luwero, Nakasongola, Mayuge, Iganga, Apac, Lira, Sironko, Mbale, Mbarara, and Bushenyi.

Working with the local council officials, our research teams compiled lists of all the households in each selected PSU. We used a random number table to select a simple random sample of sixteen households from each PSU list. After the households were identified, an interviewer visited each household and listed, by first name, all the adult citizens aged twenty-six and older who lived in each household (ate their meals there regularly), including those away from home at that time. A single individual was randomly selected from the list of household members through blind selection from a pack of numbered cards. The interview was conducted only with the selected individual. If the selected individual was not at home, the interviewer attempted to find the individual in the PSU; if unsuccessful, the interviewer made one return call later in the day. In addition, if no one was home on the first attempt, the interviewer made a second attempt later in the day. When return calls were unsuccessful—either because the house remained empty or the selected respondent was not found—then another household (not another individual from the same household) was substituted and the process of listing and randomly selecting household members was repeated. Substitution households were also randomly selected in the same method as the original households.

The survey instrument was a questionnaire containing ninety-two items. I designed the instrument based on other surveys, in-depth interviews, and focus-group discussions with a variety of Ugandans. We pretested the instrument in rural and urban locations. The questionnaire was translated into the five languages of the sampled regions: Luganda, Lugisu, Luo, Lusoga, and Runyankole. We used the technique of translation/back-translation to check for inaccuracies and to obtain congruence between the different languages. The survey was administered face to face by five teams of trained native-speaking interviewers.

APPENDIX B
Variable Names, Question Wordings, and Descriptors

TABLE B.1. Key Variables

Key Variables	Question Wording	Range	Mean	Standard Deviation
Participation activities index		0–6	1.50	1.48
	Did you attend a seminar where a member of the Constitutional Commission was present?	0, 1	0.05	0.22
	Do you personally know anyone or any group who submitted memoranda to the Constitutional Commission: Did you? Your Local Council 1? Any groups?	0–1	0.06	0.19
	Did you ever attend a meeting where people discussed these memoranda on the constitution?	0, 1	0.14	0.34
	Think back to the period before the CA elections. Public meetings (or rallies) were held at the parish level, where candidates for the Constituent Assembly spoke and answered questions. Do you remember attending a Constituent Assembly candidates' meeting?	0, 1	0.44	0.50
	Did you vote in the election of delegates to the Constituent Assembly?	0, 1	0.60	0.49
	After the Constituent Assembly delegates were elected, did you hear from or contact your CA delegate about the constitution?	0, 1	0.21	0.41
Respondent-identified participation	Between 1988 and 1995, how did you participate in the constitution-making process?	0–3	0.36	0.60
Democratic attitudes		0–5	2.96	0.93
	Choose one of the following statements. A: "Political decisions should be left to the experts." B: "All the people should participate in political decisions." [after answer] Do you agree strongly with statement A/B or just somewhat?	0–1	0.73	0.39

(continues)

Key Variables	Question Wording	Range	Mean	Standard Deviation
	Please say whether you agree or disagree with the following statement: "Even someone whose ideas you do not agree with should be allowed to organize peaceful demonstrations to express his/her point of view." [after answer] Do you agree/disagree strongly or just somewhat?	0–1	0.59	0.37
	Please say whether you agree or disagree with the following statement: "Let's go back to a traditional system of government ruled by kings and chiefs." [after answer] Do you agree/disagree strongly or just somewhat?	0–1	0.74	0.34
	If the president were to shut down the newspapers, radio stations, or TV stations that were critical of him, what, if anything, would you do about it?	0–1	0.26	0.19
	Choose one of the following statements. A: "All members of a family should hold the same opinions." B: "Every family member should be free to make up his or her own mind on political issues." [after answer] Do you agree strongly with statement A/B or just somewhat?	0–1	0.64	0.44
Political capabilities		0–10	4.93	3.13
	In general can you: (a) speak about politics in public none of the time, some of the time, or most of the time?	0–2	0.73	0.78
	In general can you: (b) lead a group none of the time, some of the time, or most of the time?	0–2	1.01	0.82
	In general can you: (c) influence the political opinions of others none of the time, some of the time, or most of the time?	0–2	0.87	0.79
	In general can you: (d) understand what's going on in government none of the time, some of the time, or most of the time?	0–2	1.15	0.74
	If elected as chair of Local Council 1, do you think you could do a good job?	0–2	1.18	0.96
Institutional trust		0–4	3.11	0.98
	I am now going to read you a list of organizations. How much do you trust each of them to do what is right: (a) the police?	0–1	0.61	0.44
	I am now going to read you a list of organizations. How much do you trust each of them to do what is right: (b) the courts of law?	0–1	0.78	0.36

TABLE B.1—Continued

Key Variables	Question Wording	Range	Mean	Standard Deviation
	I am now going to read you a list of organizations. How much do you trust each of them to do what is right: (e) the Local Council 1?	0–1	0.90	0.27
	I am now going to read you a list of organizations. How much do you trust each of them to do what is right: (f) the Electoral Commission?	0–1	0.82	0.33
Political knowledge		0–7	2.48	1.69
	How many government elections have been held in Uganda since 1986? Can you tell them to me?	0–1	0.48	0.24
	We are interested in whether or not the people in your community know their government leaders. Could you tell me the name of your elected member of Parliament?	0–1	0.75	0.43
	Other than President Museveni, can you tell me the name of any other leaders in the central government? For example, the vice president, ministers, or military leaders?	0–5	1.26	1.34
Constitutional knowledge		0–10	3.77	2.38
	Can you gell me a few things that are included in the 1995 constitution of Uganda?	0–3	0.84	1.12
	How many constitutions has Uganda had since independence? Can you tell them to me?	0–1	0.38	0.20
	Please answer these questions about what is written in the 1995 constitution. If you don't know, tell me: (a) Can a person become a member of parliament while remaining a traditional or cultural leader?	0–1	0.49	0.50
	(b) Was Buganda given a federal state under the constitution of 1995?	0–1	0.34	0.47
	(c) According to the 1995 constitution of Uganda, does Uganda have a national language?	0–1	0.27	0.45
	(d) According to the 1995 constitution of Uganda, how many positions on Local Council 1 are reserved for women?	0–1	0.30	0.46
	(e) According to the 1995 constitution of Uganda, how long is the president's term in office?	0–1	0.75	0.43
	(f) What is the total number of terms that a person can be president under the 1995 constitution?	0–1	0.39	0.49

(continues)

TABLE B.1—Continued

Key Variables	Question Wording	Range	Mean	Standard Deviation
Constitutional support index		0–4	2.73	0.84
Individual Inclusion	Are your views included in the current constitution of Uganda? Would you say: all of your views, most of your views, some of your views, or none at all?	0–1	0.42	0.34
National Aspiration	Please say whether you agree or disagree with the following statement: "Our constitution expresses the values and aspirations of the Ugandan people." [after answer] Do you agree/disagree strongly or just somewhat?	0–1	0.77	0.27
Compliance	Please say whether you agree or disagree with the following statement: "People should abide by what was written in the constitution whether they agree with what was written or not." [after answer] Do you agree/disagree strongly or just somewhat?	0–1	0.73	0.32
Attachment	Choose one of the following statements. A: "Our present constitution should be able to deal with problems inherited from the past." B: "Our constitution hinders development so we should abandon it completely and design another." [after answer] Do you agree strongly with statement A/B or just somewhat?	0–1	0.74	0.34
Propensity for Constitutional Opinions	Coded one if the respondent has a score for the constitutional support index (meaning that they answered all four questions: individual inclusion, national aspiration, compliance, attachment) and zero otherwise (meaning that they failed to answer at least one question).	0, 1	0.60	0.49

TABLE B.2. Control Variables

Control Variables	Question Wording	Range	Mean	Standard Deviation
Access to basic needs	In the last twelve months, how often have you or your family gone without (a) enough food to eat, (b) medicine or medical treatment that you needed, (c) enough fuel, and a (d) cash income? Never, rarely, sometimes, or often?	0–12	5.13	3.21
Age	How old were you at your last birthday? [if can't answer] In which year were you born?	26–93	40.12	14.43
Ankole ethnicity	What is your native language?	0, 1	0.23	0.42
Associational affiliations	Now I am going to read out a list of voluntary organizations. For each one, could you tell me whether you are an official leader, an active member, an inactive member, or not a member of that type of organization: (a) religious organization like a church or a mosque; (b) art, music, and drama clubs; (c) farmers' organization; (d) professional or business association; (e) credit and savings association; (f) women's organization; (g) sports or drinking clubs; (h) parent-teacher association; (i) other.	0–17	3.08	3.33
Baganda ethnicity	What is your native language?	0, 1	0.24	0.43
Basoga ethnicity	What is your native language?	0, 1	0.13	0.33
Close to high official	Do you personally know anyone who currently holds or formerly held a position in government of Local Council 3 or higher? How do you know them?	0, 1	0.26	0.44
Community integration	How long have you lived in this district?	1–6	5.49	1.17
Distance to headquarters	Recorded by interviewer	0–20.5	3.27	3.10
Exposure to news in meetings	How often do you get news about local or national politics from the meetings?	2–5	1.33	0.96
Exposure to news on radio	How often do you get news about local or national politics from the newspapers?	0–5	3.46	1.90
Exposure to newspapers	How often do you get news about local or national politics from the radio?	1–5	1.02	1.58
Exuberant trusting	I am now going to read you a list of organizations. How much do you trust each of them to do what is right: (a) the National Resistance Movement (NRM), (b) political parties?	0, 1	0.20	0.40
Follow public affairs	Some people seem to follow what's going on in government and politics most of the time, whether there is an election going on or not. Others aren't that interested. Would you say you follow what's going on in government and public affairs most of the time, some of the time, only now and then, or hardly at all?	0–3	2.50	0.77

(continues)

TABLE B.2—Continued

Control Variables	Question Wording	Range	Mean	Standard Deviation
Improved living conditions	When you look at your living conditions today, how satisfied do you feel compared with five years ago? [after answer] Would you say you are much more/less satisfied or just somewhat?	1–5	3.21	1.42
Interest	Choose one of the following statements. A. "I care about national politics." B: "I don't care about national politics." [after answer] Do you agree strongly with statement A/B or just somewhat?	1–4	3.54	0.75
Local council position	Are you or were you ever a Local Council member? What position(s)?	0–8	0.38	0.90
Male	Recorded by interviewer	0, 1	0.51	0.50
Mobility	In the past year, about how often did you travel outside this district? Never, once or twice in the year, every few months, about once a month, a few times a month, once a week, or more?	0–5	0.99	1.41
Nilotic ethnicity	What is your native language?	0, 1	0.18	0.38
Own consumer goods	Does anyone in this household, including you, own a bicycle, motorcycle, car, phone, watch or clock, refrigerator, radio, and TV?	0–14	2.15	2.07
Primary school education	What is your highest level of education?	0, 1	0.38	0.49
Purpose of Constitution	In your opinion, what is the purpose of the constitution? (coded as one if the respondent could give an appropriate answer, and zero if s/he couldn't)	0, 1	0.67	0.47
Road difficulties	Recorded by interviewer	0.1–1	0.43	0.18
Secondary school education	What is your highest level of education?	0, 1	0.07	0.26
Social trust	Generally speaking, would you say that most people can be trusted or that you must be very careful in dealing with people?	0–1	0.18	0.38
Support NRM	If the multiparty system was brought back, which political organization would you support?	0, 1	0.46	0.50
Urban residence	Recorded by interviewer	0, 1	0.12	0.32

APPENDIX C
First-Stage Equation Estimates for 2SLS Models

TABLE C.1. First-Stage Estimates for 2SLS Model Predicting Democratic Attitudes and Participation

	Democratic Attitudes		Participation Activities Index	
	b	se	b	se
Exogenous variables				
Male	.22***	(.07)	.64***	(.09)
Urban residence	.05	(.13)	.06	(.17)
Age	−.01**	(.00)	.01#	(.00)
Primary school education	.29***	(.08)	.47***	(.11)
Interest	.16***	(.04)	.21***	(.06)
Baganda ethnicity	−.17*	(.08)	.27*	(.11)
Instruments for democratic attitudes				
Basoga ethnicity	−.27**	(.10)	−.10	(.14)
Mobility	.06*	(.03)	.03	(.04)
Secondary school education	.22	(.14)	.10	(.19)
Instruments for participation activities index				
Access to basic needs	.01	(.01)	.02	(.01)
Local council position	.03	(.04)	.23***	(.05)
Close to high official	.13#	(.08)	.28**	(.10)
Community integration	.01	(.03)	.08*	(.04)
Associational affiliations	.00	(.01)	.08***	(.02)
Exposure to news on radio	.00	(.02)	.06*	(.03)
Exposure to newspapers	.02	(.03)	.06#	(.04)
Exposure to news in meetings	.02	(.04)	.17***	(.05)
Road difficulties	−.10	(.20)	−.50#	(.27)
Distance to headquarters	.00	(.01)	−.03#	(.01)
Constant	−2.28***	(.27)	−1.19***	(.37)
R^2	.19		.42	
Tests for efficiency of instrumental variables				
F-stat. (excluded instruments)	4.71		17.33	
Partial R^2 (excluded instruments)	.09		.35	

Source: Author's data set.

Note: N = 740.

#$p \leq .10$ *$p \leq .05$ **$p \leq .01$ ***$p \leq .001$

TABLE C.2. First-Stage Estimates for 2SLS Model Predicting Political Capabilities and Participation

	Political Capabilities		Participation Activities Index	
	b	se	b	se
Exogenous variables				
Male	1.30***	(.18)	.65***	(.09)
Urban residence	−.51	(.33)	.11	(.17)
Age	−.02***	(.01)	.01#	(.00)
Primary school education	.52*	(.20)	.49***	(.11)
Access to basic needs	.06*	(.03)	.02	(.01)
Interest	.41***	(.12)	.20***	(.06)
Local council position	.53***	(.10)	.23***	(.05)
Close to high official	.70***	(.20)	.28**	(.10)
Associational affiliations	.12***	(.03)	.08***	(.02)
Exposure to news on radio	.23***	(.05)	.06*	(.03)
Exposure to newspapers	.27***	(.07)	.07*	(.03)
Exposure to news in meetings	.29**	(.09)	.16***	(.05)
Instruments for political capabilities				
Follow public affairs	.51***	(.12)	.04	(.06)
Support NRM	.46**	(.17)	.01	(.09)
Nilotic ethnicity	−.53*	(.25)	−.11	(.13)
Instruments for participation activities index				
Community integration	.09	(.08)	.08*	(.04)
Baganda ethnicity	−.04	(.21)	.29**	(.11)
Road difficulties	−.46	(.54)	−.45	(.28)
Distance to headquarters	−.03	(.03)	−.02#	(.01)
Constant	−.42	(.74)	−1.31***	(.38)
R^2	.50		.42	
Tests for efficiency of instrumental variables				
F-stat. (excluded instruments)	11.28		4.98	
Partial R^2 (excluded instruments)	.13		.05	

Source: Author's data set.

Note: N = 737.

#$p \leq .10$ *$p \leq .05$ **$p \leq .01$ ***$p \leq .001$

TABLE C.3. First-Stage Estimates for 2SLS Model Predicting Institutional Trust and Participation

	Institutional Trust		Participation Activities Index	
	b	se	b	se
Exogenous variables				
Male	−.15*	(.07)	.64***	(.09)
Urban residence	.10	(.13)	.06	(.17)
Age	.00	(.00)	.01#	(.00)
Primary school education	.00	(.08)	.49***	(.11)
Access to basic needs	.03*	(.01)	.03#	(.02)
Interest	.06	(.05)	.21***	(.06)
Local council position	.01	(.04)	.23***	(.05)
Close to high official	.02	(.08)	.26*	(.11)
Exposure to news on radio	−.02	(.02)	.06*	(.03)
Exposure to newspapers	−.07*	(.03)	.06	(.04)
Exposure to news in meetings	−.01	(.04)	.18***	(.05)
Instruments for institutional trust				
Mobility	−.06*	(.03)	.03	(.04)
Social trust	.31***	(.09)	.02	(.12)
Exuberant trusting	.62***	(.08)	−.07	(.11)
Support NRM	.25***	(.07)	.05	(.09)
Own consumer goods	−.04#	(.02)	.00	(.03)
Improved living conditions	.11***	(.02)	−.06#	(.03)
Instruments for participation activities index				
Community integration	−.01	(.03)	.07#	(.04)
Associational affiliations	−.02#	(.01)	.08***	(.02)
Baganda ethnicity	.08	(.08)	.27*	(.11)
Road difficulties	.10	(.21)	−.47#	(.27)
Distance to headquarters	.01	(.01)	−.03#	(.02)
Constant	2.42***	(.29)	−1.08**	(.38)
R^2	.24		.43	
Tests for efficiency of instrumental variables				
F-stat. (excluded instruments)	21.87		8.96	
Partial R^2 (excluded instruments)	.22		.18	

Source: Author's data set.

Note: N = 730.

#$p \leq .10$ *$p \leq .05$ **$p \leq .01$ ***$p \leq .001$

TABLE C.4. First-Stage Estimates for 2SLS Model Predicting Political Knowledge and Participation

	Political Knowledge		Participation Activities Index	
	b	se	*b*	se
Exogenous variables				
Male	.58***	(.10)	.64**	(.09)
Urban residence	.00	(.18)	.06	(.17)
Age	−.01*	(.00)	.01*	(.00)
Primary school education	.62***	(.11)	.49**	(.11)
Access to basic needs	.08***	(.02)	.02	(.01)
Interest	.23***	(.06)	.21**	(.06)
Local council position	.24***	(.06)	.25**	(.05)
Close to high official	.39***	(.11)	.27**	(.10)
Associational affiliations	.04**	(.02)	.07**	(.02)
Exposure to news on radio	.06*	(.03)	.06**	(.03)
Exposure to newspapers	.08*	(.04)	.06*	(.03)
Exposure to news in meetings	.04	(.05)	.16**	(.05)
Road difficulties	−.91**	(.29)	−.48*	(.27)
Instruments for political knowledge				
Secondary school education	.62**	(.20)	.10	(.19)
Mobility	.13***	(.04)	.03	(.04)
Instruments for participation activities index				
Community integration	.03	(.04)	.08**	(.04)
Baganda ethnicity	.16	(.12)	.29**	(.11)
Distance to headquarters	−.01	(.02)	−.02	(.01)
Constant	.47	(.39)	−1.24**	(.37)
R^2	.49		.43	
Tests for efficiency of instrumental variables				
F-stat. (excluded instruments)	12.00		5.13	
Partial R^2 (excluded instruments)	.25		.03	

Source: Author's data set.

Note: N = 731.

#*p* ≤ .10   **p* ≤ .05   ***p* ≤ .01   ****p* ≤ .001

REFERENCES

Achen, Christopher H. 1986. *The Statistical Analysis of Quasi-Experiments.* Berkeley: University of California Press.

Adorno, Theodor W. 1950. *The Authoritarian Personality.* New York: Harper.

Africa Confidential. 2001. Ungracious Winner. *Africa Confidential* 42 (7): 1–2.

Africa Confidential. 2003. The Great U-Turn. *Africa Confidential* 44 (7): 1–2.

Afrobarometer Round 1: Compendium of Comparative Data from a Twelve-Nation Survey. 2002. Afrobarometer Paper 11. Available at http://www.afrobarometer.org/papers/AfropaperNo11.pdf. Accessed August 12, 2004.

Akabway, Stephen. 2001. Interview by author. Kampala, Uganda, August 9.

Akwi, Algresia. 2001. Interview by author. Kampala, Uganda, August 19.

Almond, Gabriel A., and Sidney Verba. 1963. *The Civic Culture: Political Attitudes and Democracy in Five Nations.* Princeton: Princeton University Press.

Almond, Gabriel A., and Sidney Verba, eds. 1980. *The Civic Culture Revisited: An Analytic Study.* Boston: Little, Brown.

Arato, Andrew. 2004. Iraq and Its Aftermath. *Dissent* 51 (2): 21–28.

Barber, Benjamin. 1984. *Strong Democracy: Participatory Politics for a New Age.* Berkeley: University of California Press.

Bardhan, Pranab. 1997. Corruption and Development: A Review of Issues. *Journal of Economic Literature* 35 (3):1320–46.

Baron, Reuben M., and David A. Kenny. 1986. The Moderator-Mediator Variable Distinction in Social Psychological Research: Conceptual Strategic and Statistical Considerations. *Journal of Personality and Social Psychology* 51 (6): 1173–82.

Barya, John Jean. 1993. *Popular Democracy and the Legitimacy of the Constitution: Some Reflections on Uganda's Constitution-Making Process.* Kampala, Uganda: Center for Basic Research.

Barya, John Jean. 2000. Political Parties, the Movement, and the Referendum on Political Systems: One Step Forward, Two Steps Back? In *No-Party Democracy in Uganda: Myths and Realities,* edited by J. Mugaju and J. Oloka-Onyango. Kampala, Uganda: Fountain.

Bates, Robert H. 1981. *Markets and States in Tropical Africa: The Political Basis of Agricultural Policies.* Berkeley: University of California Press.

Bates, Robert H. 1990. Macropolitical Economy in the Field of Development. In *Perspectives on Positive Political Economy,* edited by J. E. Alt and K. A. Shepsle. Cambridge: Cambridge University Press.

Benomar, Jamal. 2004. Constitution-Making after Conflict: Lessons for Iraq. *Journal of Democracy* 15 (2): 81–95.

Berelson, Bernard R., Paul F. Lazarsfeld, and William N. McPhee. 1954. *Voting: A Study of Opinion Formation in a Presidential Campaign.* Chicago: University of Chicago Press.

Berman, Sheri. 1997. Civil Society and the Collapse of the Weimar Republic. *World Politics* 49 (3): 401–29.

Bermeo, Nancy. 2003. *Ordinary People in Extraordinary Times: The Citizenry and the Breakdown of Democracy.* Princeton: Princeton University Press.

Besigye, Kizza. 2001. Interview by author. Kampala, Uganda, August 17.

Bianco, William T. 1998. Uncertainty, Appraisal, and Common Interest: The Roots of Constituent Trust. In *Trust and Governance,* edited by V. A. Braithwaite and M. Levi. New York: Sage.

Bowler, Shaun, and Todd Donovan. 2002. Democracy, Institutions, and Attitudes about Citizen Influence on Government. *British Journal of Political Science* 32 (2): 371–90.

Bratton, Michael. 1999. Political Participation in a New Democracy: Institutional Considerations from Zambia. *Comparative Political Studies* 32 (5): 549–88.

Bratton, Michael. 2006. *Poor People and Democratic Citizenship in Africa.* Afrobarometer Working Paper 56. Available at http://www.afrobarometer.org/papers/AfropaperNo56.pdf. Accessed January 8, 2007.

Bratton, Michael, and Philip W. Alderfer. 1999. The Effects of Civic Education on Political Culture: Evidence from Zambia. *World Development* 27 (5): 807–24.

Bratton, Michael, and Gina Lambright. 2001. Uganda's Referendum 2000: The Silent Boycott. *African Affairs* 100 (400): 429–52.

Bratton, Michael, Gina Lambright, and Robert Sentamu. 2000. *Democracy and Economy in Uganda: A Public Opinion Perspective.* Afrobarometer Working Paper 4. Available at http://afrobarometer.org/papers/AfropaperNo4.pdf. Accessed February 20, 2006.

Bratton, Michael, Robert B. Mattes, and Emmanuel Gyimah-Boadi. 2005. *Public Opinion, Democracy, and Market Reform in Africa.* Cambridge: Cambridge University Press.

Bratton, Michael, and Nicolas van de Walle. 1997. *Democratic Experiments in Africa: Regime Transitions in Comparative Perspective.* Cambridge: Cambridge University Press.

Brehm, John, and Wendy Rahn. 1997. Individual-Level Evidence for the Causes and Consequences of Social Capital. *American Journal of Political Science* 41 (3): 999–1023.

Bunce, Valerie. 2000. Comparative Democratization: Big and Bounded Generalizations. *Comparative Political Studies* 49 (1): 703–34.

Byarugaba, Foster, and Sabiti E. Makara. 1996. The Study of the Constituent Assembly Elections in Uganda: Some Key Issues and Conclusions. In *Politics, Constitutionalism, and Electioneering in Uganda: A Study of the 1994 Constituent Assembly Elections,* edited by S. E. Makara, G. B. Tukahebwa, and F. Byarugaba. Kampala, Uganda: Makerere University Press.

Calvert, Randall L. 1995. The Rational Choice Theory of Social Institutions: Cooperation, Coordination, and Communication. In *Modern Political Economy: Old Topics, New Directions,* edited by J. S. Banks and E. A. Hanushek. Cambridge: Cambridge University Press.

Carbone, Giovanni M. 2003. Political Parties in a "No-Party Democracy": Hegemony and Opposition under "Movement Democracy" in Uganda. *Party Politics* 9 (4): 485–501.

Carlson, Scott. 1999. Politics, Public Participation, and the 1998 Albanian Constitution. *Osteuropa-Recht* 45 (6): 491–507.

Carothers, Thomas. 1999. *Aiding Democracy Abroad: The Learning Curve.* Washington, D.C.: Carnegie Endowment for International Peace.

Citizen's Forum for Constitutional Reform. 1999. *Background.* Available at http://www.cdd.org.uk/cfcr/bkg.htm. Accessed March 20, 2005.

Clarke, Harold D., and Alan C. Acock. 1989. National Elections and Political Attitudes: The Case of Political Efficacy. *British Journal of Political Science* 19 (4): 551–62.

Commonwealth Human Rights Initiative. 1999. Best Practices of Participatory Constitution Making: Recommendations to Commonwealth Heads of Government Meet (CHOGM) '99. Paper presented at the Conference on Consultation on Participatory Constitution-Making, August 16–17, Pretoria, South Africa.

Cragg, John G. 1983. More Efficient Estimation in the Presence of Heteroscedasticity of Unknown Form. *Econometrica* 51 (3): 751–63.

Dahl, Robert A. 1966. Further Reflections on the Elitist Theory of Democracy. *American Political Science Review* 15 (3): 296–305.

Dahl, Robert A. 1971. *Polyarchy: Participation and Opposition.* New Haven: Yale University Press.

Dalton, Russell J. 2000. Citizen Attitudes and Political Behavior. *Comparative Political Studies* 33 (6): 912–40.

Dalton, Russell J. 2004. *Democratic Challenges, Democratic Choices: The Erosion of Political Support in Advanced Industrial Democracies.* Oxford: Oxford University Press.

Daruwala, Maja. 2001. *Civil Society Involvement in Constitutional Review: A Letter from Maja Daruwala, Director of Commonwealth Human Rights Initiative (CHRI) to Justice M. N. Venkatachelliah, Chairman of the National Commission for Reviewing the Constitution and Chief Justice of India.* Available at http://www.human rightsinitiative.org/publications/const/civil_society_involvement_in_constitu tional_review.pdf. Accessed March 20, 2005.

Deegan, Heather. 2000. Participatory Democracy in South Africa. Paper presented at the European Consortium for Political Research, April 19, Copenhagen, Denmark.

Deutsch, Karl W. 1961. Social Mobilization and Political Development. *American Political Science Review* 55 (3): 493–514.

Diamond, Larry Jay. 1993. *Political Culture and Democracy in Developing Countries.* Boulder, Colo.: Rienner.

Diamond, Larry Jay. 1999. *Developing Democracy: Toward Consolidation.* Baltimore: Johns Hopkins University Press.

Diamond, Larry Jay. 2002. Thinking about Hybrid Regimes. *Journal of Democracy* 13 (2): 21–35.

Diamond, Larry Jay. 2005. Lessons from Iraq. *Journal of Democracy* 16 (1): 9–23.

Di Palma, Giuseppe. 1990. *To Craft Democracies: An Essay on Democratic Transitions.* Berkeley: University of California Press.

Easton, David. 1965. *A Systems Analysis of Political Life.* New York: Wiley.

Ebrahim, Hassen. 1998. *The Soul of a Nation: Constitution-Making in South Africa.* Cape Town: Oxford University Press.

Eckstein, Harry. 1988. A Culturalist Theory of Political Change. *American Political Science Review* 82 (3): 789–804.

Ekeh, Peter. 1975. Colonialism and the Two Publics in Africa: A Theoretical Statement. *Comparative Studies in Society and History* 17 (1): 91–112.

Elster, Jon. 1993. Constitution-Making in Eastern Europe: Rebuilding the Boat in the Open Sea. *Public Administration* 71 (1–2): 169–217.

Elster, Jon. 1997. Ways of Constitution-Making. In *Democracy's Victory and Crisis,* edited by A. Hadenius. Cambridge: Cambridge University Press.

Elster, Jon. 1998. Deliberation and Constitution-Making. In *Deliberative Democracy,* edited by J. Elster. Cambridge: Cambridge University Press.

Elster, Jon, Claus Offe, and Ulrich Klaus Preuss. 1998. *Institutional Design in Post-Communist Societies: Rebuilding the Ship at Sea.* Cambridge: Cambridge University Press.

Emler, Nicholas, and Elizabeth Frazer. 1999. Politics: The Education Effect. *Oxford Review of Education* 25 (1–2): 251–73.

Englebert, Pierre. 2002. Born-Again Buganda or the Limits of Traditional Resurgence in Africa. *Journal of Modern African Studies* 40 (3): 345–68.

Finkel, Steven E. 1985. Reciprocal Effects of Participation and Political Efficacy: A Panel Analysis. *American Journal of Political Science* 29 (4): 891–913.

Finkel, Steven E. 1987. The Effects of Participation on Political Efficacy and Political Support: Evidence from a West German Panel. *Journal of Politics* 49 (2): 441–64.

Finkel, Steven E. 2000. Civic Education and the Mobilization of Political Participation in Developing Democracies. Paper presented at the Conference on Political Participation: Building a Research Agenda, October 12–14, Princeton,
New Jersey.

Finkel, Steven E. 2003. Can Democracy Be Taught? *Journal of Democracy* 14 (4):
137–51.

Finkel, Steven E., Christopher A. Sabatini, and Gwendolyn G. Bevis. 2000. Civic
Education, Civil Society, and Political Mistrust in a Developing Democracy:
The Case of the Dominican Republic. *World Development* 28 (11): 1851–74.

Freedom House. 2002. *Freedom of the World: The Annual Review of Political Rights and
Civil Liberties.* Available at http://www.freedomhouse.org/ratings/index.htm.
Accessed April 23, 2003.

Freedom House. 2005. *Freedom of the World: The Annual Review of Political Rights and
Civil Liberties.* Available at http://www.freedomhouse.org/research/freeworld/
2005/table2005.pdf. Accessed March 8, 2005.

Furley, Oliver, and James Katalikawe. 1997. Constitutional Reform in Uganda:
The New Approach. *African Affairs* 96 (383): 243–60.

Geist, Judith. 1995. Political Significance of Constituent Assembly Elections. In
From Chaos to Order: The Politics of Constitution-Making in Uganda, edited by
H. B. Hansen and M. Twaddle. Kampala: Fountain.

Ghai, Yash P. 1996. The Theory of the State in the Third World and the Problem-
atics of Constitutionalism. In *International Human Rights Law in Context: Law,
Politics, Morals, Text, and Materials,* edited by H. J. Steiner and P. Alston. New
York: Clarendon.

Gibson, James L. 1996. A Mile Wide but an Inch Deep(?): The Structure of Democratic Commitments in the Former USSR. *American Journal of Political Science*
40 (2): 396–420.

Gibson, James L., and Gregory A. Caldeira. 2003. Defenders of Democracy? Legitimacy, Popular Acceptance, and the South African Constitutional Court. *Journal
of Politics* 65 (1): 1–30.

Gibson, James L., Gregory A. Caldeira, and Vanessa A. Baird. 1998. On the Legitimacy of National High Courts. *American Political Science Review* 92 (2): 343–58.

Gibson, James L., and Amanda Gouws. 2003. *Overcoming Intolerance in South Africa:
Experiments in Democratic Persuasion.* Cambridge: Cambridge University Press.

Gingyera-Pinycwa, A. G. G. 1996. Constituent Assembly Elections in Jonam Con-
stituency, Nebbi District. In *Politics, Constitutionalism, and Electioneering in
Uganda: A Study of the 1994 Constituent Assembly Elections,* edited by S. E.
Makara, G. B. Tukahebwa, and F. Byarugaba. Kampala, Uganda: Makerere
University Press.

Gloppen, Siri. 1997. *South Africa: The Battle over the Constitution.* Brookfield, Vt.:
Ashgate.

Golooba-Mutebi, Frederick. 2004. Reassessing Popular Participation in Uganda.
Public Administration and Development 24 (4): 289–304.

Granovetter, Mark S. 1973. The Strength of Weak Ties. *American Journal of Sociology* 78 (6): 1360–80.

Greenberg, Douglas, Stanley N. Katz, Melanie B. Oliver, Steven C. Wheatley, and American Council of Learned Societies., eds. 1993. *Constitutionalism and Democracy: Transitions in the Contemporary World.* Oxford: Oxford University Press.

Hansen, Holger Bernt, and Michael Twaddle, eds. 1995. *From Chaos to Order: The Politics of Constitution-Making in Uganda.* Kampala: Fountain.

Hardin, Russell. 1998. Trust in Government. In *Trust and Governance,* edited by V. A. Braithwaite and M. Levi. New York: Sage.

Hart, Vivien. 2003. *Democratic Constitution Making.* U.S. Institute of Peace Special Report 107. Washington D.C.: U.S. Institute of Peace. Available online at http://www.usip.org/pubs/specialreports/sr107.html. Accessed December 10, 2006.

Hatchard, John. 2001. Some Lessons on Constitution-Making from Zimbabwe. *Journal of African Law* 45 (2): 210–16.

Hirschman, Albert O. 1970. *Exit, Voice, and Loyalty: Responses to Decline in Firms, Organizations, and States.* Cambridge: Harvard University Press.

Howard, A. E. Dick, ed. 1993. *Constitution Making in Eastern Europe.* Washington, D.C.: Woodrow Wilson Center Press.

Howard, Marc. 2003. *The Weakness of Civil Society in Post-Communist Europe.* Cambridge: Cambridge University Press.

Human Rights Watch. 1999. *Hostile to Democracy: The Movement System and Political Repression in Uganda.* New York: Human Rights Watch.

Huntington, Samuel P. 1968. *Political Order in Changing Societies.* New Haven: Yale University Press.

Huntington, Samuel P. 1991. *The Third Wave: Democratization in the Late Twentieth Century.* Norman: University of Oklahoma Press.

Huntington, Samuel P., and Joan M. Nelson. 1976. *No Easy Choice: Political Participation in Developing Countries.* Cambridge: Harvard University Press.

Hyden, Goran, and Denis Venter. 2001. *Constitution-Making and Democratization in Africa.* Pretoria, South Africa: Africa Institute of South Africa.

Inglehart, Ronald. 2003. How Solid Is Mass Support for Democracy—and How Can We Measure It? *PS, Political Science and Politics* 36 (1): 51–57.

Inglehart, Ronald, and Gabriela Catterberg. 2002. Trends in Political Action: The Developmental Trend and the Post-Honeymoon Decline. *International Journal of Comparative Sociology* 43 (3): 300–16.

Jackman, Robert W. 1972. Political Elites, Mass Publics, and Support for Democratic Principles. *Journal of Politics* 34 (3): 753–73.

Jennings, Kent M. 1998. Political Trust and the Roots of Devolution. In *Trust and Governance,* edited by V. A. Braithwaite and M. Levi. New York: Sage.

Justus, Mugaju, and Joseph Oloka-Onyango, eds. 2000. *No-Party Democracy in Uganda: Myths and Realities.* Kampala, Uganda: Fountain.

Kanyeihamba, George W. 1975. *Constitutional Law and Government in Uganda.* Nairobi, Kenya: East African Literature Bureau.

Karlstrom, Mikael. 1996. Imagining Democracy: Political Culture and Democratisation in Buganda. *Africa* 66 (4): 485–505.

Karugire, Samwiri Rubaraza. 1980. *A Political History of Uganda.* Nairobi, Kenya: Heinemann Educational.

Kasfir, Nelson. 1976. *The Shrinking Political Arena: Participation and Ethnicity in African Politics with a Case Study of Uganda.* Berkeley: University of California Press.

Kasfir, Nelson. 1995. Ugandan Politics and the Constituent Assembly Elections of March 1994. In *From Chaos to Order: The Politics of Constitution-Making in Uganda,* edited by H. B. Hansen and M. Twaddle. Kampala: Fountain.

Kasfir, Nelson. 1999. "No-Party" Democracy in Uganda. In *Democratization in Africa,* edited by L. J. Diamond and M. F. Plattner. Baltimore: Johns Hopkins University Press.

Kasfir, Nelson. 2000. "Movement" Democracy, Legitimacy, and Power in Uganda. In *No-Party Democracy in Uganda: Myths and Realities,* edited by J. Mugaju and J. Oloka-Onyango. Kampala, Uganda: Fountain.

Kasfir, Nelson. 2005. Guerrillas and Civilian Participation: The National Resistance Army in Uganda, 1981–86. *Journal of Modern African Studies* 43 (2): 271–96.

Kasozi, A. B. K. 1999. *The Social Origins of Violence in Uganda, 1964–1985.* Kampala, Uganda: Fountain.

Katorobo, James. 1996. Constituent Assembly Elections in Kabale Municipality—South Western Uganda. In *Politics, Constitutionalism, and Electioneering in Uganda: A Study of the 1994 Constituent Assembly Elections,* edited by S. E. Makara, G. B. Tukahebwa, and F. Byarugaba. Kampala, Uganda: Makerere University Press.

Katz, Elihu, and Paul F. Lazarsfeld. 1955. *Personal Influence: The Part Played by People in the Flow of Mass Communications.* Glencoe, Ill.: Free Press.

Kaufman, Robert R., Harry I. Chernostsky, and Daniel S. Geller. 1975. A Preliminary Test of the Theory of Dependency. *Comparative Politics* 7 (3): 303–30.

Kingdom of Buganda. 2001. *The Main Issues to Be Presented to the Uganda Constitutional Review Commission.* Available at http://www.bicusa.com/federo.htm. Accessed May 20, 2003.

Kizito, Dick Mutebi. 1992. Media Role in Constitutional Making Process in Uganda, 1988–1992. Thesis for Diploma in Journalism, Uganda School of Journalism, Kampala, Uganda.

Klug, Heinz. 1996. Participating in the Design: Constitution-Making in South Africa. *Review of Constitutional Studies* 3 (1): 18–59.

Knight, Jack. 1995. Models, Interpretations, and Theories: Constructing Explanations of Institutional Emergence and Change. In *Explaining Social Institutions,* edited by J. Knight and I. Sened. Ann Arbor: University of Michigan Press.

Kritz, Neil. 2003. *Constitution-Making Process: Lessons for Iraq* [testimony by director of the Rule of Law Program at the U.S. Institute of Peace before a joint hearing of the Senate Committee on the Judiciary, Subcommittee on the Constitution, Civil Rights, and Property Rights, and the Senate Committee on Foreign Relations, Subcommittee on Near Eastern and South Asian Affairs, June 25]. Available at http://www.usip.org/aboutus/congress/testimony/2003/0625_kritz.html. Accessed October 10, 2005.

Kuenzi, Michelle, and Gina Lambright. 2005. *Who Votes in Africa? An Examination of Electoral Turnout in Ten African Countries.* Afrobarometer Working Paper 51. Available at http://www.afrobarometer.org/papers/AfropaperNo51.pdf. Accessed December 30, 2005.

Kuria, Gibson Kamau. 1996. Which Institutions Should Kenya Use in Re-Writing the Constitution? In *In Search of Freedom and Prosperity: Constitutional Reform in East Africa,* edited by K. Kibwana, C. M. Peter, and J. Oloka-Onyango. Nairobi, Kenya: Claripress.

Laitin, David D. 1994. The Tower of Babel as a Coordination Game: Political Linguistics in Ghana. *American Political Science Review* 88 (3): 622–34.

Lal, Brij V. 1997. Current Developments in the Pacific: Towards a United Future: Report of the Fiji Constitution Review Commission. *Journal of Pacific History* 32 (1): 71–84.

Lal, Brij V. 2002. Constitutional Engineering in Post-Coup Fiji. In *The Architecture of Democracy: Constitutional Design, Conflict Management, and Democracy,* edited by A. Reynolds. Oxford: Oxford University Press.

Levi, Margaret. 1998. A State of Trust. In *Trust and Governance,* edited by V. A. Braithwaite and M. Levi. New York: Sage.

Levitsky, Steven, and Lucan Way. 2002. The Rise of Competitive Authoritarianism. *Journal of Democracy* 13 (2): 51–65.

Lind, Allan E., and Tom R. Tyler. 1988. *The Social Psychology of Procedural Justice.* New York: Plenum.

Linz, Juan J., and Alfred C. Stepan. 1978. *The Breakdown of Democratic Regimes: Crisis, Breakdown, and Reequilibration.* Vol. 1. Baltimore: Johns Hopkins University Press.

Linz, Juan J., and Alfred C. Stepan. 1996. *Problems of Democratic Transition and Consolidation: Southern Europe, South America, and Post-Communist Europe.* Baltimore: Johns Hopkins University Press.

Lipset, Seymour Martin. 1959. Some Social Requisites of Democracy: Economic Development and Political Legitimacy. *American Political Science Review* 53 (1): 69–105.

Lipset, Seymour Martin. 1960. *Political Man: The Social Bases of Politics.* Garden City, N.Y.: Doubleday.

Lipset, Seymour Martin. 1994. The Social Requisites of Democracy Revisited: 1993 Presidential Address. *American Sociological Review* 42 (4): 1–22.

Logan, Carolyn, Nansozi Muwanga, Robert Sentamu, and Michael Bratton. 2003. *Insiders and Outsiders: Varying Perceptions of Democracy and Governance in Uganda.* Afrobarometer Paper 27. Available at http://www.afrobarometer.org/papers/AfropaperNo27.pdf. Accessed December 27, 2005.

Lupia, Arthur, and Mathew D. McCubbins. 1998. *The Democratic Dilemma: Can Citizens Learn What They Need to Know?* Cambridge: Cambridge University Press.

Maitum, Mary. 1999. Interview by author. Kampala, Uganda, June 18.

Majome, Fungayi Jessie. 1999. The State of Constitutional Struggles in Zimbabwe: The Interaction of the Government Process with Civil Society and Citizens. Paper presented at the International Conference on Constitutionalism in Africa, October 5–8, Kampala, Uganda.

Makara, Sabiti E. 1996. Constituent Assembly Elections in Ruhaama, Ntungamo District. In *Politics, Constitutionalism, and Electioneering in Uganda: A Study of the 1994 Constituent Assembly Elections,* edited by S. E. Makara, G. B. Tukahebwa, and F. Byarugaba. Kampala, Uganda: Makerere University Press.

Makara, Sabiti E., and Geoffrey B. Tukahebwa. 1996. Politics, Constitutionalism, and Electioneering in Uganda: An Introduction. In *Politics, Constitutionalism, and Electioneering in Uganda: A Study of the 1994 Constituent Assembly Elections,* edited by S. E. Makara, G. B. Tukahebwa, and F. Byarugaba. Kampala, Uganda: Makerere University Press.

Makara, Sabiti E., Geoffrey B. Tukahebwa, and Foster Byarugaba, eds. 1996. *Politics, Constitutionalism, and Electioneering in Uganda: A Study of the 1994 Constituent Assembly Elections.* Kampala, Uganda: Makerere University Press.

Mansbridge, Jane. 1995. *Does Participation Make Better Citizens?* Available at http://www.cpn.org/sections/new_citizenship/theory/mansbridge1.html. Accessed May 10, 2002.

March, James G., and Johan P. Olsen. 1989. *Rediscovering Institutions: The Organizational Basis of Politics.* New York: Free Press.

Matembe, Miria. 2001. Interview by author. Kampala, Uganda, September 5.

Matembe, Miria R. K., and Nancy R. Dorsey. 2002. *Miria Matembe: Gender, Politics, and Constitution Making in Uganda.* Kampala: Fountain.

Mattei, Ugo. 1999. Patterns of African Constitution in the Making. *Cardozo Electronic Law Bulletin.* Available at http://www.jus.unitn.it/cardozo/Review/Constitutional/Mattei-1999/Patterns.html. Accessed June 8, 2003.

McWhinney, Edward. 1981. *Constitution-Making: Principles, Process, Practice.* Toronto: University of Toronto Press.

Melson, Robert, and Howard Wolpe. 1970. Modernization and the Politics of Communalism: A Theoretical Perspective. *American Political Science Review* 64 (4): 1112–30.

Mill, John Stuart. 1948. *Representative Government.* London: Oxford University Press.

Mishler, William, and Richard Rose. 1997. Trust, Distrust, and Skepticism: Popular Evaluations of Civil and Political Institutions in Post-Communist Societies. *Journal of Politics* 59 (2): 418–51.

Mishler, William, and Richard Rose. 2001. What Are the Origins of Political Trust? Testing Institutional and Cultural Theories in Post-Communist Societies. *Comparative Political Studies* 34 (1): 30–62.

Mugaju, Justus, and Joseph Oloka-Onyango. 2000. Introduction: Revisiting the Multiparty versus Movement System Debate. In *No-Party Democracy in Uganda: Myths and Realities,* edited by J. Mugaju and J. Oloka-Onyango. Kampala, Uganda: Fountain.

Mugisha, Anne. 2004. Museveni's Machinations. *Journal of Democracy* 15 (2): 140–44.

Mugisha, Maude. 1999. Interview by author. Kampala, Uganda, July 29.

Mujaju, Akiiki B. 1996. Constituent Assembly Elections in Fort Portal Municipality, Kabarole District. In *Politics, Constitutionalism, and Electioneering in Uganda: A Study of the 1994 Constituent Assembly Elections,* edited by S. E. Makara, G. B. Tukahebwa, and F. Byarugaba. Kampala, Uganda: Makerere University Press.

Mujaju, Akiiki B. 1999. Towards a National Resistance Movement Constitution in Uganda. Paper presented at the Second East African Workshop on Democratic Transitions in East Africa, March 29–30, Arusha, Tanzania.

Mukholi, David. 1995. *A Complete Guide to Uganda's Fourth Constitution: History, Politics, and the Law.* Kampala, Uganda: Fountain.

Mukwaya, Aaron K. 1996. Constituent Assembly Elections in Bukooli North Constituency, Iganga District. In *Politics, Constitutionalism, and Electioneering in Uganda: A Study of the 1994 Constituent Assembly Elections,* edited by S. E. Makara, G. B. Tukahebwa, and F. Byarugaba. Kampala, Uganda: Makerere University Press.

Muller, Edward N., Mitchell A. Seligson, and Ilter Turan. 1987. Education, Participation, and Support for Democratic Norms. *Comparative Politics* 20 (1): 19–33.

Mulondo, Besweri K. L. 2001. Interview by author. Kampala, Uganda, August 18.

Museveni, Yoweri Kaguta. 1997. *Sowing the Mustard Seed: The Struggle for Freedom and Democracy in Uganda.* Edited by E. Kanyogonya and K. Shillington. London: Macmillan Education.

Mutz, Diana C. 2002. Cross-Cutting Social Networks: Testing Democratic Theory in Practice. *American Political Science Review* 96 (1): 111–26.

Mutz, Diana C., Paul M. Sniderman, and Richard A. Brody. 1996. *Political Persuasion and Attitude Change.* Ann Arbor: University of Michigan Press.

Mwesige, Peter G. 2004. "Can You Hear Me Now?": Radio Talk Shows and Political Participation in Uganda. Ph.D. diss., Indiana University.

Nabli, Mustapha K., and Jeffrey B. Nugent. 1989. The New Institutional Economics and Its Applicability to Development. *World Development* 17 (9): 1333–47.

National Resistance Council. 1988. *Uganda Commission Statute No. 5 of 1988.*

National Resistance Council. 1993. *Constituent Assembly Statute No. 6 of 1993.*

Nee, Victor. 1998. Embeddedness and Beyond: Institutions, Exchange, and Social Structure. In *New Institutionalism in Sociology,* edited by M. C. Brinton and V. Nee. New York: Sage.

Nekyon, Florence. 2001. Interview by author. Kampala, Uganda, August 3.

Nelson, Joan M. 1987. Political Participation. In *Understanding Political Development: An Analytic Study,* edited by M. Weiner, S. P. Huntington, and G. A. Almond. Boston: Little, Brown.

Nie, Norman H., Jane Junn, and Kenneth Stehlik-Barry. 1996. *Education and Democratic Citizenship in America.* Chicago: University of Chicago Press.

Njuba, Sam K. 2001. Interview by author. Kampala, Uganda, September 4.

Norris, Pippa. 1999. *Critical Citizens: Global Support for Democratic Government.* Oxford: Oxford University Press.

Norris, Pippa. 2002. *Democratic Phoenix: Reinventing Political Activism.* Cambridge: Cambridge University Press.

North, Douglass C. 1994. Economic Performance through Time. *American Economic Review* 84 (3): 359–68.

Nsambu, Hillary. 2001. Law Society Petition Dismissed. *New Vision,* December 1.

Nsibambi, Apollo. 2001. Interview by author. Kampala, Uganda, August 2.

Odida, Irene Ovonji. 2001. Interview by author. Kampala, Uganda, March 27.

Odoki, Benjamin J. 1992. The Current Constitution-Making Process in Uganda. Paper presented at the Constitutional Seminar, May 21–22, Kampala, Uganda.

Odoki, Benjamin J. 1999. The Challenges of Constitution-Making and Implementation in Uganda. Paper presented at the International Conference on Constitutionalism in Africa, October 5–8, Kampala, Uganda.

Odoki, Benjamin J. 2001. Interview by author. Kampala, Uganda, September 4.

Odoki, Benjamin J. 2005. *The Search for National Consensus: The Making of the 1995 Uganda Constitution.* Kampala, Uganda: Fountain.

O'Donnell, Guillermo A., Philippe C. Schmitter, and Laurence Whitehead. 1986. *Transitions from Authoritarian Rule: Prospects for Democracy.* Baltimore: Johns Hopkins University Press.

Ogwal, Celia A. 2001. Interview by author. Kampala, Uganda, July 20.

Okeny, Tiberio. 1995. The Constitution Was Rigged. *National Analyst,* October 5–November 2, 23.

Okoth, P. Godfrey. 1996. The Historical Dimension of Democracy in Uganda: A Review of the Problems and Prospects. In *Law and the Struggle for Democracy in East Africa,* edited by J. Oloka-Onyango, K. Kibwana, and C. Maine Peter. Nairobi, Kenya: Claripress.

Okoth-Ogendo, H. W. O. 1991. Constitutions without Constitutionalism: Reflections on an African Political Paradox. In *State and Constitutionalism: An African Debate on Democracy,* edited by I. G. Shivji. Harare, Zimbabwe: SAPES Trust.

Olet, Charles. 2001. Interview by author. Kampala, Uganda, March 27.

Oloka-Onyango, Joseph. 1995. Constitutional Transition in Museveni's Uganda: New Horizons or Another False Start? *Journal of African Law* 39 (2): 156–72.

Oloka-Onyango, Joseph. 1996. Taming the Executive: The History of and Challenges to Uganda's Constitution-Making. In *Law and the Struggle for Democracy in East Africa,* edited by J. Oloka-Onyango, K. Kibwana, and C. Maine Peter. Nairobi, Kenya: Claripress.

Oloka-Onyango, Joseph. 1998. Governance, State Structures, and Constitutionalism in Contemporary Uganda. Paper presented at the Center for Basic Research Constitutionalism III Project Seminar, May 9, Kampala, Uganda.

Oloka-Onyango, Joseph. 2000. New Wine or New Bottles? Movement Politics and One-Partyism in Uganda. In *No-Party Democracy in Uganda: Myths and Realities,* edited by M. Justus and J. Oloka-Onyango. Kampala, Uganda: Fountain.

Oloka-Onyango, Joseph, and Julius Ihonvbere. 1999. Towards Participatory and Inclusive African Constitutionalism. Paper presented at the International Conference on Constitutionalism in Africa, October 5–8, Kampala, Uganda.

Oloka-Onyango, Joseph, and Sam Tindifa. 1991. *Constitutionalism in Uganda: Report on the Survey and Workshop of Organized Groups.* Kampala, Uganda: Center for Basic Research.

Olson, Mancur. 1982. *The Rise and Decline of Nations: Economic Growth, Stagflation, and Social Rigidities.* New Haven: Yale University Press.

Onegi-Obel, Geoffrey. 2001. Interview by author. Kampala, Uganda, July 22.

Oneka, Joseph A. 1999. Interview by author. Kampala, Uganda, July 22.

Ordeshook, Peter C. 1992. Constitutional Stability. *Constitutional Political Economy* 3 (2): 137–75.

Ostrom, Elinor. 1990. *Governing the Commons: The Evolution of Institutions for Collective Action.* Cambridge: Cambridge University Press.

Pateman, Carole. 1970. *Participation and Democratic Theory.* Cambridge: Cambridge University Press.

Pharr, Susan J., and Robert D. Putnam, eds. 2000. *Disaffected Democracies: What's Troubling the Trilateral Countries?* Princeton: Princeton University Press.

Przeworski, Adam, and Fernando Limongi. 1993. Political Regimes and Economic Growth. *Journal of Economic Perspectives* 7 (3): 51–69.

Putnam, Robert D. 1993. *Making Democracy Work: Civic Traditions in Modern Italy.* Princeton: Princeton University Press.

Putnam, Robert D., Susan J. Pharr, and Russell J. Dalton. 2000. Introduction: What's Troubling the Trilateral Countries? In *Disaffected Democracies: What's Troubling the Trilateral Countries?* edited by S. J. Pharr and R. D. Putnam. Princeton: Princeton University Press.

Radcliff, Benjamin, and Ed Wingenbach. 2000. Preference Aggregation, Functional Pathologies, and Democracy: A Social Choice Defense of Participatory Democracy. *Journal of Politics* 62 (4): 977–98.

Raftery, Adrian E. 1995. "Bayesian Model Selection in Social Research." *Sociological Methodology* 25:111–63.

Rahn, Wendy M., John Brehm, and Neil Carlson. 1999. National Elections as Institutions for Generating Social Capital. In *Civic Engagement in American Democracy,* edited by T. Skocpol and M. P. Fiorina. Washington, D.C.: Brookings Institution Press.

Regan, Anthony J. 1995. Constitutional Reform and the Politics of the Constitution of Uganda: A New Path to Constitutionalism? In *Uganda: Landmarks in Rebuilding a Nation,* edited by P. Langseth, J. Katorobo, E. A. Brett, and J. C. Munene. Kampala: Fountain.

Reynolds, Andrew. 1994. *Election '94 South Africa: The Campaigns, Results, and Future Prospects.* New York: St. Martin's.

Reynolds, Andrew. 1999. *Electoral Systems and Democratization in Southern Africa.* Oxford: Oxford University Press.

Riker, William H. 1995. The Experience of Creating Institutions: The Framing of the United States Constitution. In *Explaining Social Institutions,* edited by J. Knight and I. Sened. Ann Arbor: University of Michigan Press.

Rose, Richard, William Mishler, and Christian W. Haerpfer. 1998. *Democracy and Its Alternatives: Understanding Post-Communist Societies.* Baltimore: Johns Hopkins University Press.

Rose, Richard, and Neil Munro. 2003. *Elections and Parties in New European Democracies.* Washington, D.C.: CQ Press.

Rosenn, Keith S. 1990. Brazil's New Constitution: An Exercise in Transient Constitutionalism for a Transitional Society. *American Journal of Comparative Law* 38 (4): 773–802.

Rosenstone, Steven J., and John Mark Hansen. 1993. *Mobilization, Participation, and Democracy in America.* New York: Macmillan.

Rousseau, Jean-Jacques. 1968. *The Social Contract.* Harmondsworth: Penguin.

Salisbury, Robert H. 1975. Research on Political Participation. *American Journal of Political Science* 19 (2): 323–41.

Scaff, Lawrence A. 1975. Two Concepts of Political Participation. *Western Political Quarterly* 28 (3): 447–62.

Schaffer, Frederic C. 1998. *Democracy in Translation: Understanding Politics in an Unfamiliar Culture.* Ithaca: Cornell University Press.

Schmitter, Philippe C., and Terry Lynn Karl. 1996. What Democracy Is . . . and Is Not. In *The Global Resurgence of Democracy,* edited by L. Diamond and M. F. Plattner. Baltimore: Johns Hopkins University Press.

Selassie, Bereket Habte. 1998. Creating a Constitution for Eritrea. *Journal of Democracy* 9 (2): 164–74.

Selassie, Bereket Habte. 1999. Constitution-Making in Eritrea: Democratic Transition through Popular Participation. Paper presented at the International Conference on Constitutionalism in Africa, October 5–8, Kampala, Uganda.

Sen, Amartya Kumar. 1994. Freedoms and Needs: An Argument for the Primacy of Political Rights. *New Republic,* January 10 and 17, 31–38.

Sen, Amartya Kumar. 1999. *Development as Freedom.* 1st ed. New York: Knopf.

Shin, Doh Chull. 1994. On the Third Wave of Democratization: A Synthesis and Evaluation of Recent Theory and Research. *World Politics* 47 (1): 135–70.

Shivji, Issa G. 1991. State and Constitutionalism: A New Democratic Perspective. In *State and Constitutionalism: An African Debate on Democracy,* edited by I. G. Shivji. Harare, Zimbabwe: SAPES Trust.

Skach, Cindy. 2005. We, the Peoples? Constitutionalizing the European Union. *Journal of Common Market Studies* 43 (1): 149–70.

Ssemogerere, Paul. 2001. Interview by author. Kampala, Uganda, July 28.

Ssempebwa, Frederick E. 2001. Interview by author. Kampala, Uganda, August 27.

Ssewanyana, Livingston. 2001. Interview by author. Kampala, Uganda, August 8.

Stiglitz, Joseph E. 2002. Participation and Development: Perspectives from the Comprehensive Development Paradigm. *Review of Development Economics* 6 (2): 163–82.

Sullivan, John Lawrence, James Piereson, and George E. Marcus. 1982. *Political Tolerance and American Democracy.* Chicago: University of Chicago Press.

Tamale, Sylvia. 1999. *When Hens Begin to Crow: Gender and Parliamentary Politics in Uganda.* Boulder, Colo.: Westview.

Tarrow, Sidney. 2000. Mad Cows and Social Activists: Contentious Mechanisms in the Trilateral Democracies. In *Disaffected Democracies: What's Troubling the Trilateral Countries?* edited by S. J. Pharr and R. D. Putnam. Princeton: Princeton University Press.

Thompson, Dennis F. 1970. *The Democratic Citizen: Social Science and Democratic Theory in the Twentieth Century.* Cambridge: Cambridge University Press.

Tocqueville, Alexis de. 1945. *Democracy in America.* New York: Knopf.

Tripp, Aili Mari. 2000. *Women and Politics in Uganda.* Madison: University of Wisconsin Press.

Tripp, Aili Mari. 2005. The Politics of Constitution-Making in Uganda. Unpublished manuscript.

Tripp, Aili Mari, and Joy C. Kwesiga. 2002. *The Women's Movement in Uganda: History, Challenges, and Prospects.* Kampala, Uganda: Fountain.

Tukahebwa, Geoffrey B. 1996. Constituent Assembly Elections in Bushenyi District. In *Politics, Constitutionalism, and Electioneering in Uganda: A Study of the 1994 Constituent Assembly Elections,* edited by S. E. Makara, G. B. Tukahebwa, and F. Byarugaba. Kampala, Uganda: Makerere University Press.

Tyler, Tom R. 1989. *Why People Obey the Law: Procedural Justice, Legitimacy, and Compliance.* New Haven: Yale University Press.

Tyler, Tom R. 1998. Trust and Democratic Governance. In *Trust and Governance,* edited by V. A. Braithwaite and M. Levi. New York: Sage.

Tyler, Tom R., Jonathan D. Casper, and Bonnie Fisher. 1989. Maintaining Allegiance toward Political Authorities: The Role of Prior Attitudes and the Use of Fair Procedures. *American Journal of Political Science* 33 (3): 629–52.

Uganda Constitutional Commission. 1989. *Programme and Timetable of the Constitutional Commission.* Kampala, Uganda: Uganda Constitutional Commission.

Uganda Constitutional Commission. 1991a. *Guidelines on Constitutional Issues.* Kampala, Uganda: Uganda Constitutional Commission.

Uganda Constitutional Commission. 1991b. *Interim Report on Adoption of the New Constitution.* Kampala, Uganda: Uganda Constitutional Commission.

Uganda Constitutional Commission. 1992a. *The Report of the Uganda Constitutional Commission: Analysis and Recommendations.* Kampala, Uganda: Uganda Constitutional Commission.

Uganda Constitutional Commission. 1992b. *The Report of the Uganda Constitutional Commission: Index of Sources of People's Views.* Kampala, Uganda: Uganda Constitutional Commission.

Uganda Constitutional Review Commission. 2001. *EnterUganda.com.* Available at http://enteruganda.com/constitution/. Accessed May 27, 2003.

United Nations Development Programme. 1994. *Placing the People First: Elections to the Constituent Assembly.* New York: United Nations Development Programme.

United Nations Development Programme. 2002. *Human Development Report 2002.* New York: Oxford University Press.

United Nations Security Council. 2001. *Security Council Condemns Illegal Exploitation of Democratic Republic of Congo's Natural Resources.* Press Release SC/7057, Security Council 4317th and 4318th Meetings. Available at http://www.un.org/News/Press/docs/2001/sc7057.doc.htm. Accessed May 21, 2003.

U.S. Agency for International Development. 2000. *Improving Democracy Promotion: FY 2000.* Washington, D.C.: U.S. Agency for International Development, Center for Democracy and Governance.

U.S. Department of State, Bureau of Democracy, Human Rights, and Labor. 2002. *The Country Reports on Human Rights Practices—2001.* Available at http://www.state.gov/g/drl/rls/hrrpt/2001/af/8409.htm. Accessed May 21, 2003.

U.S. Institute of Peace. 2005. *Iraq's Constitutional Process: Shaping a Vision for the Country's Future.* Special Report 132. Washington, D.C.: U.S. Institute of Peace.

Van Cott, Donna Lee. 2000. *The Friendly Liquidation of the Past: The Politics of Diversity in Latin America.* Pittsburgh: University of Pittsburgh Press.

Verba, Sidney, Nancy Burns, and Kay Lehman Schlozman. 1997. Knowing and Caring about Politics: Gender and Political Engagement. *Journal of Politics* 59 (4): 1051–72.

Verba, Sidney, Norman H. Nie, and Jae-on Kim. 1978. *Participation and Political Equality: A Seven-Nation Comparison.* Cambridge: Cambridge University Press.

Verba, Sidney, Kay Schlozman, and Henry E. Brady. 1995. *Voice and Equality: Civic Voluntarism in American Politics.* Cambridge: Harvard University Press.

Waliggo, John M. 1995. Constitution-Making and the Politics of Democratization in Uganda. In *From Chaos to Order: The Politics of Constitution-Making in Uganda,* edited by H. B. Hansen and M. Twaddle. Kampala, Uganda: Fountain.

Waliggo, John M. 1999. Interview by author. Kampala, Uganda, June 8.

Walker, J. L. 1966. A Critique of the Elitist Theory of Democracy. *American Political Science Review* 15 (3): 285–95.

Walubiri, Peter. 2001. Interview by author. Kampala, Uganda, August 11.

Wapakhabulo, James F. 2001. *Uganda's Experience in Constitution Making.* Available at http://www.kenyaconstitution.org/docs/07d042.htm. Accessed May 16, 2003.

Weimann, Gabriel. 1994. *The Influentials: People Who Influence People.* Albany: State University of New York Press.

Weingast, Barry R. 1997. The Political Foundations of Democracy and the Rule of Law. *American Political Science Review* 91 (2): 245–63.

Widner, Jennifer A. 2001. *Building the Rule of Law.* New York: Norton.

Widner, Jennifer A. 2005a. Africa's Democratization: A Work in Progress. *Current History* 104 (682): 216–21.

Widner, Jennifer A. 2005b. Constitution Writing and Conflict Resolution. *Round Table* 94 (381): 503–18.

Wilson, Masalu Musene. 2001. Interview by author. Kampala, Uganda, August 7.

World Bank. 2002. *World Development Indicators* [CD-ROM]. Washington, D.C.: International Bank for Reconstruction and Development.

Yablokova, Oksana. 2001. Constitution Turns Eight, Public Still Ambivalent. *Moscow Times,* December 11. Available at http://www.cdi.org/russia/johnson/5593-10.cfm. Accessed April 9, 2003.

Young, G. E., K. S. Suresh Rao, and Vijay R. Chatufale. 1995. Block-Recursive Identification of Parameters and Delay in the Presence of Noise. *Journal of Dynamic Systems, Measurement, and Control* 117 (4): 600–607.

Zaller, John. 1992. *The Nature and Origins of Mass Opinion.* Cambridge: Cambridge University Press.

INDEX

235